IMAGE AND PRESENCE

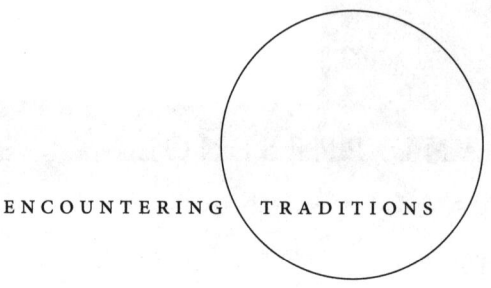

ENCOUNTERING TRADITIONS

Stanley Hauerwas, Peter Ochs, Randi Rashkover, and Maria Dakake
EDITORS

Nicholas Adams, Rumee Ahmed, and Jonathan Tran
SERIES BOARD

IMAGE AND PRESENCE

A Christological Reflection

on Iconoclasm and Iconophilia

NATALIE CARNES

STANFORD UNIVERSITY PRESS
STANFORD, CALIFORNIA

Stanford University Press
Stanford, California

© 2018 by the Board of Trustees of the Leland Stanford Junior University. All rights reserved.

No part of this book may be reproduced or transmitted in any form or by any means, electronic or mechanical, including photocopying and recording, or in any information storage or retrieval system without the prior written permission of Stanford University Press.

Printed in the United States of America on acid-free, archival-quality paper

Library of Congress Cataloging-in-Publication Data

Carnes, Natalie, author.

Title: Image and presence : a Christological reflection on iconoclasm and iconophilia / Natalie Carnes.

Other titles: Encountering traditions.

Description: Stanford, California : Stanford University Press, 2017. | Series: Encountering traditions | Includes bibliographical references and index.

Identifiers: LCCN 2017028670| ISBN 9781503600348 (cloth : alk. paper) | ISBN 9781503604223 (pbk. : alk. paper) | ISBN 9781503604230 (electronic)

Subjects: LCSH: Jesus Christ—Iconography. | Jesus Christ—Presence. | Image (Theology) | Iconoclasm. | Idols and images—Worship. | Christian art and symbolism.

Classification: LCC BT590.I3 C37 2017 | DDC 246/.53—dc23

LC record available at https://lccn.loc.gov/2017028670

Typeset by Bruce Lundquist in 10/14 Minion

For Matthew

CONTENTS

	Preface	ix
	Acknowledgments	xiii
	Introduction: Our Life with Images	1
1	*Born of the Virgin Mary*: Arriving Presence	19
2	*Came Down from Heaven and Was Made Human*: Abiding Presence	57
3	*Crucified, Died, and Was Buried*: Riven and Riving Presence	87
4	*Rose Again on the Third Day*: Abiding Presence	121
5	*Will Come Again in Glory*: Arriving Presence	153
	Conclusion: The Image of the Invisible God	181
	Notes	189
	Works Cited	217
	Index	229

PREFACE

In spring 2010, Marina Abramović sat across from an empty chair in New York's Museum of Modern Art (MoMA). Viewers waited in line, sometimes for hours, for the chance to sit with the woman called the grandmother of performance art. To many who did sit with her, the experience was gripping. A series of photographs by Marco Anelli testifies to the range of emotions evoked in the sitters: serenity, searchingness, defiance, fragility, surprise, hopefulness. But the reaction most striking—and strikingly common—was weeping.[1]

While the exhibition was open, a group of New York artists handed out badges that read, "I cried with Marina Abramović." After it closed, photographs of the sitters were collected on a blog titled "Marina made me cry." Her performance seemed to have hit a cultural nerve, reverberating emotionally and intellectually well beyond the museum's walls. From those who sat with Marina, those who watched the sitting, and those who followed the event from afar, responses poured forth as essays, books, blogs, and even a documentary, titled, like the performance piece itself, *The Artist is Present*.[2]

Why did Marina's being-present inspire such extraordinary response? Why did the weepers weep? At the time of the performance, I lived in North Carolina, hundreds of miles from MoMA, and waves of excitement billowed even there. I observed the swells of enthusiasm in the writings of the now-late Arthur Danto, first in his *New York Times* piece on Marina's performance. It was not his first essay on the subject. Before Marina had performed *The Artist is Present*, before it was even quite clear what the piece would be, Danto had written a catalogue essay anticipating the exhibition by meditating on the title's invocation of presence. "Presence," he writes, connotes the mystical presence of icons, and he discerns what he calls a "resonance in the metaphysics of art" between the presence of a saint to an icon and the presence of an artist to her performance.[3] There is an echo, or harmony, between Marina's presence and a tradition of claimed mystical presence that may, Danto seems to aver, account for the power of her performance.

After he sat with her, Danto wrote the *New York Times* article I read. The tone of that piece is different. His prose is expressive, almost rhapsodic, as it bears witness to his transformative encounter with Marina. He narrates the way she leans back and fixes her eyes on him without seeming to see him, "as if she had entered another state." She grows "translucent" and "luminous." Danto's short essay soars into the ecstatic as he concludes: "Those who do get lucky enough to sit with Marina will not be disappointed, because the light I noticed will be there, even if they are not ready to see it."[4] With this general evocation of light, is Danto tiptoeing into theological terrain? His follow-up essay published a few days later removed any doubt. There he borrows more definitively theological language, as he exhorts the reader to remember Christ at Emmaus, or at the Last Supper, and so to consider the significance of sitting and presence as a "ritual moment" in which Marina, like Christ, honors the sitters.[5] Across these three essays on Marina, then, Danto's writings claim there is something about Marina's presence in her performance that is like a saint's presence to an icon, like Christ's presence to his disciples. It is a presence that confers light. Danto's turn to the language of religion is repeated by Marina herself, who observes in an interview that her performance became for many a "religious experience" in which MoMA was, for a while, transformed into something like Lourdes.[6]

Marina grasps at the language of religion and Lourdes. Danto seizes upon icons and light. The more I read about Marina, the more theological language I detected. Both academic and popular articles on her performances consistently conjure her background in a strict Serbian Orthodox home and reference her great uncle, once Patriarch of the Serbian Orthodox Church—even though Marina herself disavows the claims of any religion.[7] The writers of these articles, like Danto and Marina, strain for a language to express the power of Marina's performances, to communicate something of what makes them so compelling. And it is not just Marina who inspires religious terms. The thickly theological language I read in articles about Marina attuned me to the ubiquity of theological vocabulary in writing about art and images more broadly.

I saw that Marina's is not the only art that edges writers into theological ground. Writing on modernist art in the 1960s, art historian and critic Michael Fried broached religious language to express art's surplus of presence. Fried begins his famous essay "Art and Objecthood" with a quotation from a biography of preacher and theologian Jonathan Edwards. The epigraph ends, quoting Edwards, "'[I]t is certain with me that the world exists anew every moment; that the existence of things every moment ceases and is every moment renewed.'

The abiding assurance is that 'we every moment see the same proof of a God as we should have seen if we had seen Him create the world at first.'"[8] The perpetual newness of the world testifies for Edwards to God's presence to the world as Creator. For Fried, such divine presence typifies an excessiveness that contrasts with literal, bare existence. It proposes that an object can be more than a mere object, that it can communicate something beyond its materiality. Fried calls this communication *presentness*, and he memorably ends his essay with a return to the theological key of his epigraph. "We are all literalists most or all of our lives. Presentness is grace."[9]

Fried's essay foreshadows the importance the category of presence acquires in visual studies in the ensuing decades. It also signals the need for renewing the concepts for invoking such presence. The more I read in visual studies, the more I realized that the field is wrestling with a dilemma. After years of describing images as inert, lifeless objects that point to a vitality beyond them, what resources do visual studies and its sister fields have for describing images that are more than tokens?

In his own attempts to move beyond the tokenist paradigm for images, Horst Bredekamp argues that images bear an agency (a presence) that is reducible neither to the projections of the viewer nor the intentions of the maker.[10] In this, he is representative of many contemporary picture theorists who want to exorcise what they see as Platonist or Kantian understandings of the image as pointing beyond itself to some distant meaning.[11] Seeing this approach as denigrating the image, these picture theorists work to recover the significance of the image as a presence to be encountered. For his efforts at correction, Bredekamp has been called an animist and totemist—a kind of idolater, really.[12] There is something wrong here when the attempt to displace tokenism is received as a form of idolatry. There is something missing in the world of visual studies when it swings between the poles of total absence and total presence, as if the image must be a token or an idol, either pointing to a distant vitality or claiming to possess its own presence. The language has been depleted, blanched by years of discussing images as lifeless objects. No wonder writers discussing art and images forage theological fields.

I believe writers like Danto and Fried glean words from theology because a rich imagination of presence persists in Christianity, developed through efforts to render coherent the church's own claims about the ongoing presence of Christ in the world. Theologians attempt to articulate what the church means when it says, "*There* is Christ," when *there* could indicate the Eucharist, a martyr, a priest, a saint, the afflicted, or two or three gathered in Christ's name. Each of these bears Christ's presence, even as it is distinct from both Christ and each of the others.

Elaborating these claims of Christ's presence in the church presses larger questions of divine presence. How is God's presence to all as Creator different from God's presence to Israel as Yahweh, and how are both of these different still from God's presence in Christ? How does Christ continue to be present after the ascension, and in what way do we wait for the fullness of God's presence, even as we claim not to be abandoned by God? What is unique about God's presence (and apparent absence, forsakingness) on the cross? These questions exert a pressure internal to Christian theology to develop differentiated descriptions of how the divine is present, and the Christian theological imagination is steeped in these claims of variegated presence. It is a storehouse of wealth for describing the presence images bear.[13]

It is there, in this storehouse of the Christian imagination, that I labor in the pages that follow, gathering material to weave the wispy evocations of theological presence in the likes of Fried, Bredekamp, and Marina into a more substantial tapestry. What alternatives to tokenism and animism do they want to conjure with their theological language? I am wary, as I work, of Hans Belting's accusation that early Christian theologians "were satisfied only when they could 'explain' the images."[14] Attempting to resist this spirit of explanation—a wholly iconoclastic attitude—I aim instead to *respond* to images from a theologically-formed imagination, recognizing the distinctiveness of their own modes of communication. I proceed in the conviction that an imagination formed through reflection on Christ the Image of the invisible God keeps faith with the presence of images, with even the cultural reverberations of Marina's performance.

By way of keeping faith with those reverberations, I wonder about the power of Marina's performance, about the way sitters fell under the spell of Marina when she sat with them as the present artist. Why did the weepers weep? Perhaps they wept from the difficulty of bearing the excess of what Danto called her light and Fried might call her grace. Perhaps when Danto described sitting with Marina in terms of Christ at the Last Supper or on the road to Emmaus, he did not merely contrive a metaphor. Perhaps he also issued a call for theological reflection to enrich descriptions of that event, to give content to the claim that to sit in her presence in that exhibition was to catch some vestige, some flash of the divine that comes to us in Christ. This book is one answer to that call.

ACKNOWLEDGMENTS

As the years go by, I find it more difficult to name my debts, not because they diminish but because they multiply. Like wild and tangled vines they grow, and I recognize my work as their fruit.

Looming large in my thicket of debts is the Louisville Institute, which awarded me a sabbatical grant for the 2015–16 school year. Baylor University supported this sabbatical and also offered summer sabbaticals (in 2012, 2013, and 2016) as well as research leave in spring 2017. I am grateful for this institutional support and the individuals who advocated for me to have it, especially my chair Bill Bellinger and then associate dean Robyn Driskell.

Together with the Institute for the Studies of Religion (ISR), the Louisville Institute also supported a symposium I convened titled *Image, Idol, Christ*. I am thankful to ISR and the insightful symposium speakers, Dmitri Andreyev, Matthew Milliner, and Carole Baker. This book is better for their conversation.

Father Maximos, Father Silouan, and Father Parthenios from Holy Cross Monastery spoke at a second set of image discussions at Baylor, convened by Carlos Colón. The monks impressed me with their kindness and wisdom, and they also nuanced my understanding of the living iconographic tradition in important ways.

One of my happiest debts is to the Some Institutes for Advanced Study (SIAS) Summer Institute of 2013 and 2014: Scenes in the History of the Image, organized by Thomas Pfau and David Womersley. I am grateful for the many generative conversations hosted there and for constructive feedback on what became my fourth chapter. In the summer 2014 workshop in Berlin, I also met Horst Bredekamp, whose interpretations of images inspired me at a crucial juncture. I do not expect he agrees with all my arguments, but his tour through the Bode Museum opened new worlds of insight for me. For all our sakes, I hope his writings will one day be widely available in the English-speaking world.

Other groups have given feedback on various pieces of the book. I am grateful to participants in the National Endowment for the Humanities 2016 summer seminar Problems in the Study of Religion, convened by Chuck Mathewes and Kurtis Schaeffer, for reading and commenting on the Preface and Introduction; to the Society for the Study of Theology for allowing me to present and receive feedback on a piece of Chapter 4; and to the University of St Andrews Theology, Imagination and Arts colloquium, the University of Edinburgh Theology and Ethics colloquium, and the University of Glasgow Literature, Theology and the Arts colloquium for feedback on a draft of Chapter 5 in fall 2014. Ralph Wood led a theology and ethics colloquium on Flannery O'Connor and Walker Percy at Baylor in spring 2012, and it introduced me to material that became important to Chapter 2. The graduate students in my 2015 seminar on Christology helped me probe connections between Christology and imaging. And I am also grateful to the *Scottish Journal of Theology* for giving me permission to publish a revised version of an article I wrote for them as a piece of Chapter 3.

Throughout my writing process, I have benefited from the assistance of talented graduate assistants. David Cramer improved Chapter 3 by lending his expertise on John Howard Yoder. Matthew Crawford's research helped lay the groundwork for Chapter 5. Jon-Michael Carman did some helpful background research for me. And Nicholas Krause has copyedited this entire manuscript with scrupulosity and good spirits.

I also want to thank my colleagues Cat Jonathan Tran and Paul Martens. Cat has been reading pieces of this manuscript since I began stammering toward it, and conversations with him have marked the book in ways I cannot fully fathom. Paul helped straighten out Chapter 3 as it was going awry, and it is a better work for his intervention. I realize how fortunate I am to have colleagues like these. Graduate students are also colleagues, and the ones at Baylor have been important for me. Thomas Breedlove, Tom Millay, Brandon Morgan, Cody Strecker, and Rachel Toombs all read and commented on the entire manuscript over one Christmas break, and I am grateful for the care and intelligence they brought to the project.

There are many other colleagues who have read sections of the manuscript or listened to me as I tried to work out my ideas. I am thankful to Carole Baker, Candi Cann, Sean Larsen, Sheryl Overmyer, Thomas Pfau, Bharat Ranganathan, Judith Wolfe, and many others for conversations, comments, critiques, and encouragement. Particular thanks are owed to Stanley Hauerwas, who asked me a question years ago that lit the spark for Chapter 1; to Paul Griffiths, whose recommendations, advice, and confidence in the project helped see it to completion; and to Ben Cowan, who has been a fellow sojourner in the academic life longer than anyone else. I became a scholar through conversations with him and will always be grateful for his generosity and friendship.

I am also grateful to Stanford University Press for its support and particularly to Emily-Jane Cohen, who helped me find a clearer voice; to the Encountering Traditions series board, who offered support and encouragement; and to the reviewers, whose suggestions have made this a better book.

And then there are other debts, of a less academic variety. It takes a village to raise a child, and that village gets a little more taxed when the child's parents are both writing books. My extended family, children's teachers, and babysitters have offered support for my husband, my children, and me. They have made my writing possible, my children happier, and our lives richer. Thank you.

Even the casual reader will quickly discern the ecumenical context of this book. The roots of such conversations run deep for me. They are earthed in efforts to negotiate an ecumenical marriage with my husband, Matthew, as we work to cultivate a religious life for our children, Chora, Edith, and Simone. May such soil, however poorly tilled, prove fertile for you girls, that you may grow loving and joyful and courageous.

In more ways than one, this hope would ring empty without Matthew. Daily he encourages me to be a better writer, scholar, and person. Often his support is verbal, and just as often it is not—coming to me instead through the way he models the attention, conviction, and love I hope one day to emulate.

IMAGE AND PRESENCE

INTRODUCTION
Our Life with Images

TWO ARMED GUNMEN entered the offices of the French satirical magazine *Charlie Hebdo* early in 2015. Over the years, the magazine had published cartoons lampooning the Prophet Muhammed, and on that January day, the gunmen sought vengeance. They killed twelve and injured more.[1] France, along with the rest of the world, was stunned.

As horrific as the clash was, it was not unfamiliar. It reminded many of the controversy that had swirled years earlier around the Danish newspaper *Jyllands-Posten*. After the paper published cartoons of Muhammed, cartoonists there received death threats; journalists at other outlets debated reprinting the cartoons; and Muslims around the world fasted, prayed, and protested.[2] The cartoon images spawned dramatic and dramatically clashing responses.

The charged controversies at *Charlie Hebdo* and *Jyllands-Posten* did not mark the climactic conclusion to two opposed views of images. They augured still more violence. Among the latest image attacks has been the massive destruction of art and images by the Islamic State in Iraq and Syria (ISIS)—images ISIS deems idols and art it calls "an erroneous form of creativity."[3]

This brief litany of image crises originates in the headlines of the last few years. As a group, the stories sketch a picture of an unassimilated, image-breaking Islam threatening an image-making, image-celebrating Modern West.[4] This picture often governs how each individual story is narrated.[5] We, the enlightened Modern Westerners, laud the image (or at least protect it as free speech), while the image-intolerant Islamists refuse to open their views to critique. This has been our guiding picture for the image crises of our time. This is the picture that both captivates and deceives us.

The picture deceives in part because it homogenizes both Islam and the Modern West, eliding Islam with violent Islamists and the Modern West with a particular, secularized brand of modernity. The picture sustains this homogeneity by representing certain image attacks and eclipsing others. In particular, it obscures controversies in which Christians or Modern Westerners assume a more overtly iconoclastic role. In some cases, these episodes of iconoclasm mirror the type of iconoclasm practiced by the likes of ISIS. For example, in 2011, four self-professed Christians entered an exhibit displaying Andres Serrano's photograph *Piss Christ*. Arriving with hammers, they threatened the guard, smashed the protective glass, and slashed the image.[6] This was a case where an image deemed religiously offensive was physically destroyed, and in that way (though not in the scope of destruction), it is similar to the ISIS attacks.

Not all attacks on the image in the Modern West have been so straightforward. Over the years, lawmakers in France have sought to enforce the separation of church and state and diminish religious violence by legislating the circulation of religious symbols. They proscribed headscarves, yarmulkes, turbans, and crucifixes in public schools (2004). They outlawed wearing full face coverings in public (2010). They prohibited the display of large religious symbols by private day-care workers (2015).[7] These image fighters did not come with hammers but with laws; they did not physically destroy an image but circumscribed its appearance in the world. It is a different kind of iconoclasm.

It might be that the Modern West has bred new strains of iconoclasm. It did, after all, give rise to the museum, which arguably attenuates images' political force. Pivotal in this history was the transformation of the Louvre Palace into a museum for housing political and religious artifacts of the old regime as objects of formal value.[8] Just so, the museum both protected images from physical harm and enshrined images as objects of specifically *aesthetic* admiration.[9] Though the museum can be a powerful place of encounter and transformation, the Louvre of the late eighteenth century, like many art museums today, did not treat images as political or religious objects, even if it attended to their political and religious histories. Ironically, the result is that those attacking images as blasphemous or idolatrous—like the Christians vandalizing *Piss Christ* or the Islamists protesting cartoons of Muhammed—often take the claims of images more seriously than those protecting the images do. The image attackers damage an image because they disagree with it; museumgoers do not attack even when they disagree with an image, in part because they are not as impressed by the seriousness of the image's claims. It is this strange dynamic of iconoclasm that inspired art historian Horst Bredekamp's paradoxical observation, "The iconoclasts are the real iconophiles."[10]

In mentioning Christian and Modern Western iconoclasm here, I am not equating it with the iconoclasm in the litany above. Ignoring an image's claims is not the same as destroying it, nor is it congruent with harming image-makers and image protectors (though this is not to say that Christians and Modern Westerners have not destroyed images and harmed people as well). I cite these examples neither to absolve image violence nor to minimize cruelty on excuse of its ubiquity. Instead, I point out Christian and Modern Western iconoclasm to illustrate that Christianity and the Modern West are complicated and manifold regarding images—much more so than the distorted picture I first sketched. Within the traditions of Christianity and the Modern West, the image has been divisive. In the case of Christianity, the image even marks the divisions among its major ecclesial families.

For relations among Catholics, Protestants, and Orthodox, the question of the image has been vexed. In the wake of the Byzantine iconoclastic controversy, the Orthodox privileged icons as sites of sacred revelation in a way the West has not fully embraced, and that has, in turn, left the Orthodox rather cold on Western image traditions. As for the Protestant-Catholic divide, Protestants' exit from the Catholic Church was announced with acts of iconoclasm intended to symbolize and enact the purification of the church. In the sixteenth and seventeenth centuries, Protestant mobs shattered stained glass images of saints, tore down and mocked crosses and crucifixes, and vandalized paintings. Since then, Protestant churches have developed a range of positions on images, but a suspicion of the role of images in worship is generally a distinctively Protestant (and often anti-Catholic) impulse. More than other Christians, Protestants worry about the temptation to idolatry, about the subtlety of difference between image and idol. Catholics, meanwhile, remain as a group much more sanguine about images. Not only do images fill Catholic churches, but canon law even requires some of them—the empty cross, the crucifix, and the stations of the cross.

Even today, these various Christian churches do not agree on the role of images in their life together as the people of God. Differences persist in twentieth- and twenty-first-century theology. While Catholics like Hans Urs von Balthasar and Pope Benedict XVI have insisted on the indispensability of images to Christianity, Protestants like John Howard Yoder and Robert Jenson have called for continued iconoclasm as a form of fidelity to Christ.[11] Meanwhile, those like Leonid Ouspensky and Paul Evdokimov in the Orthodox tradition have defended the importance of holy icons by opposing them to what they call *Roman art*.[12] The image marks the distance of these ecclesial families from one another.

Here, then, is one reason the us-versus-them picture of images cannot be sustained. It presumes a more unified *we* in the Christian and post-Christian Modern West than exists. *We* who live in a world shaped by Christianity are much more plural than a simple opposition to "unassimilated" Islam implies. *We* include image worriers, image lovers, and icon venerators. *We* admit a range of practices and attitudes toward the image.

But there is a still more fundamental problem with this opposition, one centered on what an image is. The problem is not just that *we* both affirm and negate the image. The problem is also that the image negates itself. Negation is internal to how images mediate to us the presence of the imaged. To put the point more polemically, I claim that images possess an iconoclastic structure: From negation, presence.

Image and Likeness

What counts as an image? Or better: how does something become for us an image? To illustrate how I am using the term *image*—and ultimately defend my claim about the iconoclastic structure of imaging—I propose we imagine a small child who has recently mastered the art of holding tools for drawing. Our child picks up a yellow crayon and presses it against a piece of construction paper, running it back and forth across the paper's rough surface, exploring the materiality of her medium and coating the sheet with the waxy residue of her efforts. As a wonder-driven experiment with new media, these yellow scribblings are not an image. They are a picture. They are not an image because they do not signify something to the child but simply mark her delight in making—for the moment. Soon an adult approaches the picture and begins interpreting it to the child. "What a lovely drawing! What is it? Have you made the sun?" The child observes the adult beaming her approval and agrees; she has made the sun. Now the picture has been negotiated in a new relationship, one that overlaps with but remains distinct from pictures. It has become for the child an image.

There are two aspects of this vignette that I want to highlight. First is the way the image is constituted in relation to a beholder. What is simply an object (yellow waxy residue) for one person or at one moment can become an image (of the sun) for another or at another moment. An object can become an image when a person's relationship to it changes. And as an object can become an image, so can an image become an idol, spectacle, token, or illusion—all deteriorations of the image I will explore in the chapters that follow. The image is never safe from the threat of degradation, for identities like idol and image do not inhere in a thing; they name a relationship mediated by communities, institutions, histories, and desires. One person's image is another person's idol.

The second aspect I want to underline is the specific difference between a picture and an image.[13] A picture becomes an image when it is an image *of* something. For, an image is first and foremost a type of sign, which a picture need not be. When a young child scribbles on a paper, her scribblings do not necessarily point beyond themselves. They are traces of the child's work with certain materials. But an image does point beyond itself; it has a signified. Any child's drawing is a picture, but as they grow, children learn to make images insofar as their pictures are *of* something. This is not to claim that pictures are failures or unrealized images. It may be the case that a work of great art, like the child's scribblings, is also a picture rather than an image. I mean simply to distinguish these categories of images and pictures, which form a kind of Venn diagram. In one way, an image may be said to be a certain kind of picture: a picture that is also a sign. But as there are pictures that are not images, so also are there images that are not pictures, for images need not be visual.[14]

While often visual, images encompass a highly diverse set of phenomena, including sound images. For example, onomatopes like *sizzle*, *slurp*, *beep*, and *hush* are word-images. That is, they are signs twice over, for they signify both as words and as images signify. As words, they signify as groupings of letters taken to mean certain things. One could say, "I slurp my lemonade," or "I drink with a loud, sucking sound my lemonade," and the meaning in both cases is, at one level, interchangeable. *Slurp* means "drink with a loud sucking sound" because that is what we take that grouping of letters to denote. But *slurp* has another, more visceral level of signification. It *sounds like* the action it denotes, and in this way *slurp* signifies in the same way images do: by its *likeness* to the signified.

Likeness to the signified is the essential and distinctive feature of images, distinguishing them from all other species of signs, including words and symbols.[15] It names at a broad level the relationship between image and imaged, and as a term, *likeness* accommodates considerable diversity. An image might bear, for example, the likeness of sound, as in onomatopes, or of a certain type of physical resemblance, as in most photographic portraits. Likeness of substance, person, and name have all been named by Byzantine image defenders (*iconodules*) in their efforts to distinguish image veneration from idol worship. Likeness is a capacious criterion for images.

For the Byzantine iconodules, likeness also signifies the presence an image bears. Each type of likeness corresponds to a distinct presence, and the type of presence an image bears justifies the attention or service given it. An icon is said to bear *hypostatic* presence (the presence of a person) because it is hypostatically like the imaged—so the ancient argument goes—and therefore worthy of veneration.[16] Because the photographic portrait of my mother bears a likeness to her we name "physical resemblance," her physical resemblance is present to me through the photograph. A presence of physical resemblance is much weaker than that of *hypostasis*, so while I treat my mother's photograph with respect, I would not, say, prostrate myself before it.[17] The various likenesses of an image correspond to the registers of presence it bears.

To claim the centrality of likeness to imaging raises the question of unlikeness. John of Damascus, the great seventh-century iconodule, describes an image as "a likeness and pattern and impression of something" that is, however, "certainly not like the archetype . . . in every respect."[18] Of course, an image cannot be like the archetype in *every* respect. If it were, it would be the archetype itself. It must be both like and unlike the archetype, for if likeness names the distinctive feature of imaging, unlikeness names the distinction between image and what John of Damascus calls archetype and others call prototype, signified, or imaged. Both likeness and unlikeness are essential to what an image is.[19]

For images, the structure of presence echoes the structure of likeness, which signals but does not exhaust this presence. As likeness appears in a stratum of unlikeness, so presence dawns in absence. In itself—in its own literal existence—the image is not this presence. The light-sensitive chemicals and glossy finish of the photograph, for example, are not the same as the presence of my mother. Her presence is other than these media. In mediating to me my mother's presence, an image gives more than it is. It confers a presence beyond itself. It mediates, that is, presence-in-absence. Absence, then, names the condition for the possibility of imaging.[20] The image presents what it is not, and in the presentation of the "is not," the "is"—the literal image—recedes.[21] This is the negation at the heart of imaging.

Here we come to iconoclasm. An image, to be an image, is broken open to mediate a presence beyond it. And this breakingness, this negation internal to the image, is homologous with certain iconoclasms external to an image. As many forms of external iconoclasm break images to insist that the images are not identical with divine presence, so the image negates its own literal existence so it can mediate a divine presence with which it is not identical. Many iconoclasts want to claim that the image does not circumscribe the divine, that the divine cannot be located in the image. But the image—when it is not functioning as an idol—also makes this claim in the way it negates itself to present the divine that it is not. When a person concerned about idolatry does not perceive that negation, she may respond with her own negation, an external iconoclasm.

Images need negation to be images. The negation at the heart of imaging is not an eradication nor an erasure. Neither is it a degradation of the image. It is a breaking open that leads to greater revelation. It is a way of saying images mediate presence-in-absence and likeness-in-unlikeness. When absence and unlikeness are elided, the image becomes an idol. This is a failure of negation, and without the negation, the image ceases to be an image.

The negation internal to the image becomes notably important in communities with a heightened anxiety about idolatry. In the Christian tradition, for example, many artworks dramatize the negation to accentuate the image's distinction from the divine it presents. Horst Bredekamp argues that it was through artists exaggerating the internal negations of images that Christianity was able to tolerate a tradition of image-making. In the teeth of a command not to make images, artisans justified Christian image-making by expressing that prohibition in the image itself. These images, then, communicate the iconoclast's critique. Bredekamp points to Niclaus Gerhaert van Leyden's fifteenth-century statue known as the Dangolsheim Madonna, created during a time of image anxiety.[22] In it, Mary looks down toward the Christ child, who holds the edge of Mary's head covering across her neck so that it cuts off her head visually, the way an iconoclast might sever it materially. The Dangolsheim Madonna internalizes and expresses anxiety about images by anticipating the critique of the iconoclast and so discouraging idolatry. The statue thus reminds the beholder that it is just an image, that it can be destroyed and so should not be confused with the heavenly Madonna and child, who are beyond the reach of the iconoclast's hammer. Just so the Dangolsheim Madonna works to render the negation of the image—the sense in which it "is not" what it images—highly legible. In attempting to stave off idolatry and external iconoclasm, it dramatizes the iconoclasm internal to the image. The negation of the image thus simultaneously chastens the image (it is not the imaged) and testifies to its power (it commands a dangerous authority).

Caroline Walker Bynum describes multiple medieval art pieces that work similarly. She describes, for example, Pietàs with a polished finish that "call attention ... to the stuff of which they are made" to "underline the paradox of life and death, grief and triumph, they manifest."[23] Looking at one such Pietà, the viewer is reminded by its glossy shine that it is an image, and in remembering it is an image, the person observes a theological commitment to life in not-life. God in Christ came by what God is not. And in emphasizing that it is not identical to what it signifies, the Pietà suggests the power of what it signifies, the divinity that cannot be reduced even to the most precious materials of the world. For another example, Bynum points to a cradle for a Christ doll. Shaped like a cathedral, the architecture of the cradle "announces that it is in several senses a place for the God-man, complicating what 'presence' means in a way it would take paragraphs of words to explain."[24] The negation of the object as purely a cradle or only a cathedral suggests the complexity of divine presence, the way that God can be present by different means and in various ways.

Such negations, then, do not deny the possibility of the image but respect and underscore those possibilities, resonant with the way apophatic language opens up words. These negations name an internal iconoclasm (a breaking) that makes an image an image. And there can be external forms of iconoclasm similarly faithful to what an image is. Such iconoclasm attempts to recuperate an image that has become an idol, as an image. Not all—nor perhaps most—iconoclasm falls under this description, yet iconoclasm that does remains an important mode of fidelity to images. For all images, to the extent that they image, invite the gaze to open to a signified beyond them. Images like the Dangolsheim Madonna call attention to what all images do: by their likeness, they mediate what they are not. This is what I have called the iconoclastic structure of imaging, and it is surpassingly revealed—as I display in the chapters that follow—in Christ the Image.

The Language of Iconoclasm

It may raise the hackles of some readers to see iconoclasm discussed appreciatively. Such appreciation may sound like heresy revival or unnecessary provocation. After all, why use the term *iconoclasm* to describe the structure of imaging? Is it not like arguing for a quasi-divine God? Why not just write of a negation or, better still, stick to the language of recession and *kenosis* that phenomenologists use to describe a similar feature of imaging? In fact, why not take a cue from those phenomenologists who disavow iconoclasm all together?[25] I cannot promise to soothe every reader's anxiety about iconoclasm, but I can assure readers that I use the term advisedly. There are some historical and etymological reasons for feeling less squeamishness about the term, and some modern-constructive ones for embracing it. First the former.

Iconoclasm is not an ancient term, nor even a Greek one. It first appeared as the Latin word *iconoclasmus*, used by a sixteenth-century writer trying to describe the actions of a ninth-century bishop. In the late eighteenth century, *iconoclasm* appeared occasionally in English to describe actions of French revolutionaries and certain Protestant groups, but it was not until 1953 that it was first employed to describe the Byzantine image controversy—and it has spawned a vast literature in the decades since.[26] The word *iconoclast* has a longer history. Its first recorded use is found in Greek in 720 (*eikonoklastes*), to rebuke a bishop, and it does have a place in the iconodules' literature. But the term Byzantine contemporaries most often used to describe the image controversy was *iconomachy*, the image struggle, a term more literally fitting to the controversy, which did not involve breaking images so much as removing them and legislating against them.[27]

When I invoke iconoclasm, then, I do not mean to straightforwardly identify with the Byzantine iconomachs. I intend to capture a sense of "breaking" an image, but I want to draw from the wide spectrum of cultural associations with the term. *Iconoclasm* is a complex term today, in part because the images iconoclasm targets have diversified and changed over time, from material and concrete images to increasingly immaterial and abstract ones. James Simpson has traced this evolution in the Anglo-American tradition in his book *Under the Hammer*, where he argues for what he calls the dynamic of iconoclasm.[28] Iconoclasm, as he displays, has an expansive appetite that moves from deposing images to exposing ideologies. The dynamic he traces sheds light on the use of the word today. Iconoclasm for most people names a wide set of practices, and I use it in keeping with that ordinary sense.[29]

As one example of the ordinary, capacious use of the word, *iconoclast* has become a sometimes laudatory term for someone who challenges entrenched beliefs or cultural institutions. Robert Mapplethorpe, for example, was an image-maker whose provocative photographs earned him the epithet iconoclast. And Pope Francis, when he washed what some considered the wrong feet on a Maundy Thursday—those of women, Muslims, and convicts rather than priests—was called by some an iconoclast.[30] These contemporary uses of iconoclast insinuate the way that making and projecting images can also break other culturally valorized images. In this use of iconoclast, the acts of making and breaking images can be coeval, just as in the case of the museum, protecting and muffling them can be. It is in this sense of iconoclast that I have set up this book as one kind of iconoclastic project—liberating us from a picture of us versus them that has held us captive—even as I attempt to resist other kinds of iconoclasm, like reducing the significance of images to verbal explanation, a project that is iconoclastic because it attempts to unmask images as simply imprecise words.

The popular use of iconoclast is important not just because it helps identify the ambivalences of iconoclasm. The description of an iconoclast as a breaker of cultural images—a blasphemer—is additionally important because it resonates with Scriptural descriptions of Christ as a *skandalon* or stumbling block (1 Corinthians 1:23).[31] These accusations of blasphemy leveled at Jesus by some of his contemporaries figure him as an iconoclast, in the modern sense that Mapplethorpe and Pope Francis are called iconoclasts. All three break cultural expectations and institutional mores. In some cases, iconoclastic breaking injures; in others, it renews. Distinguishing between the two is important, and I do not mean to claim all instances of iconoclasm as positive. Throughout this book, I will attempt to name and discern both iconoclasms of fidelity and iconoclasms of temptation. Retrieving iconoclasm in all its ambivalence lays the groundwork for making such distinctions, and for drawing lines of continuity between the way Jesus images the divine and the restorative forms of iconoclasm in our modern life with images.

There is another reason for using the language of iconoclasm. It helps to dissolve the us-versus-them narrative perpetuated against those we regard as our "others," notably Islam. In the days following the *Charlie Hebdo* attacks, millions gathered in Paris both to mourn these horrific shootings and to rally in support of the magazine and those who had died there. The discussion that followed in the streets and newspapers spilled over into a conversation among University of Chicago professors, hosted by the Divinity School's online forum *Sightings*.[32] Phenomenologist Jean-Luc Marion inaugurated the conversation, expressing his outrage at the *Charlie Hebdo* shootings by interpreting them not only as murder but also as themselves a kind of iconoclasm. The shooters attacked more than an image or set of images, though. For Marion, they attacked the French tradition of satire. Though careful to criticize the possible oppressions of what he calls "French-style secularism," Marion explains French society's support of *Charlie Hebdo* in spite of the latter's often offensive content by invoking the "fundamental and ancient trait of French society" to think and speak freely.³³ Thus he builds to a call for Islam to open itself to critique, that by which "religions demonstrate their excellence" and "[test] . . . their religious validity."³⁴ In this line of thought, the attack on *Charlie Hebdo* was uncommonly vicious because it targeted both individual citizens and also an institution that was part of making France *France*. Iconoclasm is located here in the attacks on the culturally important institution of free critique.

What interests me about this response is not the harsh condemnation of the attackers. That sentiment is broadly shared, well beyond French nationals. What intrigues me is the strong us-versus-them opposition that comes across in the article. Marion does not narrate a fight in which certain Islamic attackers respond to particular images. He describes a contest between France and Islam. The cartoon images stand for a culture that is distinctively French, such that to attack the image-makers is to attack France. And the attackers stand for an unassimilated Islam—an Islam that has not opened itself to critique or tested its religious validity, as have other, properly assimilated religions. Thus the us versus them emerges: *they* are the iconoclasts who have not opened themselves to critique. *We* are the iconophiles who make, permit, and circulate images under the banner of free speech. And so, Marion announces: "France is at war."

Two of Marion's colleagues at the University of Chicago Divinity School responded to his article. Bruce Lincoln and Anthony Yu name as the iconoclasts, not the Islamic attackers, but the *Charlie Hebdo* writers and cartoonists who attacked a religious icon. In their article for *Sightings*, they do not endorse *Charlie Hebdo*'s iconoclasm, which falls short of "courageous" iconoclasm. It mocks the weak, they claim, not the powerful.³⁵ It is one thing, they write by way of example, for *Charlie Hebdo* to mock the Pope; another to ridicule Muhammed. The iconoclasm of *Charlie Hebdo* amounts to "cheap bullying," for the cartoonists attack the cultural icon of a marginalized group within France.³⁶

In identifying the cartoonists as iconoclasts, Lincoln and Yu reframe the story around *Charlie Hebdo*. It is not just us (iconophiles) versus them (iconoclasts), for both writers and attackers operate out of iconoclastic impulses. And just as both are iconoclastic, so both are, contra Marion, *critical*. Lincoln and Yu point to Talal Asad as they claim critical self-reflection as internal to both Christianity and Islam—even as that tradition is differently expressed in each.³⁷ The hope is not to *equate* the iconoclasm of the cartoonists and those who attacked them but to call us into the murkier work of distinguishing the two more subtly, identifying the darkness, integrity, viciousness, and hopefulness in each. By seeing the ways that iconoclasm is internal to both Christianity and the Modern West, we can cease from using the label as an easy way to distance others. We have to reckon with our own iconoclastic impulses and sort through what we want to affirm about others' iconoclasm. For while Modern Westerners might laud the iconoclasm of Robert Mapplethorpe or Pope Francis, connections are not often drawn between their iconoclasm and the image crises of our times. We Modern Westerners hold them apart when we condemn the iconoclasm of Islamists.

In general, I admire Marion's work on images. Readers of his work and of the phenomenologists he has influenced will notice vibrant affinities between my approach to images and theirs—for example, in the way that images open to an excess beyond themselves. What Marion and other phenomenologists describe as recession is like what I describe as negation. Several other similarities will be highlighted throughout this book. But the way I most starkly diverge with this tradition is over the language of iconoclasm.[38]

Marion condemns iconoclasm as the inverse of idolatry. If the problem of our image-saturated age is, for Marion, that images become disconnected from their prototypes, iconoclasm simply entrenches this "tyranny of the image" more completely.[39] It reinforces the disconnection of images from the invisible, of icons from the face of God, by attempting to privilege the invisible and do away with images all together. Marion writes: "a number of religious movements have tended toward this radical response [that is, iconoclasm] . . . not only Islam or Judaism."[40] But iconoclasm is not, for him, the way of the church, which combats problematic forms of imaging with an iconic approach to images.[41]

I cannot help but wonder whether Marion's insistence that iconoclasm opposes true imaging, that iconoclasm is something external to the church, that it is found in Islam and other places outside the church, also funds his us-versus-them narration of *Charlie Hebdo*. It seems, that is, to become a way of splitting the world into us and those who ought to become more like us. One reason for using the language of iconoclasm, for insisting on iconoclasm's internality to proper imaging, then, is to resist the consolations such narratives offer.

Christ the Image

The approach of this book is to generate other, less consoling but perhaps more hopeful narratives of imaging. Rather than a problematic polarity of us (iconophiles) versus them (iconoclasts), I want to discern iconoclasms of fidelity and resist iconoclasms of temptation by reflecting on the ambivalences of Christ the Image. In this Image, the seemingly competing impulses of iconophilia, iconoclasm, and icon veneration are all affirmed, the differences separating the ecclesial families—on this one issue, at least—dissolved. Christ negates to reveal.

As the Son, Christ perfectly images the Father (John 14:9)—revealing the Father by saying *Not my will but the Father's*. The Son, that is, reveals the Father by effacing himself. The Son accomplishes the Father's will (John 5:36–38, 8:19, 28–9; Luke 22:42; Mark 14:36; Matthew 26:39, 42), establishes the Father's kingdom (Luke 11:2; Matthew 6:10), glorifies the Father's name (John 12:28, 17:1), and performs the Father's works (John 5:36, 10:32) and word (John 14:23). Like the Dangolsheim Madonna, the Son recedes—minimizes or negates himself—to reveal the Father. The Son's negation does not erase himself, for in effacing himself to reveal the Father, the Son ultimately reveals himself. When the Son says *Not my will but the Father's*, he not only reveals the Father; he also reveals who he is as the Son and what that Sonship means. In effacing himself as the Son, Christ fulfills his Sonship, revealing Sonship as the obverse of Fatherhood.[42]

This way that the Son images the Father sustains, in the incarnation, a new form of imaging—a new way that humanity can image divinity. In Christ, humanity reveals divinity by expressing the divine life of God. That is, in Christ's desires, possibilities, and *telos*, humanity expresses not only what it is (humanity) but also what it is not (very God). In Christ, humanity mediates a unique divine presence (one consubstantial with the Father), even though such presence is not circumscribed by Christ's humanity. In revealing divinity, Christ also reveals himself as the most perfectly human one. Humanity is negated in Christ, ordered beyond itself to reveal very God, and in revealing very God, the very human is also revealed. For what could be more human than to reveal God? The end of the Genesis 1 creation story implies that humanity was created to do just that, to bear the distinctive image and likeness of the divine throughout the earth. Thus, in the incarnation, humanity is negated—opened beyond itself as "mere humanity"—to reveal divinity and ultimately to reveal true humanity.

This negation-revelation dynamic comes more specifically into the orbit of the image conversation when it is cast in terms of likeness and presence. The Son is like the Father in having the same substance as the Father. They are, in the traditional language, *homoousios* or consubstantial, and they are more like one another than any image on earth.[43] But the Son is, importantly, not the Father. The Son is unlike the Father at the level of person, of *hypostasis*. Then, in another way, Christ (the God-human) is like the invisible God in that Christ is *homoousios* with the invisible God, but unlike the invisible God in that Christ is (also) visible. Or to put it in language redolent of the Council of Chalcedon: Christ is *homoousios* with Father with regard to his divinity, and *homoousios* with us with regard to his humanity. This "is" and "is not," "likeness" and "unlikeness," "presence" and "absence" that makes an image *image* is the negation at the heart of imaging, the negation that, in our life with images, translates into the centrality of iconoclasm to iconophilia.

This book probes that strange intertwining. Each chapter focuses on a creedal claim about Christ and a controversy or ambivalence around imaging to sketch the negations and presences of a Christological grammar of imaging. Woven with a textured account of our life with images, each chapter traces the way an image negates itself to give more than the image itself is. And in each of the chapters, Christ is the Image who limns the structure of imaging.

In Chapter 1, controversies around images of the nursing Mary—as well as images of art, pornography, and Muhammed—come into focus through the way Christ who was "born of the Virgin Mary" mediates desire.[44] This chapter treats Christ's *arriving* presence. Chapter 2 puts the image concerns of the Byzantine iconomachs together with those of Walker Percy and Flannery O'Connor to consider the hybridity of the visible and invisible that characterizes and connects humanity, images, and the Christ who "came down from heaven and was made human." It ponders Christ's *abiding* presence. Chapter 3 traces several images and types of images—including paintings of the crucifixion, the photograph *Piss Christ*, the statue Cristo Negro, and the written lives of cruciform female mystics—together with Reformation iconoclasm, and illumines them through reflection on the broken Image who breaks false images, the Christ who "was crucified, suffered death, and was buried." It explores Christ's brokenness and breakingness, that is, Christ's *riven* and *riving* presence. Pulling together sundry forms of resurrection images—icons, representations of "the least of these," and images made without human hands—Chapter 4 reflects on the Christ who "rose again on the third day" to inaugurate a new relationship of the visible and the invisible. It meditates again on Christ's *abiding* presence. Then the fifth and final chapter focuses on an image of waiting and failing to wait for divine presence—Sinai and the worship of the golden calf. It reflects on two families of modern iconoclasm, which I call the Baconian and the Wittgensteinian, while working through the claim that Christ "will come again in glory." Revisiting the theme of desire, this chapter explicitly reflects on discerning iconoclasms of fidelity and iconoclasms of temptation in our life with images. It returns to Christ's *arriving* presence. The chapters thus form a chiasm of presence: arriving, abiding, riven and riving, abiding, arriving.

Reflecting on Christ helps us to reflect better on images, for the Christological grammar of negation and presence is the grammar of imaging, even if certain kinds of images disclose that grammar more clearly than others. In this book, I trace the grammar of all imaging by traveling deep into Christological claims. At times that means focusing on sacred images or even a class of sacred images (like icons), and at times that means surveying other kinds of images to see how the structure works there, too.

There are, then, several levels of argument about images at work in this book. The first maintains that iconoclasm is generally intrinsic to iconophilia, as negation is to revelation and presence. The second identifies a peculiarly modern thorniness to the entanglement of iconoclasm and iconophilia, generated by the institutions and cultural forms that shape image relationships in modernity. The third articulates the intertwining of iconoclasm and iconophilia represented by Christ the Image that is determinative for the Christian imaging tradition and echoed at some level in all images. The book treats all three levels of argument, though it spends the most time elucidating the third, for it is this third level that helps to make sense of the other two. The hope is to provoke reexamination of the global images crises of our day by also stimulating reassessment about the role of images and the unity of the church.

By tracing the way the image itself has an iconoclastic structure, I hope to articulate the intimacy of iconophilia and iconoclasm in such a way as to promote a fresher politics of imaging. By identifying the way iconoclastic and iconophilic logics are at work in Christology, I want to dissolve some of the ecclesial differences over images and propose an ecumenical hope—one that affirms a Catholic love for images, a Protestant anxiety about them, and an Orthodox priority of the icon. In affirming the fundamental impulses of these different communions and demonstrating the way these impulses need not conflict with one another, I hope these Christological reflections on images, iconoclasms, and iconophilias might open up conversation that works toward the unity of Christian churches.

Distinguishing iconoclasms of fidelity from iconoclasms of temptation is a nebulous task. Often the two look almost identical. I hope this difficulty nudges Christians from different churches to view one another's lives with images more sympathetically, to see both iconoclasms of fidelity and faithful images as aspiring to faithfulness to Christ the Image. In the end, I want to show strange depths to Christians' and Modern Westerners' lives with images. We are, perhaps, not exactly who we thought we were, and our complex identity cannot sustain an easy opposition with those who once seemed wholly other to us. I hope in the pages that follow to release us from the thrall of the distorted picture of ourselves as a monolith we can pit against others, by sketching several other pictures of the complexity of our life with images. A strong polemic about the iconoclastic structure of imaging energizes the chapters that follow, but it is one that I hope makes us strange and strangers kin in a way that prepares us for greater ecclesial unity and perhaps even goads us one faltering step toward earthly peace.

FIGURE 1. Lorenzo di Credi, 1459–1537, *Madonna and the Nursing Christ Child*. Pinacoteca, Vatican. Photo by Saliko. Public domain (Wikimedia).

1 BORN OF THE VIRGIN MARY
Arriving Presence

THE WOMAN IS FAIR and dressed modestly. Her head is covered, her hair pulled back, and her heavy dress obscures the contours of her body. In her left hand, she holds her breast, high, conical, and exposed to the nipple. Poised to nourish the plump infant on her lap, the breast occupies the woman's gaze and partially blocks the face of the infant, whose lips part to take it even as his eyes remain locked on the viewer. He is naked, and the generous folds of his large baby body testify to the quality of the nourishment he has received.

The image is Lorenzo di Credi's *Madonna and the Nursing Christ Child*, painted some time before di Credi's death in 1537. It is one of many visual depictions of *Maria lactans*, which became a popular subject beginning in the fourteenth century. Another, painted by Antonio da Correggio around the time of di Credi's, is *Madonna of the Milk* (1524). Set in the high contrast of a dim background and luminous figures, a dark mantle slips from Mary's shoulders as she finds an opening in her red dress for her breast, held by a hand that supports her breast without covering it. The infant for whom she holds the breast also exposes his nakedness as he opens his body for the viewer, letting the white blanket fall free to confirm his maleness.[1] With one hand on his mother's body, just above her breast, the infant turns his head to follow the reach of the other arm toward the naked cherub at his side. Perfectly at ease interacting with the angelic world, it seems the infant will nevertheless turn in a moment to receive life from the human one.

Madonna of the Milk is, following his painting of Mary Magdalene, Correggio's second depiction of a woman's exposed breast, and it is not his last. In the following year, he finishes a naked Venus and a few years following that, bare-breasted mythological figures of Danae, Leda, and Lucretia, as his corpus moves from mostly Christian to mostly Greek and Roman scenes. The two Marys' nakedness seem to make a way for Correggio to depict the nakedness of other women, a nakedness that is more complete and more sexually charged.[2]

By the eighteenth century, even as nude images had become more common generally, images of Mary nursing the Christ child had all but disappeared.[3] How and why *Maria lactans* disappeared is, like most histories, complex. An anxiety about nudity in painting is registered in the final session of the Council of Trent (1563), which expressed worry about the possibility of "lasciviousness" and "beauty exciting to lust."[4] Nearly 450 years later, in summer 2008, the Vatican newspaper *L'Osservatore Romano* ran two articles calling for the artistic rehabilitation of the semi-nude nursing Mary. The authors wanted to move beyond what they saw as Protestant-inflected anxiety that such images were unseemly.[5]

That same year, in December—the month that includes the feast days for the Virgin of Guadalupe, the Immaculate Conception, and the Nativity of Christ—the cover of *Playboy* in Mexico ran an image of a woman named Maria, set in front of a stained glass window, draped in a white cloth covering her head and partially exposing her breast, with one hand cupped toward the breast as if to point to it. The headline read, "Te Adoramos, Maria." Many Catholic officials and laypersons, including the president of the Catholic League for Religious and Civil Rights, publicly voiced offense. Playboy Mexico apologized but denied the image depicted the Virgin of Guadalupe or any other religious figure.[6]

∽

Reflecting on Correggio's Mary, writer J. M. Coetzee's heroine Elizabeth Costello remembers baring her breasts for Mr. Phillips to paint.[7] The memory is occasioned by an argument with her sister, Blanche, now Sister Bridget, whom she has recently seen for the first time since their mother's death. Sister Bridget is a religious of the Marian Order who administers the Hospital of the Blessed Mary on the Hill, called Marianhill, in Zululand. They argue about the Greeks and Sister Bridget's version of the Christians, who stand for humanism and anti-humanism, respectively. Elizabeth contrasts the beautiful bodies depicted by the Greeks and the Greeks' broad development of the human to the Gothic ugliness of the crucifix and the narrowness of vision she sees encouraged by Blanche. (Sister Bridget remains "Blanche" in Elizabeth's narration.[8]) The sisters part ways, with Blanche getting the final word, making a case against the Greeks based on their rejection by the people of Zululand and "ordinary people" the world over. Ordinary people want a god familiar with suffering and acquainted with grief, she claims.[9] Blanche maintains that if Elizabeth had put her hope in a different Greek, Orpheus instead of Apollo, she might have had a chance, but she lost because, in Blanche's estimation, she went for the wrong Greeks.[10]

A month later Elizabeth sits down to write a letter in reply to her sister's argument. Answering Blanche's charge that she has forgotten the Greek Orpheus, Elizabeth claims, implicitly, that Blanche has forgotten her Order's namesake, Mary. She tells a story aimed to depict and advance a kind of humanism found, not exactly in the Greeks but in the Greek-inspired Renaissance, and especially in the Renaissance interpretation of Mary. It is a story from a time when Elizabeth is much younger, though not quite young, a middle-aged woman who has borne two children. She recalls spending an afternoon with Aidan Phillips, a special romantic friend to her mother in old age. At her mother's request, Elizabeth is sitting for Mr. Phillips that he might paint her, to cheer him up after a throat operation. Unable either to paint or to speak, he puts down his brush and writes out his thoughts, telling Elizabeth that he would have loved to paint her nude. Elizabeth interprets this as an expression of discouragement at having lost his virility, his creativity, so she helps Mr. Phillips awaken his manhood by loosening her wrap, and like Correggio's Madonna, letting it fall about her to expose her breasts to him. He begins to paint. She calls this breast-offering a blessing, a gift of life in a place "of withering away and dying."[11] The blessing, she writes in her letter to Blanche, "revolved around my breasts . . . around breasts and breast-milk," and she locates the blessing she exudes both with Correggio's Mary and the model for Correggio's painting.[12]

The letter ends the story here, though there is more that Elizabeth does not write, even in this letter she knows she will never send to Blanche. The story picks up in a setting with which her sister is much more intimate than Elizabeth. It is a hospital, to which Mr. Phillips has returned after radiation treatment. He is shriveled, pained, and waiting for death. He writes a message thanking Elizabeth for the day he painted her breasts. Then for the second and final time, Elizabeth removes her clothes and exposes her breasts for him. She is less certain about this blessing, but it is what happens next that she feels she cannot tell Blanche. Unable to awaken his sense of his own virility at a distance, she begins to stroke his penis and ends up taking it in her mouth. How would the Greeks describe such an act? It is too grotesque for *eros*, she decides, and *agape* does not fit, either. She settles upon *caritas*, a word she recognizes as distinctively Christian.

Eros Literal, Literalized, and Anxious

What do these exposed breasts of Mary, Maria, and Elizabeth express? What divine presence is their baring supposed to bear to us? And what does it mean that these verbal and visual depictions of breasts communicate to many a desire besides *caritas*, that they convey some meaning other than their capacity to nourish the Christ-babe?

The argument of this chapter is that the Christ born of the Virgin Mary summons and negates—without eradicating—a literal desire, which then becomes more than literal. In this negation, literal *eros* is not replaced but rather opened, deepened to become the divine *eros* that bears the arriving presence of Christ to us. It bears to us the God who arrives naked into the exigencies and extinctions of human desire.

The human desire in which God arrives is Christ's, Mary's, and our own. The objects of that desire are likewise multi-layered. To describe this multi-layered desire and what it means to receive God in the midst of it, I develop a lexicon of desire, for which a few clarifying notes are in order. First, I use *desire* and *eros* interchangeably. I take these two terms as bringing into view disparate aspects of a single phenomenon. Both aspects are important: desire because it is the more ordinary term we use for wanting and loving in everyday life, and *eros* because it suggests that desire is a form of love. I use them interchangeably because I take this love and this wanting to be two faces of the same event.

If desire and *eros* sound more dissimilar than they are, the opposite is the case for two other terms I use—*literal desire* and *literalized desire*. The suffix marks an important distinction in the phrases, for *literal* identifies a good desire, *literalized* a perverse one. Literal desire, on the one hand, simply names desire for a material good, like sex, food, or sensual delight. It is a consumptive desire—an appetitive desire for nourishment or pleasure that terminates in its consumption of a good. To call it a good desire is to affirm its importance for the life of a material creature and note its capacity to open up and become a desire that is more than literal. To call it good, then, is not to claim it is virtuous or noble, any more than one might call hunger virtuous or noble. Literal desires like hunger are good because they maintain material life, but their character is undetermined. Literalized desire, on the other hand, is definitively vicious. It carries a negative valence, for it names desire that has been reduced to or equated with its consumptive forms; it is desire that forecloses or attempts to foreclose any non-consumptive meanings. Literalized desire is literal desire that has been disconnected from the non-literal, or from any end other than gratifying the one who desires. It attempts to cut off pleasure and sensory gratification from any higher good.

That pleasure and sensory gratification can be ordered to higher goods implies a further distinction, between literal and non-literal forms of desire. This distinction corresponds to something like the traditional literal and non-literal meanings of Scripture. The non-literal meanings of desire refer, that is, to a spiritual sense, which finds its most robust form in desire from and for the divine—though non-literal desire, too, may go astray, as Chapter 5 explores. And as in the interpretation of Scripture, so with the hermeneutics of desire: much hangs on the configuration of the literal and non-literal senses. Does the non-literal extend and augment the literal? Or displace it?

The Christ-babe of *Maria lactans* arrives amidst desire that neither reduces to the consumptive nor leaves it behind. Literal *eros* is not eradicated, and neither is non-literal *eros* sundered from the literal. The arriving Christ negates, without ever being sanitized of, literal desire. This is what makes *Maria lactans* a source of anxiety: it figures together the desire for nourishment, pleasure, and the divine. Images of the Christ-babe nursing at Mary's breast suggest the slipperiness of desire that feeds the anxiety threaded through the string of vignettes I beaded together—an anxiety about communication, about saying and being heard rightly, showing and being rightly seen. It is a worry about exposure and failure and the costs of success. The anxiety is made explicit in the ending of J. M. Coetzee's short story alluded to earlier, "The Humanities in Africa." Elizabeth Costello writes a letter she knows she will never send. She writes it, anyway, for the words will not come unless she mentally addresses them to her sister, Blanche.

After she ends the letter, Elizabeth continues the story of the second breast-baring as she speaks to Blanche in her head, but when she arrives at the end of that story, she has blocked Blanche from sharing her remembrance. The memory continues without further audience. At last hitting upon the word *caritas* to describe her action, Elizabeth knows the word is right by "the swelling in her heart," even though she realizes that what a nurse or her mother would see if they were to walk into Mr. Phillips's room right then would bear an "utter, illimitable difference" to that feeling in her heart.[13] That the difference cannot be overcome by transforming the visual image into a verbal one is implied by Elizabeth's decision to end her mental address to Blanche. If the difference does not correspond to the difference between visual and non-visual communication, neither does it correspond to the difference between the perception of the event by others and the perception of the event by herself. For Elizabeth worries most, not about what others might make of the event, but what she will make of it when she leaves the hospital, when it is the next day or week or year. "What can one make of episodes like this, unforeseen, unplanned, out of character?" she wonders. "Are they just holes, holes in the heart, into which one steps and falls and then goes on falling?"[14]

She does not want to fall. Where is someone who can prevent such a fall, who might even mend her heart's hole? She turns back to the memory-figure of her sister. "*Blanche, dear Blanche . . . why is there this bar between us? Why can we not speak to each other straight and bare, as people ought who are on the brink of passing? . . . [O]f the world we grew up in, just you and I left. Sister of my youth, do not die in a foreign field and leave me without an answer!*"[15] It is on this desperate plea, this unfulfilled desire to make herself known and so know herself without holes, that the story ends. She has groped for something— expression? recognition?—that she has not found.

Desire, whether we name it *eros, caritas,* or *agape,* leads us into versions of ourselves we do not know and are perhaps afraid to know. In the desire she expresses and inspires, Elizabeth Costello finds a vulnerability that renders this desire still more precarious: our selves are known through others who might misunderstand (or too fully understand) what we are expressing. Perhaps it is better to silence those desires and live with our opacity. Elizabeth never sends the letter, nor does she finish it. Rather than risk the exposure of her desires, she chooses death in a foreign field without an answer.

Elizabeth performs a certain kind of iconoclastic response—one that attempts to curtail the contingencies involved in expressing desire by truncating the expressions themselves. She enacts an iconoclasm of temptation, a fear-governed attempt to suspend the presences an image might loose into the world.[16] The slipperiness of desire generates in her an anxiety similar to the Tridentine and the Protestant worries about images that excite lust and cultivate desire for shameful activities. In the end, Elizabeth suppresses her memory-image and stifles even her desire to know her own desire. She eliminates the possibility of exposing her shame by eliminating the expression of her desire.

Even though she has some hope that exposing this image of herself might lead to some healing, she conceals it instead, fearing it will disappoint her. She hides herself in despair. Thus is her response an iconoclasm of temptation: she suppresses an image out of fear that it might not do what she hopes; she denies desire and its ambiguities.

(We readers of Coetzee's story can only wonder what Sister Bridget, well-educated anti-humanist that she is, might have made of Elizabeth's story. Would she have recognized in it the ancient tale *Caritas Romana*, in which a woman secretly breastfeeds her father who has been jailed and sentenced to starvation? Would she remember the way Caravaggio, centuries later, interprets this daughter's action as exemplary of one of the corporeal works of mercy in his painting *The Seven Works of Mercy*? And the way John Steinbeck also recalls the story for his final scene in *The Grapes of Wrath*?)

I hope to show how iconoclasms of temptation are misguided, unfaithful even. They cannot achieve what they want to achieve, and they betray both the commitments of Christ the Image and the desire of the iconoclast herself. Still, it is also important to acknowledge the truth of these iconoclastic impulses: that expressions of desire can get away from us, that desires can literalize (and idolize) when they should open to the divine. The slipperiness of desire, after all, means desire can turn both toward and away from the divine.

The histories surrounding *Maria lactans* expose our temptation to avoid living with the slippery vitality of desire—our temptation to deny the erotic or literalize it. When we deny literal desire, we enact an iconoclasm of temptation. When we literalize desire, we relate to the image as an illusion that is both more and less real than the prototype. Both responses attempt to protect our independence, our autonomy, by denying the way our desire makes us dependent upon life beyond us. This chapter traces those temptations, and it marks the path *Maria lactans* illumines through them at the level of church doctrine, philosophical commitment, and life with our modern image-serving institutions. First I ask: What renders *Maria lactans* so fitting for helping us navigate desire? The answer begins with the breast.

Why Breasts? Lovers and Mothers

In fourth-century theologian Gregory of Nyssa's hagiography of his older sister, Macrina, Macrina's breast takes a curious, prominent role in the narrative. Most of the *Life of Saint Macrina* tells the story of the death of Macrina, as

Gregory stages a tableau of her dying. Macrina is surrounded by religious sisters mourning the loss of their spiritual mother and founder of their community. After she dies, one of them, Vetiana, works with another sister to prepare Macrina's body for burial and lays bare the breast of their venerable teacher and founder. The two women interpret Macrina's body to her brother Gregory, who in turn interprets it for the readership of the hagiography. As she exposes Macrina's breast, Vetiana draws Gregory's attention to a small scar. It marks the former location of a cancerous growth, dangerous both to cut out and to let spread. Vetiana tells the story of that scar: Macrina had resisted treatment because it would require unclothing her breast before a physician. Against her mother's desperate entreaties and arguments about God's gift of medicine, Macrina determined she would rather be ill than bare her breast to a strange man. The story, at this point, might sound like a story about another iconoclasm of temptation, about fearing to expose what might be misunderstood. But then it takes another turn.

Macrina mixed a salve of prayer-born tears and mud onto her affliction and asked her mother to make the sign of the cross. Without exposing Macrina's breast even to her small community of religious sisters, her mother placed her hand inside Macrina's robe and signed the cross. The tumor disappeared, and Macrina's breast remained unseen until Vetiana exposes it to Gregory, who exposes it through his literary descriptions to his readership. When Macrina's body is later covered again, in the dark mantle that had belonged to her mother, her body glows divinely from beneath the robe, hidden no more.[17]

Of the two major ways that breasts embody dependence and the slipperiness of desire, Macrina declines one and embraces the other. To demur the possibility that her breasts might elicit sexual desire, Macrina turns to her mother, whose own breasts were the object of Macrina's infant desire. She asks the woman whose breasts gave her life to restore her to the fullness of life by healing her own breast. Macrina's response to her cancer draws attention to the life that comes from beyond her—from God, of course, but more materially, from her mother, whose role in the story underscores Macrina's vulnerability, her need of another. Even though her mother dies years before Macrina does, her presence at Macrina's death is signified by her mantle, through which Macrina's luminous body shines in testimony to the God Macrina names her Bridegroom.[18] Her refusal to bare her breast to a strange man is, as she sees it, an act of fidelity for this Bridegroom, whose light finally illumines her body for all to see.

Breasts draw attention to our dependence upon mothers and lovers. They recall both the infant's desire for nourishment and the sexual desire of adults. In both these ways, they remind us of our vulnerability to a life and love that is beyond us. To try to receive a divine presence that comes to us in and as desire is to expose ourselves, like Macrina, like the Christ-babe, to the contingencies of desire. It is to realize our dependence upon others, to refuse the illusion of total sovereignty. Breasts expose our exposure. That we desire means that we can be destroyed.

In what follows, I illustrate the multiple meanings that cluster around the breast in order to prepare for further exploration of why the Christ-babe's need of Mary's breast can be so unsettling and yet so crucial to Christ the Image. This is both an attempt to give an account of the rise and disappearance of *Maria lactans* and an attempt to come to terms with the proliferation of meanings around the breast and its significance for our life with images.

A Thumbnail Sketch of Shifts in Cultural Meaning Around Breasts

In the Scripture called both the Tanakh and the Old Testament, one of the names for God is El Shaddai, the "God with breasts" or "God who suckles."[19] It is an early indication of the intense cultural significance of breasts, one presented visually in the sacred statues of gods covered in breasts in some ancient cultures, like the famous Artemis of Ephesus statue.[20] But there are two meanings of *suckle*. The mother suckles the infant when she feeds him from her breast, and the infant suckles the mother when he feeds from her breast. Images of *Maria lactans* highlight the less obvious interpretation for El Shaddai. In them, God suckles creation, not by giving life to the world, Artemis-like, through divine breasts, but by suckling the breast of another, receiving life through the milk of a human mother. As *Maria lactans* makes plain, God does not just give sustenance as Creator; God also needs nourishment as a creature. The God who suckles the world suckles Mary. Images of *Maria lactans* reinterpret for Christians what it means that they worship El Shaddai.

It seems unlikely any of the painters of *Maria lactans* thought of themselves as reinterpreting their religious and cultural heritage in this way. Theological discussion of the history of religions was not exactly the context from which they painted. Their more immediate context in high medieval Florence—and Europe more generally—was governed by its own local concerns, two of which likely influenced the rise of *Maria lactans*: food shortages and wet nurses. The images of *Maria lactans* appeared as anxiety about childhood nourishment and maternal intimacy were on the rise.[21] Crop failure compounded by waves of the plague disrupted the food supply and exacerbated malnutrition. For the lower classes especially, hunger was everywhere, and children were ill-fed. At the same time, maternal breastfeeding had declined among the upper classes. From the year 1300, records of contracts with *balía* (wet nurses) increased among the wealthy of Florentine society, the very context into which painters of *Maria lactans* were born.[22] It may be, then, that the prevalence of images of *Maria lactans* express a longing for maternal intimacy that the artists did not themselves know, or for a stable food supply that could nourish Florentine children into the chubby health the Christ-child enjoys.[23] That it is Mary's breasts that express these desires and anxieties links physical nourishment and human intimacy with the divine—a strong connection that continues as the Middle Ages end and the Renaissance begins.

As the church lost its role as the dominant commissioner of images, it also lost its grip on the cultural narratives around breasts—a loss registered as artists depict breasts other than Mary's. The naked breasts of mythological figures like Venus, Diana, Europa, and Io appeared in paintings, not as sources of nourishment but as evidence of these women's physical perfection. These Renaissance breasts were more naturalistically and less symbolically rendered than the breasts of the early and high Middle Ages. The new anatomy textbooks also depicted the breast more naturalistically, as a scientific interest in the breast and the human body more generally grew. As the breast was increasingly secularized, the church that had once commissioned so many images of the bare-breasted Mary articulated in the last session of the Council of Trent (1563) a worry about inappropriate images and lustful beauty.[24]

By the time of the French Revolution, the breast was so thoroughly secularized that it could be aligned with the emerging secular nation-state over and against the *ancien régime* of the church-authorized crown. One of the most famous images of the French Revolution, Eugène Delacroix's *Liberty Leading the People*, allegorizes Liberty as a bare-breasted woman waving the flag of the French Revolution as she marches over the corpses of fallen fighters. Though the painting dates from 1830, it draws on a tradition dating to the Revolution itself, when the allegorical figures of Reason and Liberty merge into Marianne, who, with one breast bared, figures the new republic by 1793. As the body and physical health become a metaphor for the health of the state, the bare-breasted allegorical female rallies political energies in France and beyond, and the breast begins to bear political meanings.[25] Its role in nurturing young life in a family is connected with nurturing the life of the state.

The political significance of the breast has not disappeared, though it has receded in the present situation in the United States, where the breast carries primarily sexual associations. Or perhaps it is better to say that the politics of the breast have focused on the politics of women's sexuality. In 2012, a *Time* magazine cover tapped into current cultural anxieties around the breast by featuring a twenty-six-year-old model and mother nursing her three-year old son, both of them looking directly at the camera.[26] Both the visual cues of the photograph—the selection of a model as the representative nursing mother, the body-skimming clothes in which she is dressed, the way mother and son are posed standing, their bodies pressed against one another—and the shrill reaction it elicited insinuate the dominance of the breast's sexual meanings.[27] And the breast is regulated as a sexual object. In some places, public breastfeeding is still forbidden or frowned upon, even as lingerie stores display ten-foot posters of cleavage in their windows. Where and to whom do breasts belong?

Though the sexual meaning of the breast dominates today, it is not the only cultural meaning, nor is it necessarily divorced from other cultural meanings. Sigmund Freud inaugurated a discourse that contributed to both the dominance of the sexual meaning of the breast and the connection of that meaning to other meanings. By claiming the child's relationship with the breast as the prototype of all later sexual relations, psychoanalysis proliferated the breast's meaning in a way that connected the breast's sexual, maternal, and religious significances, even as it elevated the sexual valence of the breast as its most fundamental meaning.[28] In breastfeeding, according to psychoanalysts like Melanie Klein, the child comes to recognize the mother's body as distinct from his own, and with the cessation of breastfeeding, the child experiences the loss of the breast as the loss of paradise, an ejection from the Garden of Eden. Not only are the maternal and the sexual connected in this discourse; so are the religious and the secular.

In the psychoanalytic tradition, the desire for the divine, for the mother, and for the lover all intertwine with one another, as pleasure, nourishment, and security mingle. In this, the psychoanalytic tradition resonates with the theological tradition communicated in *Maria lactans*—though the two traditions diverge over how to understand the nature of this mingling and which desire is primary.[29] If these traditions are right about the intertwining of desire, then it is difficult to see how divine desire can be excised from the desire for mothers and lovers without mutilating it. These literal desires for nourishment and pleasure inaugurate, figure, and fund desire for the divine. They teach us how to desire the divine and make our own divine desire intelligible to ourselves. We are, as divine desirers, acutely dependent on our desire for mothers and lovers.

Desire is slippery. It is plural. One desire slips into the next, and exposes our powerful dependence in the world. The breasts of mothers and lovers remind us of that dependence. And so it is unsurprising that attempts to deny the dependence of divine desire often entail a denial of a mother, who figures our dependence to us.[30] To illustrate thought gripped by the denial of desire and its plurality—and the mother as one symbol of that plurality—I turn to one premodern and one modern example of mother denial. These mother denials attempt to shield the denier from the ambivalences of desire by sundering literal from non-literal desire.

Nestorius's Mother Denial

Early in Christian history, some Christians attempted to secure divine desire from the perils of literal desire. Nestorius was one such Christian, and his efforts resulted in the heresy we today name Nestorianism—the denial of the Mother of God. (Nestorius might retort that he denies only that Mother of God is a thoroughly appropriate term for Mary.) His uneasiness about divine desire places Nestorius in good heretical company, though the iconoclastic form his heresy takes is more distinctive. Many heresies affirm something about Christ the church deemed incorrect. Nestorianism is a heresy that denies something about Christ the church deemed correct. Nestorius, that is, became a heresiarch because of his ambition to sanitize Christian speech of any possible misinterpretation. He worried that referring to Mary as the Mother of God might lead someone to believe that God's origin was in Mary—a false dependence of the divine upon the human. He stumbled into heresy as he tried to uproot it. It is another case of an iconoclasm of temptation, when fear overrules hope. The fuller story illumines what went wrong.

One important context for Nestorius is the centuries-prior dispute over Gnosticism. Incarnational anxieties, expressed as worries about Christ's dependence upon Mary, are famously recorded in Irenaeus's second-century reply to those he names Gnostic, those who claim Christ only "passed through" (*dielthen*) Mary, like water through a tube.[31] Such a "passing through" displaces the birth that would have marked Christ's humanity, thus generating a disjunction between what Christ appears (human) and what Christ really is (divine). To "pass through" Mary became a way for certain thinkers to express Christ's divine intactness, his self-sustenance, his independence from all of creation, including his mother. This Christ is *docetic* (from *dokein*, "to seem") becomes he only seems human, whereas his true nature is divine. Even as a fetus, the docetic Christ did not need Mary; she was simply the pod by which he entered the world. Irenaeus, by contrast, wanted to affirm that Christ truly took flesh from Mary in order to truly recapitulate perfect humanity. He was less worried than those he attacked about describing God's mingling with creation, both because he did not believe matter to be evil and because his imagination of divine possibility was more expansive.

A few centuries after docetic Christologies were deemed heretical by most Christian churches, a dispute over naming Mary erupted into a new Christological controversy. It began when Nestorius was named Patriarch of Constantinople, and he determined to bring the "hammer of orthodoxy" down on heresies.[32] Did he imagine himself to be a kind of fifth-century Irenaeus, with the power of the patriarchate to supplement the power of the pen? Did he dream of securing the church from the danger of heresy? Did he think it possible to eliminate any whiff of heterodoxy? It seems clear, at least, that he arrived in his new seat in Constantinople ready to clean house. He began by moving against the Arians, a group already officially anathematized. Nestorius set about planning the demolition of the last Arian chapel in the city—an apparently dangerous move considering the Byzantine army's reliance on Arian German mercenaries to defend their northern borders. It was also a move that earned him the nickname "Torchie."[33]

Nestorius found himself in the midst of the controversy for which he was to become infamous as a heresiarch when he was asked to mediate a dispute between two factions, one monastic and the other possibly led by Nestorius's chaplain Anastasius. The monastics were under fire for their practices of venerating Mary as *Theotokos*, the Mother of God. Those attacking them insisted that Mary was properly *Anthropotokos*, the Mother of the Human, for God pre-existed Mary even though the humanity of Christ was indeed birthed by her. In a private meeting with both parties, Nestorius claimed that either title for Mary could be interpreted in an orthodox fashion and that neither party's claim that the other was absolutely heretical was correct. However, he claimed that "strictly speaking" (*akribos*), both titles were inaccurate and capable of generating heretical thought. "Strictly speaking" was apparently a verbal tic of Nestorius's that, according to John McGuckin's descriptions, defined his distinctive style, which exuded an anxiety for "semantic exactness."[34] Such verbal scrupulosity occasioned his downfall.

In this case, Mother of God was not *strictly speaking* accurate, Nestorius believed, because Mary did not give birth to God but to the human recognized as divine and thus called God; Mother of the Human was not *strictly speaking* accurate because it could be taken to mean that Mary gave birth to a *mere* human. Nestorius thus proposed a third term as a compromise that satisfied his criteria: *Christotokos*. This term was in every way accurate, and could generate, so he claimed, no heretical interpretation, for it located Mary's motherhood specifically in the event of Christ, who was himself both God and human. The term *Christotokos* was supposed to eradicate the possibility of heresy. Where *Theotokos* might suggest God's dependence upon Mary, as if God were drawing life from her, *Christotokos* was safe from such construals of the divine. Nestorius worried about the term *Theotokos* not because it was false but because it might loose into the church false ideas about God. His worry about *Theotokos* is thus another iconoclasm of temptation, a temptation to secure Christian speech and worship from potential misuse or misinterpretation. Could naming Mary as God's mother verbally compromise God, leaving God exposed to misconstruals? Could it lead worshipers to believe that divinity found its origin in Mary, that God in God's divinity desired, even needed, a mother? In a way, Nestorius's anxiety is not unlike Elizabeth Costello's: a worry about how communication exposes a person to a desire that gets away from her.

Far from settling the dispute, Nestorius opened up what would become one of the most acrimonious debates in the history of a faith tradition that is not short on acrimonious debates. It was fought through sermons and public lectures and letters (including letters to the pope), and it ended with the man determined to rid Constantinople of heresy being himself exiled as a heretic. The monastic faction interpreted his refusal to endorse Mary as *Theotokos*—a refusal that escalated into an injunction against *Theotokos*—first as a denial of her Son's divinity and then as an attempt to split Christ into two subjects.[35] At one point, Nestorius's main opponent, Cyril, associated him with the docetic heresy by pointing out that Nestorius claimed God "passed through" Mary.[36] The word Nestorius actually used was not the Gnostics' *dielthen* but *parelthen* (a term similar in sense, but without such a compromised history), and he was using it not to deny Christ's humanity but to protect (as he saw it) Christ's divinity. Nevertheless, the rhetorical blow was well-calculated. Nestorius became associated with a docetic queasiness about Mary, a discomfort with God's nearness to her. He has come through history as the one who denied God's Mother.

For Cyril, the urgency of affirming Mary as God's Mother was bound to the soteriological importance of affirming God's death.[37] For if one cannot rightly claim that God was born of Mary, then one cannot rightly claim that God died on the cross. And if it was not God who died on the cross, then how is that death salvific? The desire of God for Mary—for humanity—as an infant means that God becomes vulnerable to humans and their desires. God's desire for Mary means that God can die.[38] To depend on Mary is to desire her in some way, and to desire and depend on her is to be vulnerable to loss, to sadness, and ultimately to death.

It was Cyril who won the day. Nestorius's impulse to protect God from intimacy with the messy births and extinctions of human desires ended in his exile. *Nestorianism* came to signal the error of disjoining Christ's divinity from his humanity. It was anathematized in a series of councils and became an epithet used to discredit faulty Christologies, as seen in the way both the iconomachs and the iconodules hurled that charge in the Seventh Ecumenical Council.[39]

The story of Christian discomfort with the humanity of God does not end with Nestorius. Followers of Cyril also found a way to deny that God was subject to the exigencies of humanity, by claiming that the divine nature wholly absorbed the human one. Still later, the Julian heresy tried to affirm the incorruptibility of God's body. The orthodox response to these heresies was not just to reaffirm Christ's humanity in doctrine, but to develop a new liturgical image of Christ that also affirmed the fullness of Christ's humanity. Records at least as far back as the sixth century testify to the Marian icon *Galaktotrophousa* (Milk-Giver).[40] These images show Mary nursing Christ with a bared breast, similar to the *Maria lactans* of the Middle Ages and Renaissance. *Galaktotrophousa* is meant to affirm the full implications of Christ's birth into the creaturely world. Christ comes to us amidst literal desire and to deny those desires—to deny the Mother who was the first object of those desires—is to deny the full reality of the incarnation and undermine the hope of salvation.

Galaktotrophousa witnesses to a tradition that affirms that in Christ, the invisible God was birthed by Mary as an image, appearing to the world first as a bulge in a woman's belly. From a bulging belly to a full-swollen one, the *Theotokos* bore God into the world, laboring to give the infant God a life independent of her womb. As a newborn, God was not yet independent of Mary's body. For the next several months, God would grow stronger through the nourishment of Mary, her milk giving God human life. It was not only that God died at the hands of humans; God lived by them, too. God, who spoke and speaks the world into existence, God who was and is the eternal Word, could only gurgle and babble, dependent upon Mary to interpret and tend to the Divine One's human needs. As *Galaktotrophousa* displays: before the scandal of the cross, there was the scandal of the breast.[41]

Philosophy's Mother Denial

The scandal of the breast continues, even in our more secular age. However much we might see ourselves as having sloughed off the sexual prudery of early modern Europe, anxiety about desire and its slipperiness persists in the Modern West. The worry about desire rendering God dependent that haunts early Christianity's attempt to come to terms with God-in-Christ parallels an anxiety that characterizes much of modernity: a worry about desire rendering the human dependent and vulnerable. Anxiety about how desire can overthrow, wound, and open us remains central to the Modern Westerner's relation to images and the world. The iconoclasm of temptation that tries to uproot desire from our doctrine of God thus finds analogs in modern philosophy. Philosopher Stanley Cavell turns to Freud's descriptions of the loss of the mother's body to identify anxiety about dependence in the dawn of modern philosophy. Specifically, Freud helps Cavell to interpret the attempt to secure the certainty and reason of philosophy as pathological mother-denial, a refusal of our humanity.

One way that Cavell diagnoses the denial of the humanness of knowledge in philosophy is by turning to the plays of Shakespeare, that dramatist of modernity's birth pangs. For Cavell, Shakespeare's characters Coriolanus and Hamlet express a skeptic's disgust or disappointment with our (human) knowledge. Both believe their knowledge to be inadequate, to fall short of the certainty they desire. Their knowledge is not secure enough. Could Coriolanus's disappointment with the uncertainty of knowledge register the loss of his mother's body? Cavell rejects this directly psychoanalytic reading of the play.[42] Instead, he turns to *Hamlet* to draw out a more subtle relationship between philosophy and the mother's body.

Cavell reads *Hamlet* as a drama about separateness. We are separate from both the world and other minds because they are different from us. Knowledge of their existence is always vulnerable to the insinuation of doubt. To try to defeat this separateness is pathological; to come to terms with it, according to Cavell's reading of *Hamlet*, requires two kinds of acceptance. First it requires "acceptance of one's mother as an independent sexual being whose life of desire survives the birth of a son and the death of a husband, a life that may present itself to her son as having been abandoned by her."[43] To accept his mother as an independent, desiring person is to accept that her desire exists beyond funding his own life. Even after Hamlet's birth and his father's death, Hamlet's mother continues to desire in a way that makes clear she does not belong only to her son, that he cannot claim her and secure her presence for himself. Her life of desire exceeds him. Second, accepting one's separateness in the world requires "an acceptance of one's father as a dependent sexual being whose incapacity to sustain desire [Hamlet] cannot revive, which may present itself to his son as having to abandon him."[44] The death of Hamlet's father is the death of his own erotic claim over Hamlet's mother; he has neither the rights to her desire nor the ability to generate it, thus leaving Hamlet's own claim on his mother vulnerable to displacement. As Hamlet's mother's life of desire exceeds him, so Hamlet's life of desire exceeds his father. In his interpretation of *Hamlet* as the drama of the separateness of personhood, Cavell concludes that taking one's place in the world entails a kind of mourning or loss that comes from accepting one's parents as desiring persons. We live unsecured, and the desire of our parents points to the way their—and thus our—humanity is open, vulnerable, mortal. Desire coexists with what Cavell calls *separateness*, a condition that generates the possibility of what I refer to as *distance*.

To refuse to accept the separateness, the independence and dependence, of one's mother and father is to refuse the human condition in which we do philosophy. It is to deny, in a way, the humanness of philosophy—and to succumb to a Nestorian-like temptation. If Nestorius denied the Mother of God in order to safeguard the independent infinitude of God and secure Constantinople from the threat of heresy, Hamlet and Coriolanus face the temptation of denying the independent finitude of their mothers in order to secure their worlds from the threat of abandonment. And as Hamlet does not want to face a father subject to the exigencies and extinctions of desire, so Nestorius denied *Theotokos* in order to present God as free from desire. Hamlet's way of denying desire, though, is not to deny its existence but to deny the separateness of the object by reducing desire to its consumptive forms. Desire, for Hamlet, is that which assimilates the desired to the desirer (the mother to the father), such that one's desires need not lead to loss. According to Cavell's interpretation of *Hamlet*, to take one's place in the world is, in contrast to the desire that tempts Hamlet, to come to terms with both the persistence and the exhaustion of the human desires that fund one's own existence, even as the rolling and tumbling and ceasing of these desires may leave one feeling abandoned. It is to relinquish the fantasy that we can shield ourselves from loss. Modern philosophy that clings to the fantasy of such shielding, that attempts to secure the human against the world, etiolates desire by displacing the mother's body. As Nestorius's mother denial attempts to secure God by eradicating Christ's desires, those strands of modern philosophy that deny the mother attempt to secure the human by privileging a reason untainted by desire.

How can one find another way? How does one learn to reason *amidst* these unsecured desires? How does philosophy resist the temptation to mother (and father) denial? Cavell proposes that we learn to accept "having been a child" as the inescapable condition of philosophy, which means, among other things, that reason comes to us through and in desire, that we cannot secure reason from the losses and gifts of desire.[45] We might paraphrase this by saying that the condition of philosophy is having needed and desired the milk of another, or that it is having a mother. Reason is, in multiple senses, birthed from desire. We learn to reason because two people desired one another and gave us life, because we were desired and so nourished, because we desired that nourishment, and because we desired to know the world that we loved even before we understood it. As I will explore next, that desire is the condition of reason remains suppressed in much philosophy, naturalized in our (Modern Western) language of critique and in our relationship to images. We continue the Nestorian and modern philosophical projects of keeping desire at bay. In our life with images, we have found ways to maintain the illusion that we can remain insulated from the winds and waves of desire.

Blasphemy and Free Speech:
Images of Critique, Images of Consumption

The denial of the mother—and the suppression of the plural desire she symbolizes—is registered and naturalized in our Modern Western life with images, a life recently made more visible through a series of pitched image crises. Among these is the Danish cartoon controversy of the early 2000s. Caricatured images of the prophet Muhammed, published in 2005 by the Danish newspaper *Jyllands-Posten* and reprinted in 2008 by several other publications, inspired adverse and diverse reactions around the world, including peaceful protests, violent protests, violent threats, demands for an apology, and special Friday prayers. The flood of Western media reports that followed typically discussed the controversy over the images as one of blasphemy versus free speech, thus inspiring the co-written volume from Talal Asad, Wendy Brown, Judith Butler, and Saba Mahmood *Is Critique Secular?: Blasphemy, Injury, and Free Speech*, a book that probes ways in which the Danish cartoon controversy reveals the formations and commitments of Modern Western secularity.[46] Mahmood's and Asad's contributions are especially illuminating on the relationship of images to desire. They trace divergent—though ultimately complementary—roles of desire in Modern Western life with images: one where desire plays a minimal role, lest it compromise the integrity of the image relationship; and one where desire plays a dominant role, because the significance of that desire is curtailed. In other words, one strategy for containing the slipperiness of desire is for the image to deny desire; the other is for it to deny desire's plurality.

Mahmood traces the first of these, noting how the Modern Western imagination of images holds them at a distance from desire. She argues that the pervasive description of the Danish cartoon controversy in terms of free speech versus blasphemy entails a judgment about what kind of moral injury the publication of the cartoons caused and how that injury might be addressed. Relying on a semiotic ideology in which signs are arbitrarily linked to their signified, the Modern West codes the violation as blasphemy and so renders the cartoons primarily an offense against an abstract moral command.[47] But this analysis fails to make sense of the claim of personal injury and loss expressed by many (especially Eastern Muslims) in the wake of the publication of these cartoons. What loss do the mourners lament? Why do the faithful pray as if they have been hurt? These reactions do not express a violation against an abstract edict; they express the violation against a certain structure of affect. They witness to a "living relation" among faithful, image, and prototype similar to that described in Byzantine Christianity.[48]

The view of images as sharing a substantive relationship with both the faithful and the prototype is not the dominant one in the Modern West. Mahmood suggests that it is, perhaps, not even readily intelligible to many Modern Westerners. To the extent that the image and the prototype are understood to be linked arbitrarily, the image simply conveys information or misinformation about the prototype. There is no living relationship; rather, beholder, image, and prototype are three distanced nodes in an informational network. This distance, according to Mahmood, models a secular form of critique, one understood in opposition to religious belief, which lacks the distance critical rationality requires. According to this view, religious belief names the giving of oneself over to the nearness of desire; it identifies an irrationality that compromises the rationality of secular critique. Desire is critique's other; it girds religious extremism and aligns with what is "uncritical, violent, and tyrannical" over and against critique, which aligns with what is "tolerant, satirical, and democratic."[49] Thus the book title's question: Is critique (need critique be) secular? Are there other forms of critique? Or is religion hopelessly irrational? Is desire? In figuring the Danish cartoon controversy as one of religious taboo (blasphemy) against freedom of expression, Western media outlets assume affirmative answers to the last two questions. They write as if those Muslims who express injury from the cartoons are offended by the breaking of an irrational religious rule, as if they value that rule above the freedom of expression essential to democracy. Desire signals here an encroachment on democracy; it names what has been improperly disciplined by secular freedom, insufficiently displaced by rational critique. This desire identifies an image relationship that has gone awry. By contrast, the image relationship coded as rational and free by the Modern West operates as though religious desire compromises critique. In what follows, I call the images disciplined by these desire-minimizing formations of the secular *images of critique*.

One way of framing the exclusion of desire by images of critique is to see these images as iconoclastic in a certain way. In an essay introducing Mahmood's, Wendy Brown attributes this model of image, critique, and critical distance to Protestant Christianity.[50] Brown diagnoses Protestantism as offering a version of religious authority as "distant and command-based," and thus as generating this relationship to image, freedom, and critique.[51] We might interpret Brown's rather broad characterization of Protestantism as speaking to the Protestant anxiety about images that are held too close and loved too much, which can translate into a version of Protestant iconoclasm. The claims of blasphemy and free speech both derive, according to Brown, from a specifically Protestant way of viewing the world.

Asad's essay extends these insights by figuring both blasphemy and free speech as iconoclastic. He points out the way both blasphemy and critique attempt "to create spaces for new truth . . . by destroying spaces that were occupied by other signs."⁵² If, as Wendy Brown contends, secular critique is birthed by Christianity, then critique descends from blasphemy, for according to Asad, it was Jesus's blasphemous claim of divinity that began the movement. (Asad quotes Alain Cabantous: "blasphemy *founded* Christianity."⁵³) And this genealogical relationship between blasphemy and free speech redounds in their conceptual similarity: Like critique, blasphemy attempts to break other signs to clear the ground for new ones, and in this way, blasphemy and critique may be less polarized than they initially appear. They share a buried iconoclastic structure where they clear out signs and desires. Casting the Danish cartoon controversy in terms of blasphemy and free speech exposes Modern Westerners' own iconoclasm and the way it figures critique in opposition to desire.

There is another kind of image relationship in the Modern West, one much less concerned with excluding desire. Asad brings this image relationship into view as he excavates the commitments of the valorization of free speech in the Modern West. He interrogates the relationship between free speech and desire through the lens of Modern Western society's diverging attitudes toward rape and seduction.

In modern liberal society, rape is a serious crime but seduction—even the seduction of one pledged to another—is not.⁵⁴ Whereas rape violates the integrity of another by acting against her desires, seduction manipulates desires to align with an end of the seducer. The seducer cultivates the seduced one's desire. Because the seduced one's desires are coaxed rather than violated, seduction in modern liberalism is not a crime. Asad compares this understanding of seduction to that which existed in ancient Greece, which he characterizes as treating seduction as the more serious crime. Seduction, after all, claims the victim's affections as well as her body.⁵⁵ The seducer coaxes the seduced to open up his or her "innermost self" to the instruments of seduction (words, images, sounds) in order to lead the seduced, unwittingly, into ends of the seducer, thereby, for ancient Greek society, stealing something more valuable and difficult to recover than the rapist does.⁵⁶

Asad's point, as I take it, is not to claim that we should take rape less seriously than seduction. It is to point out how difficult it is for the Modern West to make sense of the harms of seduction. In the Modern West, a seduced person sustains no very substantive injury—at least, not in comparison to the conception of injury sustained by the seduced person (and that person's former beloved) in ancient Greece. It is this view of seduction and desire that is expressed in the Modern West's valorization of free speech. Protecting images under the banner of free speech suggests that whatever desire images elicit cannot do real harm to a person. Arousing and seducing desire is trivialized. Images that seduce are neither seen as violating a person nor conceived as constituting any real threat. That is to say, they seem not to imperil democracy; rather, they just arouse a desire that terminates in consumption of its object.

As Asad and Mahmood help us to see, there is an interesting ambivalence in Modern Western life with images. On the one hand, the constructed polarity of blasphemy and free speech insinuates the importance of maintaining a distance between image and beholder that is not compromised by desire: the image of critique. These are images for a reasoning public. On the other hand, the elevation of free speech as the banner under which images are protected communicates unconcern with the way those images may in fact work on desire. Because images' arousal of desire is not considered harmful, the public permits the second model of image and desire: the image of seduction. The image of critique eradicates or ignores desire; the image of seduction minimizes it (and its harms) by, as we shall see, literalizing it. The image of seduction often becomes the image of total consumption.

Where do these two conflicting images exist in Western society? What produces the desire-free image Mahmood locates at the heart of critique and the desire-manipulating image Asad locates in debates over free speech? I want to suggest that in the Modern West, these two types of images—or better, these two ways of relating to an image—are produced and sanctioned by different, though mutually reinforcing, institutions. They are produced and found in the institutions of art and pornography—including, in the latter case, pornography's kin, advertising.

Two Models for the Image in the Modern West: Art and Pornography

The two types of image relationship—critique and consumption—emerge from the two image models dominating the Modern West: the model of critical distance denies the erotic; the model of total consumption literalizes it. Both express anxieties about how desire threatens our sovereignty, with each offering divergent strategies for containing it. Disciplined through institutions like the museum and the academy, the model of critical distance, on the one hand, attempts to secure autonomy by denying or managing the erotic pull images might exert over a person. In the critical distance model, a person relates to an image as an object of scrutiny or disinterested contemplation. On the other hand is the model of total consumption, cultivated by institutions like advertising and pornography. This image model also liberates a person from the erotic force of image, not by denying but by literalizing it, so that it terminates in consumption. This model refuses the separateness of the image. The image is given for the beholder's consumption; its reality, its life, and its presence all move toward assimilation to the beholder. Thus, the model of critique refuses desire by insisting on distance; the model of total consumption literalizes desire by refusing distance. The slipperiness, the fullness of desire in both models is occluded. A person's sovereignty over herself remains unthreatened by the fissures of desire.

One way to tell the story of how these image models came to dominate the Modern West is through attending to the emergence and separation of the museum and the secret museum. The development of these two institutions and the forms of imaging they support—fine art on the one hand and pornography and advertising on the other—cultivate certain dispositions toward desire and distance in images. They are not always successful in their cultivations. Artworks can and frequently do overcome their institutional situations to elicit desire. Certainly images of *Maria lactans* can elicit multiple forms of desire, just as advertising images can provoke philosophy.[57] However, the place of images in the Modern West is disciplined by the pedagogy of desire and distance these institutions promote. In what follows, I want to probe the museum and the secret museum, art and pornography, as institutions that train us into certain relationships with images, that form us to regard images with certain types of desire or to engage them philosophically.[58] We begin with the modern histories of these institutions.

ART: IMAGES OF CRITIQUE

To many of us children of late modernity, the Council of Trent's worry that images like those made by Michelangelo or those of *Maria lactans* could "excite lust" sounds rather quaint. These images, after all, belong to the category of fine arts, a category for which the reaction of lust might seem absurd to many in our world. "Images that excite lust" look to us Modern Westerners like the image with the headline "Te Adoramos, Maria," on the cover of *Playboy* Mexico that incited such controversy. They are, that is, usually photographs rather than oil paintings; displayed in a form like a magazine, a DVD, or a computer screen, where they can be privately rather than publicly consumed; and purposed exclusively toward sexual arousal rather than entwined with any political or religious argument. However obvious that may seem to us now, the fine arts were disembarrassed of *eros* through a series of distinctively modern philosophical and institutional developments. Chief among the philosophical developments was the consolidation of certain arts under the rubric of the *fine* or *beaux* (beautiful) *arts* and an understanding of the emerging paradigm of disinterestedness. That is, the proper way to respond to these arts was understood to be a form of appreciation distinct from any benefit it might confer to the individual beholder. The art object here is not something to be needed or desired. It is not *for* the beholder. Her engagement with it must instead be disinterested, evacuated of desire.[59]

At the same time that fine arts were being delimited, the *aesthetic* was also being coined in modern language and elaborated in European (and especially German) philosophy. Paramount to the emergence of this category was the freedom of the imagination. Aesthetic perception (through which one engaged the fine arts) was located in the faculty of the imagination (or as Kant put it, in a free play between the imagination and the understanding), which grew in importance along with the categories of the aesthetic and the fine arts. The fine arts both presupposed and fostered the imagination's freedom, to the extent that they did not operate on erotic desire.[60]

These philosophical developments were promoted by two institutions, one new and one medieval, though much transformed in modernity. They are the museum and the university. The museum had a definitive moment during the French Revolution, when the revolutionaries discovered an alternative to vandalizing the images and icons of the old regime: neutralizing them by placing them in the Louvre, which was transformed from a palace into a museum. Thus, in 1793, a year after the revolutionaries' assembly voted to destroy all signs of the old regime, the Louvre Museum opened, muffling the political and religious claims of these objects while leaving them physically intact. *Art* named a category divorced from overtly political or religious agents, one that could be approached disinterestedly, apart from the agendas and desires of the beholder. Of course, it was nevertheless, as Mahmood's and Asad's essays on images and secularity indicate, a crucially political category. Still, art named a new way of relating to the public, distinct from politics and religion and set apart from *eros*.[61] As for the university, as it became increasingly independent of the church, it also promoted, produced, and proliferated secular images, like the anatomists' drawings of the breast. These were images for study, scrutiny, or contemplation—not for desire. Eliciting desire became the province of a new set of institutions purposed toward consumption rather than contemplation: pornography and advertising.[62]

PORNOGRAPHY: IMAGES OF CONSUMPTION

As the institution of the museum began spreading over Europe, secret museums also developed. The first-known secret room was recorded in 1795. At the Herculaneum Museum, room number 18 held "obscene" antiquities from the excavation of Herculaneum that could be visited only with a permit.[63] Pompeii's secret museum developed about three decades later and included erotic frescoes locked in metal boxes and available to gentlemen (and *only* men of the gentry) willing to pay a small fee. Mirroring this secret museum, the Secretum of the British Museum was officially created in the early 1860s to store materials deemed obscene.[64] The secret museum contains the pornographic that maps onto the "private" over and against the "public" of the rest of the museum's art and artifacts. In this way, the secret museum contributed to the creation of modern pornography as a visual form. But as a literary genre, pornography had been established for some time.

Before the secret museum, in the early decades of the sixteenth century, two new genres of writing were beginning to appear: propaganda pamphlets and illustrated accounts that would later be named "pornography." Initially, pornography did not primarily name a set of visual images. It named a type of narrative, set in brothels.[65] Called both the "father of pornography" and the "father of journalism," Pierre Aretino (1492–1556) trafficked in this written genre, while remaining disdainful about sexually or anatomically explicit images: for example, Michelangelo's naked figures in *The Last Judgment*.[66] Claiming his pornographic dialogue *Nanna* was more modest than Michelangelo's painting, Aretino deemed Michelangelo's figures suitable for a voluptuous bathroom, not the choir of the holiest chapel.[67] Aretino thus exhibits more worry about visual than verbal eroticism and a sense of propriety about where such eroticism is displayed. This "father of pornography" is unlike what we might expect of a pornographer today. Pornography had to undergo a few more stages of evolution before it arrived at its modern form.

In its early days, pornography was a self-consciously political and philosophical genre. During what some scholars refer to as the "golden age" of pornography, from 1650 to 1800, pornographic publications were referred to as "philosophical books," and they used sex to expose and attack perceived hypocrisies of the church, the crown, and other institutions of power.[68] The protagonists might be "freethinkers" whose actions and discourses critiqued sexual mores as well as religious doctrines.[69] This form of pornography, which presents the body as belonging to the individual rather than traditional institutions, constitutes a rhetoric persuading the reader of the freethinkers' claims for the autonomous, self-owning individual.[70] Pornography thus flourished for a time as a self-consciously political act, a rhetorical form that fit with the explicit arguments the freethinking characters made in these "philosophical books" of the seventeenth and eighteenth centuries: A person owns her mind by expressing beliefs condemned by institutions like the church; and a person owns her body by expressing with it similarly condemned acts. The sexual acts express sovereignty over oneself.

For a time, then, philosophical debates often went together with descriptions of sexual escapades. Things began to change around the same time the word *pornography* appeared in a modern language to describe a type of literature. In 1769, Restif de la Bretonne used the word *pornographe* (coined from the Greek *pornographos*) to describe writing about prostitutes.[71] In France in 1806, just a few years after the Louvre was established as a museum, a man named Charles Peignot used the category of pornography as a subset of "moral obscenity," as he was cataloguing and censoring books. He meant to refer to erotic literature that existed purely for the purposes of erotic arousal and masturbation.[72] As such literature proliferated, so, too, did obscenity laws, and by 1857, the *Oxford English Dictionary* included *pornography* among its entries.[73] As the museum was solidifying the category of fine arts, pornography was gaining its modern sense and being used as a category for culling certain books from libraries.[74] Pornography's purpose of erotic arousal meant that it shared little in common with the books of the library deemed fit for more contemplative and more cerebral forms of consumption.

By the nineteenth century, art and pornography named their own realms of images, distinct from the political and the religious. And they were near inverses of one another. Pornography was to be consumed; art contemplated. Pornography was erotic; art aesthetic. Pornography was private, while art was public.

New technologies helped carve out and sustain these distinct image realms. On the one hand, the printing press and the secret museum enabled private forms of consumption in which the category of pornography developed. The category of art, on the other hand, developed through the establishment of new public institutions like the museum and the opera house. In these public spaces, the beholder was encouraged to engage artworks with disinterested contemplation—a form of contemplation devoid of *eros*. While not identical to cognitive or intellectual contemplation, the disinterested contemplation of aesthetics is kin to it in its engagement of the imagination and understanding. Art, while not the same as philosophy, could be philosophical in the sense both of provoking philosophy and of engaging philosophical questions.[75] It achieved this philosophical nature by maintaining a critical distance from the beholder—a metaphorical distance symbolized in the physical distance between the museumgoer and the painting that she must not touch.

Pornography, which began as a form of critique, has since lost that function. Over the years, it was increasingly shorn of any purpose other than the creation and gratification of desire for pleasure. It required no ostensible social engagement, much less critique. In these ways, the pornographic image is both a mirror to and the inverse of the artistic image, which invites critical engagement, though in politically marginal locations. The artistic image is for contemplation; the pornographic, like the advertising image, is for consumption. Both pornographic and advertising images' desires terminate in the assimilation of the image to the beholder. While the art image controls desire by excluding it, the pornographic image controls desire by consuming the cause of that desire. It contains desire by assimilating the desired object to the desiring one.

This analysis of art and pornography speaks not to a quality that inheres in an image but to the institutional catechesis into an image relationship. It is not, in other words, that images produced as art and those sold as pornography cannot be read otherwise; certainly they can be and are. Aretino's judgment on Michelangelo is one example of an image produced as art and read as pornography. The claim here is that we Modern Westerners are trained by our institutions to relate to images as either images of consumption or images of critique—with either literalized desire or no desire. This is how, despite their differences, the advertising image is kin to the pornographic: they both catechize for consumption and arrest literal desire from its transformations.[76] Our social structures, reinforced by advertising images, teach us to separate desire and critique, protecting the latter from the potential irrationality and violence of the former.

But there is a significant tradition, dating at least as far back as Plato, of seeing desire and contemplation more fruitfully ordered. In this tradition where desire can open up into love of wisdom, the image can have a more complex role. And it is as a version of this tradition that *Maria lactans* yields to the beholder who yields to the arriving Christ.

Breasts and the Disjunctions of Desire

We return to Elizabeth Costello. Moved by compassion to reconnect the sick and dying Mr. Phillips to a sense of his own vitality, she bares her breasts as a Marian blessing to him. She understands this gift, which "revolved... around breasts and breast-milk," to be a way of conferring humanity on Mr. Phillips in a place of death. Yet Elizabeth remains torn between her confident claim of this act as a Marian blessing, as one of *caritas*, and another, unnamed description—the one that she worries would come more readily to the mind of a nurse who walked in or her mother or perhaps a later version of herself. That the alternative description remains unmade hints at the depth of Elizabeth's shame. It relates to the question of how to see her attempt to elicit *eros* from Mr. Phillips. Does Elizabeth write to her sister Blanche, as she claims, to refute Blanche's valuation of the "Gothic ugliness" of the crucifixion by claiming the life-giving beauty of the nursing Mary? Or does she write to Blanche, Sister Bridget of the Marian Order, who has spent her life in hospitals, because she is the one who might help Elizabeth understand her act as one of *caritas*? Might it be that Elizabeth momentarily hopes Sister Bridget can help her overcome the disjunction between the two descriptions of her desire, the one in which she participates in a kind of divine desire and the one in which she selfishly elicits sexual arousal from her mother's romantic friend? It seems to be this fracture that has created a hole in her heart. Can Sister Bridget, her sister Blanche, help Elizabeth beyond this break to find a language to mend it?

I have already named one discourse that overcomes the disjunction between desires: Freudianism. However, it does so by rendering sexual desire as the most fundamental desire—as primary both in the sense of being the first desire, in the proto-sexual life of an infant, and of lending other desires intelligibility.[77] Elizabeth would seem unmoved by this possibility for overcoming the holes in her heart; her rejection of *eros* as a grotesque description for what she has done also entails a rejection of a Freudian configuration of desire.[78] She wants to see her act as expressing a desire to bless her mother's romantic friend, not as performing a sexual desire born from infant desire for her mother. The quasi-deterministic descriptions of Freudian desire, further, seem to betray the self and the world she hopes for, where people lead lives worthy of humanistic inquiry. And so, rejecting *eros*, Elizabeth finds a fitting description in the word *caritas*, but she has no way to secure this description, no way to attach it firmly to her activity such that the nurse will see *caritas* when she walks into the room or even that she herself will see *caritas* when she looks back on the event in her mind's eye. Thus she worries that when the wave of desire that has carried her to that place with Mr. Phillips recedes, "the swelling in her heart" that tells her the description is right will also subside, proving to be an ephemeral feeling that cannot keep her description of *caritas* in view. Sister Bridget represents Elizabeth's hope for a community that can render *caritas* a more stable description, something more than a fleeting feeling. But Elizabeth has not the faith—in her activity, her sister, or herself?—to risk the shame of exposure. Elizabeth dramatizes a literal desire that can open onto divine desire, though it is not clear to her that it has done so, or how much it has opened, or how steadily. Is it literal desire tending toward openness to divine desire, or toward its own literalization?

Desire Literal, Literalized, and Divine

Images of *Maria lactans*, like Elizabeth Costello, represent and summon a literal desire that attempts to deepen into divine desire, and they do so in a tradition rich in resources for negating without eradicating literal desire. One common strategy of this tradition is to depict Mary's bared breast non-naturally—by painting only one breast on an otherwise flattened chest and by presenting that breast higher on the body than is natural and more geometrically shaped. This painterly trope is commonplace in medieval paintings and Orthodox icons like *Galaktotrophousa*, which communicate in a symbolic idiom and often occupy a liturgical space, perhaps near the altar. The very setting of the paintings—connecting Christ's feeding from Mary with the faithful's feeding in the Eucharist—presses a non-literal interpretation of desire. As potential settings for paintings proliferate and more naturalistic depictions of Mary come into style, painters search for new forms of negation so that *Maria lactans* will continue to image and invite non-literal desire.

In the di Credi painting described in the opening of this chapter, *Madonna and the Nursing Christ Child*, the infant Christ gazes at the viewer even as he prepares to take the somewhat geometric breast. He invites the viewer's identification with him, to desire as he desires and be nourished as he is nourished. The flesh and blood viewer, who is likely not an infant, cannot feed in the same way that the infant of the painting can feed from Mary. The differences in the material existence of the painted infant and the fleshly viewer negate a purely material interpretation of the Christ-babe's invitation. The kind of nourishment the viewer is invited to seek—while issuing from a material invitation and rooted in material practices—is ultimately spiritual nourishment. In the viewer-directed gaze of the Christ-babe, the literal opens to the non-literal, as the viewer is invited to feed from Mary spiritually, to desire her spiritually, as a way of desiring the divine.

The negation works somewhat differently in Correggio's *Madonna of the Milk*. The Christ-babe gazes, not at the viewer, but down toward the cherub, as if wrapped in thought, imitating, it seems, the gaze of his mother. His splayed body stretches between Mary and the little cherub beside him whose glance is directed up, toward Mary's more naturalistic breast. As the eyelines of Mary and Christ direct the viewer downward, toward the angel, it is the angel's gaze the viewer follows back to the breast. The presence of the cherub signifies to the viewer the angelic realm Christ knows as home, thus reminding the viewer of Christ's divinity, and it also frames the line of sight by which the viewer's own eyes return to Mary's breast. Through this circulation of glances, the viewer is, first, reminded that while Christ in his humanity desired Mary's milk, in his divinity, Christ did not need it. Second, the viewer is invited to gaze at Mary's breast with her own spiritual nature, to share the cherub's angelic gaze at Mary's breast. The presence and gaze of the cherub produces the negation of a literal desire that can become more than literal.

In some of Correggio's other paintings of nudity, there is a much weaker negation, sometimes no clear negation of literal desire at all, and so it is telling that Elizabeth Costello identifies with Correggio's Mary rather than di Credi's or some other artist's. It is not always as clear in Correggio's paintings, notably his mythological scenes, how literal desire does open to divine desire. Even so, in receiving his paintings of Mary, the Renaissance viewer has been formed by the church to interpret a negation in the painting, however weakly cued by the painting itself. After all, the sexual meaning of Mary's bared breast is negated by the perpetual virginity of Mary, and the nutritive meaning by the divinity of Christ. The religious training of the viewer pushes her to non-literal interpretations of *Maria lactans* even when individual paintings do not visually nudge the reader in that direction.

In both the formation of its viewers and the innuendos of the image itself, the *Playboy* cover "Te adoramos, Maria," promotes a contrasting interpretation of its subject's bared breast. Maria's nakedness is offered up for the viewer's consumption with every visual cue confirming the viewer's instinct to respond to it in the ways he has been trained to respond to pornography. The image represents and elicits a desire that terminates in consumption by the viewer. In so giving itself over to consumption—in such readiness for complete absorption to the viewer—the image elicits a desire infected with the lust to dominate and control desire's object. It is an effort to foreclose divine or non-literal desire, and it is this attempt at foreclosure that literalizes the desire. Without opening to non-literal desire, literalized desire is closed to the transformation divine desire effects. Sexual desire so sequestered from the divine runs the dual dangers of exhaustion and perversion. Determined solely by its consumptive structure, it becomes corrupted by the lust to dominate, possess, and control. Such lust terminates in its assimilation of its object. It may then find a new object, but it risks exhaustion by not opening to a stream of desire that can continue to fund it.

The reduction, or literalization, of desire for Maria's breast is what it means to say that *Playboy* is pornography while *Maria lactans* is not.[79] Whereas the *Playboy* image presents itself as an image of consumption, *Maria lactans* is an image that lures the beholder toward contemplation. It is an image of and for desire; it invites the viewer into a desire that is vulnerable rather than dominating, a desire over which she is not sovereign. It is not a purely consumptive desire that terminates in assimilation that masters and controls the object. It is a desire that opens up to meanings and forces beyond itself. It is the desire of one who does not generate and sustain her own existence; it is the desire of one who has a mother. It is the desire, as Cyril of Alexandria knew, of one subject to death. For when desire is placed before and directed toward the one who is perfect Charity, that desire takes on the characteristics of Charity's own desire. To desire God is to become like the desiring God. *Maria lactans* images can dramatize the mystery of how our literal desires, like sexual desires, remain open to their non-literal meanings such that we can receive the Divine One who arrives in the midst of human desire.

One way to see pornography, then, is as rendering desire and the desiring one static and, in a way, safe: the desire safe from transformation by openness to the divine and the desiring one safe from transformations by desire and desire's object. If literal desire is not opened to non-literal desire, it cannot be changed, purged, or augmented by it. If literal desire tends toward its literalization, then the desiring one is not exposed to a desire or object that can change her—strengthen her, extend her, transform her, hurt her, destroy her. Desire that has not been literalized risks suffering and death. The pain of Mary's desire for Christ is famously represented in the Pietà; that of Christ's for the world on the cross. In contrast to these treacherous desires, pornography attempts to yield desire without risk.

But if "image of consumption" names a way of relating to an image, then can any image be finally literalized? If, that is, pornography names a catechesis toward images, then can any image ever foreclose the possibility of disruption by divine desire? Doesn't the arriving Christ come into a world where much desire has been literalized, precisely because humans have idolized and consumed what should point them toward God? If God first arrived as an image into a world of literalized desire, what image could ever foreclose the possibility of divine arrival? How could any image ever be safe from the transformations of divine desire, any catechesis toward literalization ever finally be complete?

Perhaps it is more accurate to claim that the pornographic image identifies a way of relating to an image that treats images as illusions. We might say that these images of literalized desire help train the viewer into relating to them as illusions. The illusion is cast, first, by the literalization of desire it communicates and elicits, which is itself illusory. Literalized desire tends toward its own destruction, betraying its very nature as desire. And it creates this illusion, second, because it attempts to obscure the negation, the "is not" of imaging. Its failure to negate literal desire betrays a failure to effect any sort of negation, such that the viewer accepts the image as if it is the reality. The second illusion comes as the pornographic image seeks to present itself as the prototype rather than the image. In this way, the pornographic image attempts to be both more and less than an image: seeking to substitute itself for the prototype (more) and closing itself off from transformation beyond itself (less). Like most illusions, the pornographic image is both more and less real than it should be. What forms of iconoclasm might restore these illusions to fidelity to Christ and to their nature as images? And when does an iconoclasm of fidelity entail suppressing these illusions that pretend to be images?

If pornographic images are never finally successful in literalizing desire and absenting the divine, neither, on the other hand, are images of literal desire ever finally safe from worries that they tend toward the pornographic. We have already seen multiple examples of this: images of *Maria lactans* provoke anxiety they previously did not; the Council of Trent expresses a worry about lustful images the church a century prior did not; and the so-called father of pornography, Pierre Aretino, accuses Michelangelo of producing pornography in his church commissions. Elizabeth Costello's interactions with Mr. Phillips similarly dramatize the complexity and ambivalence of literal desire. In her first sitting with him, she is confident that the literal desire she summons opens to divine desire. She thinks of herself as an image akin to Correggio's *Maria lactans*. But in her second breast-baring, with death even more imminent, she finds it difficult to know how to confer blessing as image, and so she quits her pose to arouse Mr. Phillips by touch rather than sight. To Mr. Phillips, she is now more than an image; is she also less? Can touch open to the divine the way the sight of Mary's breast does in Correggio's paintings?

Elizabeth does not answer these questions. Instead, by writing, she turns herself and Mr. Phillips into an image together, one she puts before her imaginary audiences of the Greeks, the Christians, the nurse, her mother, and herself. What would they think of this image? She answers for her imagined spectators. The Greeks would find it grotesque, and she fears what the nurse, her mother, or her later self would say of it. It is the Christians who give her the word *caritas*, which names the image of herself and Mr. Phillips by a literal desire opening onto divine care. She has no confidence in the stability of literal desire's negation or divine care's presence, and so she worries about her future self's interpretation. She withdraws the image from the eyes of her imagined audience, sealing off the expression of her desire from exposure. In attempting to close off this desire, she treats this mental image as an image of consumption, a pornographic image, and so protects her heart from the pain of mending its holes. There will be no transformation of her person.

Macrina, too, worries about how her body will be received and interpreted. Keenly aware of the possibilities of the breast for eliciting sexual desire in another, Macrina responds to her mother's pleas that she see a physician with prayers and weeping, laying before God all the conflicting desires pulling at her: her anxieties about baring her breast to a strange man, her mother's desire that she see a physician, her own desire to respect her mother, her desire to remain chaste for her Bridegroom, Christ. She knows the dangers of desire from the story of her own mother, who longed as a young woman to commit herself to the celibate life but whose beauty was so compelling to male suitors that she was married off for her own safety. Macrina came near the same fate, as her parents foresaw a similar danger that her beauty would occasion violent male desire in her own future. However, she was allowed to pursue lifelong celibacy when her fiancé died. Later, as she lived in an all-female community, knowing her vulnerability and the possibility of being held captive to the literalized desire of a man who might seek to possess her, she decides to live still more completely into desires that will open toward the divine. Baring her desires before the God whose desire has claimed her, Macrina discovers in Christ's desire a way for the transformation and alignment of all the desires surrounding her breast. Her tears, prostration, and mother-love are taken up into the healing miracle Macrina asks her mother to perform. Her concealment of her breast, unlike Elizabeth Costello's, is an attempt at fidelity to divine love.

So integrated are Macrina's desires with divine desire that her body at the last becomes itself divine, glowing with light that invites the purgation and transformation of others' *eros*. The small scar that marks the absence of the tumor testifies to the way her love for her mother is taken up into her love for God, the way even her refusal to deny her mother became a new source of divine desire. At the end of her life, her breast scar on her luminous body expresses a mother dependence that imitates Christ's. Her scar is a site of desire (motherly, daughterly, and divine) that invites contemplation.

It is only when Macrina is a corpse that her naked breast can be an image that unquestionably opens onto the divine. And that is because she is not just a corpse; she is an image of the spiritual body that all people (her hagiographer brother believes) will become in the end, when all shall rest in a perfect union with Christ. In death, Macrina has become an image of Christ's second arrival, an arrival to be further explored in Chapter 5. Any final success of opening onto divine desire can come only in this second arrival. Before then, the transformation into the divine will always be incomplete, as we live suspended between these two arrivals.

There is another reason that Macrina's breast can generate less anxiety in death than in life. In death, her body becomes an image of herself. In life, her body might image many things—for example, God or the cosmos—but it does not image Macrina, though we might say it images her soul. She *is* her body. In death, her body both is and is not Macrina, and the strength and obviousness of the "is not" pushes toward a non-literal interpretation of her breast. It negates literal desire so that it might deepen into divine desire. This negation internal to imaging itself mirrors the negation of literal desire that images may elicit, thus opening such desire to the divine.

We live literally in the world most of our lives, and images extend to us the opportunity of connecting the literal with the non-literal; they help us open our desires beyond the literal without forsaking the literal all together. Michael Fried's much more eloquent, though elliptical, way of putting this is to say, "We are all literalists most or all of our lives. Presentness is grace."[80] For most of their lives, the breasts of Elizabeth Costello and Macrina may arouse a literal desire that tends toward literalization. But in moments when they become, however fleetingly, an image with a clear negation—for Elizabeth through painting, for

Macrina through death—the literal tends toward the non-literal, and they can mediate divine desire, the presence of the arriving Christ. To receive these images, to receive *Maria lactans*, is to resist our catechesis into the polarities of images of consumption and images of critique. It is to accept the separateness of the image (and of the Image) that coexists with the desire it arouses, and in this way to accept that we are not sovereign over ourselves. In this acceptance, in this mode of image relationship, we can receive a grace of divine presence.

Human Desiring and Divine Desiring

The mother dependence that imitates Christ's—Macrina's and others'—exemplifies the openness of human desiring to divine desiring and of the literal to the non-literal. It is an openness into which Israel was trained through its sacrificial systems and which Christ consummated through arriving as a helpless babe.[81] Ephrem the Syrian meditates on this openness in his hymns to the mystery of Christ's nativity:

> He Who is Lord of all, gives us all,
> And He Who is Enricher of all, borrows from all.
> He is Giver of all as one without needs.
> Yet He borrows back again as one deprived.
> He gave cattle and sheep as Creator,
> But on the other hand, He sought sacrifices as one deprived.[82]

Arriving into the world he created as one who needed this world to sustain him, God enters into the economy of human desiring to take it up into the economy of divine desiring. Because Christ, without ceasing to be God, entered fully into human desire in the incarnation, sharing in the literal *eros* that characterizes dependent life, Christ draws such desires into God's own life, making intimate the literal and non-literal desires of humanity. Christ thereby orders the economy of human desiring to that of divine desiring. In El Shaddai's suckling of Mary, we learn to suckle El Shaddai. Through the negation that opens literal to non-literal desires, the arriving Christ is made present to us.

The drawing together of these two economies of desire is expressed in an image Lorenzo Monaco painted during the late fourteenth or early fifteenth century in Florence, the epicenter of *Maria lactans* images during the age of their immense popularity. In Monaco's painting, called *The Intercession of Christ and the Virgin*, a group of the faithful kneel before Christ, making supplication to him. Christ is one of three figures who dominate the painting. He, too, is kneeling, as he gestures with his right hand toward the large figure of Mary, positioned behind the praying faithful to whom she gestures as she bares her breast to the adult Christ. She says, in a speech written onto the painting, "Dearest son, because of the milk I gave you, have mercy on them."[83] As Christ's right hand acknowledges Mary's gift, his left hand points to the wound in his side as he looks up to the third large figure, the Father, and says, "My Father, let those be saved for whom you wished me to suffer the passion."[84] The Father, holding one hand in blessing toward the Son, releases the dove of the Holy Spirit, who descends to the Son, who presumably will send the Holy Spirit to Mary and the faithful supplicants in response to their prayers.

This economy of desire which binds together Father, Son, and Spirit, now in Christ binds Son, Mary, and the faithful, drawing them into Trinitarian desire. Humanity participates in such desiring through the tracing of debts, the remembrance that our life comes from beyond us, that we are dependent (and more concretely, that we depend upon Mary). Remembering, like Christ, our debt to the nourishment of the breast allows us to desire like Christ, which is to desire the presence of the Father given by the Holy Spirit.

It is unsurprising that Monaco's painting was commissioned as an altarpiece, for it is on the altar that the faithful receive spiritual nourishment by physical nourishment. In the Eucharist, the faithful remember and trace debts in imitation of the figures in Monaco's image. The prayers celebrating the Eucharist (*anaphoras*) themselves contain an anamnesis responding to Christ's words of institution, *Do this in memory of me*. In this moment, Christians ingest and remember Christ to become like Christ. Memory of a life beyond us, which precedes us, prepares us to enter a desire similarly beyond us and preceding us.

In the Eucharist, Christians remember who they are—creatures dependent upon bread—and what the Word became: bread to feed them everlasting life. Consuming the bread, the communicant's consumptive desire for food is ordered toward that which is never entirely consumed. The literal is ordered to the non-literal, as the bread by which Christ comes to us is also negated as bread in the words of institution, "This is my body." Remaining bread in its appearance, the host opens into the presence of Christ, binding the literal to the non-literal.

As the one who becomes bread, the nursing Christ-child beckons us into a life of desire that he models at the breast of Mary. God in the infant Christ is joined to not-God, and what was not-God (creation) is taken up into God (Creator) without obliterating the difference between them. It is in God's joining with not-God that God most fully reveals Godself to all that is not-God. And that first moment of revelation, that first sign of visibility, began with a woman's body. For like all babies, God began human life invisible to the naked eye, secreted in a woman's body in the moment she became two lives instead of one. Gradually, God became visible through her, as she gave her belly as the first image of God's humanity in the world. Born from her womb, Christ nurses at the breast of Mary, entering the world as an image of and for desire.

FIGURE 2. Fra Angelico, *Annunciation of Cortona*, 1433–34. Museo Diocesano in Cortona. Photo by the Yorck Project: 10,000 Masterpieces of Painting. Public domain (Wikimedia).

2 CAME DOWN FROM HEAVEN AND WAS MADE HUMAN
Abiding Presence

IT IS THE MOMENT Mary becomes two lives instead of one—the hour her belly receives the promise of a bulge.

They bend toward each other, the girl Mary and the angel Gabriel. Each is haloed in gold visually reprised in the trim of their luxuriant gowns, the arched wings of Gabriel, Mary's throne-like chair, and the light encircling the dove. The bird hovers over Mary, near a relief sculpture of an older man turned toward the dove, his hand raised as if sending or blessing it. The stone man and the brooding dove symbolize the Father and the Holy Spirit. The missing Trinitarian member is the Son, who, in the very moment the painting depicts, becomes flesh. The script of Mary and Gabriel's speech fills the space between them to confirm this as the hour of incarnation. *Ecce ancilla domini, fiat mihi secundum verbum tuum*, Mary says in the painting. "Behold the handmaid of the Lord, let it be done to me according to your word." The *fiat mihi* echoes the *fiat lux* of the first creation and announces the second, when God enters the visible world by the womb of Mary. In the painting, the words *fiat mihi* are indiscernible, hidden, it seems, behind the pillar of Mary's home. No matter how earnestly the viewer strains to discern the graced words that mark this wondrous miracle, her eyes meet only the stony ordinariness of a pillar. This painted altarpiece stages a scene shot through with divine presence, even as the pillar denies a glimpse of the Word coming to dwell among us.

Fra Angelico's altarpiece at Cortona is a gorgeous tribute to the visible that also insists on its limits. In its sumptuous colors, exquisite detail, and light-catching gold, the painting entices the gaze. In the stony pillar obscuring the *fiat*, it blocks it. The relief of the Father and the dove of the Holy Spirit suggest a glance into the divine, and still the stubbornly ordinary pillar chastens claims to divine sight. The painting affirms and negates the visible, for it both reveals and veils the divine workings in the world. It sounds an ambivalence toward the visible in tune with both iconophilic and iconoclastic refrains. Like iconophiles, Fra Angelico makes images of the divine. Like iconoclasts, he identifies limits of what can be seen in an image. Where the Byzantine iconomachs replaced images of Christ with crosses, Fra Angelico gives us a pillar.[1]

Fra Angelico's much-loved image of the incarnation admits a sympathy with the iconomachs because the logic of the abiding presence of Christ entails both an affirmation and negation of the visible world. This chapter teases out such ambivalence, while incorporating it into a robustly incarnational approach to images. It is not that the iconomachs' arguments are correct, but that they are serious. They express profound insight into the temptations and possibilities of images. The interlocutors who can aid us in elucidating precisely *how* the iconomachs' insight can be recovered for the modern world are unlikely ones: twentieth-century American Catholic fiction writers Walker Percy (principally) and Flannery O'Connor (secondarily).

Percy and O'Connor advance the conversation about images by extending ancient conversations linking the human, Christ, and images—linguistic connections forged in the conciliar disputes of the first few centuries of Christianity. For the Byzantine iconomachs and iconodules, Christology determined the fate of the image; their debate centered on questions of who and what Christ is. During the debates about who and what Christ is in the earlier councils centuries prior, anthropology provided the crucial examples for settling language about Christ; these debates drew from descriptions of the human as composite to illumine something about the composition of Christ. Anthropology points to the plausibility of orthodox Christology, which then either legitimates images (as the iconodules aver) or proscribes them (as the iconomachs protest). Is there some logic uniting these three categories of human, Christ, and image? Yes, and Percy and O'Connor help articulate it: They share a logic of what I call *amphibiousness*. Christ is human-divine, the human is animal-spirit, and the image is visible-invisible. Fidelity to the dual natures of these amphibians requires certain forms of iconoclasm—particularly, apophaticism and confession, which recuperate idols by making them proper images, faithful to Christ the Image, who renders God visible without reducing God to that visibility, who becomes flesh without being exhausted by flesh, who abides in the world while transcending it.

Byzantine Iconomachy

In the iconomachy (literally, "image struggle") surrounding the Seventh Ecumenical Council (in 787), the icon of Christ became the test case for Christian images, and prior Christological disputes supplied the criteria for validating and invalidating icons.[2] Both the iconomachs, who codified their doctrine in their council of 754, and the iconodules, who anathematized that council in what is now remembered as the Seventh Ecumenical Council (Nicea II), waged their battle by invoking labels of heresy generated at the previous councils.[3] They hurled "Arian" and "Nestorian" and "Monophysite" as epithets that could devastate the claims of their opposition.[4]

According to the iconomachs, the iconodules were Arian because, by insisting that Christ could be depicted as an image when God clearly could not, they ruled out the possibility that Christ could be God. What is represented as Christ is not God, they claimed, but a "mere man"—at best a demoted divinity.[5] Or perhaps, as the iconomachs accused, the iconodules erred like Eutyches, who mixed the two natures in a heresy known as Monophysitism.[6] The image, in this charge, represents divinity as if it were humanity, thus confusing the two natures and vitiating their integrity. Then again, the iconomachs argued, the iconodules blunder like Nestorius, who did not refute Christ's divinity but set it aside, compromising its union with Christ's humanity.[7] As Nestorius verbally separated the two natures, the iconodules—so the iconomachs claimed—visually disjoined them, depicting only Christ's humanity and so sundering it from his divinity. The iconomachs' triple charge amounts to this: to draw (or in the case of icons, to write—in Latin, *scribere*) a person is to claim she is circumscribable, and so what is uncircumscribable is either discounted (Arianism), confused with the circumscribable (Monophysitism), or separated from the circumscribable (Nestorianism).[8] These strangely contradictory charges express a fundamentally similar anxiety, that imaging is simply incompatible with divinity. To make an image of God is either to attenuate the reality of Christ's divinity or erode its bonds to his humanity. For the iconomachs, the image-makers did not present the one true Christ with their icons; they supplanted him with idols.

In one way, the iconomachs' various contradicting charges against the image resonate with the conversations today in visual studies. As the iconomachs and iconodules of Byzantium struggled over whether the image can be reconciled to the divinity and humanity of Christ, so contemporary image conversations struggle over the immanence and transcendence of the image. Picture theorists like Gottfried Boehm, Hans Belting, Horst Bredekamp, and W.J.T. Mitchell worry about a Platonic or Kantian (or Hegelian) approach to the image that reduces the image to *meaning*—to how, that is, the image points beyond itself to a significance located elsewhere. The image, in the view these picture theorists criticize, is oriented toward the transcendent in a way that devalues it. Their correction is to value the image in terms of its immanent significance, to regard the *presence* of the image itself. Sometimes image theorists make this correction by disavowing transcendence all together. Douglas Hedley positions his book *The Iconic Imagination* as an intervention in this discussion, as he attempts to display the way the Platonic emphasis on the transcendence of the image need not devalue the image. Believing the anxieties of the image theorists to be overblown, Hedley argues that in rejecting the transcendence of the image, contemporary image theorists actually vitiate the grounds for valuing the image.[9] As the Byzantine iconomachs worried about the inability of the image to hold together the divinity and the humanity of Christ, so contemporary conversations around the image exude anxiety about the image holding together immanent encounter and transcendent meaning. There is a resonance in these Byzantine and late modern conversations.

The other major argument that the iconomachs brought against the image has no parallel in contemporary image discussion, for this argument concerns the Eucharist. According to the iconomachs, it is the Eucharist alone that makes Christ present to the faithful. Instituted by Christ himself, the Eucharist is the paradigmatic image that reveals, they claimed, the criteria for all true images: consubstantiality with Christ and opacity to human eyes.[10] Painted icons are inadequate and therefore false, not to mention superfluous. The Eucharist mediates the real presence of Christ; what could an icon add to that?

Given the arguments of the iconomachs, the iconodules faced two major fronts in the battle over images: Christological heresy and the Eucharist. For the latter, their argument was largely defensive and negative. They repudiated the claim of the Eucharist as an image—Christ did not call it one—and so claimed an image need not be consubstantial with what it represents.[11] There was little else they said about the Eucharist's relation to icons. This chapter displays that there is more that might be said. In what follows, Walker Percy and Flannery O'Connor help to develop a theology of icons that affirms an iconophilic stance while identifying a more positive role for the Eucharist in a theology of icons. The centrality of the Eucharist, in fact, strengthens iconophilia by guarding it against the threat of idolatry.

As for the arguments over Christological heresy, the iconodules argued along both defensive and offensive lines. They staked the orthodoxy of their argument on the incarnation of Christ. If God is not circumscribed by being wrapped in swaddling clothes and laid in a manger, then God is not circumscribed by being written (inscribed) in an icon.[12] As Father Maximos Constas beautifully puts the point, "Byzantine defenders of icons affirmed that Christ's depictability . . . was a necessary corollary of his embodiment. The reverse is also true: artistic representation is itself an act of embodiment, a kind of birth, but also a kind of death. . . . To consent to have a body means to be framed by the narrow edges of the manger, confined to the lap of the mother, fixed to the arms of the cross, and figured in a work of art."[13] The image makes Christ visible in a way similar to how Christ makes God visible. As God in Christ abides in the world, so Christ abides in the icon. The argument then turns from the defensive to the offensive, shifting from the idea that images are justified because Christ became incarnate to the idea that renouncing images is renouncing Christ incarnate.

To declare that God abides with us in Christ and Christ abides with us in a special way in the icon is to claim that the divine inhabits the ordinary visible world as the divine. Scripture witnesses to this complexity of Christ's abiding as well as the visibility and invisibility it entails. For example, Christ presents himself as an image of the invisible God in his conversation with Philip, who asks Jesus to show him the Father. "Have I been with you all this time, Philip, and you still do not know me?" Jesus asks. "How can you say, 'Show us the Father?' Anyone who has seen me has seen the Father" (John 14:8–9). To see Christ is to see, in some sense, the invisible Father, who nevertheless remains distinct from Christ. The difficulty for Philip is that God becomes visible as an ordinary-looking human. God abides within the everyday, and as Christ tells his disciples, when he ascends, he, too, will be invisible to all but those who have learned to see him in the world that is yet not him (John 14:19, 16:10). What does it mean to discern Christ's abiding presence in the complexity of this visibility and invisibility, presence and absence? How, as both iconodules and iconomachs asked, is an image of Christ possible? How does one receive the abiding presence of Christ, who may appear in and as the everyday? This last question is urgent, though hidden, in the lives of fictional characters Jack "Binx" Bolling in Walker Percy's *The Moviegoer* and O. E. Parker in Flannery O'Connor's "Parker's Back"—two iconophilic seekers who help to elucidate the visible-invisible image that finds its paradigm in the God made human.

Binx and Parker, Iconophiles and Seekers

Everydayness is the enemy for Jack "Binx" Bolling, the hero of *The Moviegoer*. It defeats what he calls "the search," which then dissipates into malaise. Binx is an iconophile of sorts, an attitude the novel telegraphs in its title by identifying him as a gazer of the moving image.[14] The image, for Binx, both opens onto the search and betrays it, handing it over into the malaise of everydayness. The narrative arc of *The Moviegoer* traces Binx's search, from its beginnings through its seeming successes and apparent failure to its eventual transformation. *The Moviegoer* is the tale of a seeker who does not know exactly what he is seeking.

Beyond defeating everydayness, the search's object remains unknown to the reader. Though it is tempting to claim the object is the divine or the transcendent or meaningfulness, Binx rejects any attempt to name it. The object of the search remains obscure; its directionality does not. Binx narrates both a vertical search and, following its failure, a horizontal one. The vertical search—sometimes called simply the search—moves upward toward a unifying formula for all things, a "key to existence" (the search's proximate, not final, object) that Binx pursues through "'fundamental' books" on "key subjects."[15] After reading one such book and watching the movie *It Happened One Night*, he finds that "though the universe had been disposed of, [he him]self was left over."[16] The vertical search, it turns out, may abjure the everyday, speak to humanity's higher nature, and soar high into invisible and transcendent ideas that unite the universe, and still inevitably fail. For, even if it discards the universe, it cannot ditch the seeker. More concretely, it cannot expunge the seeker's physicality, which can only be ignored so long. Eventually, the materiality of life reasserts itself.

With the burden of the self unrelieved, Binx embarks on his horizontal search.[17] Rather than moving upward into the heights of the transcendent and invisible, the horizontal search moves outward, into the everyday and the visible. Binx calls this search "the little way." It chases "the sad little happiness of drinks and kisses, a good little car and warm deep thigh." If Binx cannot abolish the everyday, then in his "little way" he seeks fleeting reprieve from the malaise that makes the everyday so unbearable.[18] Intersecting with the vertical search in its goal to overcome malaise, the horizontal search differs from the vertical in that it surrenders aspirations to transcendence. It is a search within an immanence shorn of transcendence. In some ways the two searches are one another's inverse—the vertical oriented toward the transcendent and the horizontal toward the immanent. In another way, they resemble one another, for images help to sustain (and transform) both.

These are separate activities: images sustain the vertical search, on the one hand; on the other, they transform it. Then again, they sustain the horizontal search and transform it as well. How and why can images work so divergently? Thicker, richer answers come into view by drawing *The Moviegoer* into conversation with O'Connor's "Parker's Back." In that story, O. E. Parker is, like Binx, an iconophile who avoids his given name. As a young boy, he goes to the circus and is captivated by a man covered with a tattooed arabesque of paradisal creatures.[19] Seeing those tattoos rippling on the muscles of the circus man fills Parker with wonder. It is the first time he, an extraordinarily ordinary boy, becomes dimly aware that the fact of his existence may be anything other than wholly ordinary. The awareness is so dim that O'Connor compares it to that of a blind person turned gently in a new direction. He has not yet grasped that his path has an altered end.[20]

The end nonetheless finds him, in the form of an apocalyptic tractor accident. It has been years since the tattooed man filled him with wonder, and in the intervening years, he has covered his own body with tattoos and married a woman who hates those tattoos. His wife, Sarah Ruth, is severe in her religiosity, and like the tattoos, she seems to promise a satisfaction she never fulfills. Parker wants them both without understanding why. After the accident, Parker stumbles from the rubble and keeps walking until he reaches a tattoo parlor. His life's two strong desires—for the love of his plain and pregnant wife Sarah Ruth and for the splendor of the tattooed man—converge in his decision to get a tattoo of God on the one untattooed part of his body: his back. Flipping past the familiar images of Jesus in the tattoo book, Parker chooses one that is strange to him—he has never before seen a "Byzantine Christ"—at the same time the image is familiar. The "all-demanding eyes" remind him of the "icepick eyes"[21] of Sarah Ruth, whose piety is so stringent she believes churches are idolatrous. Parker does not understand why he is so compelled by his wife, though he knows he is. He does not show tenderness toward her, but he does tell her his first two names, which he has not told anyone else. And he desperately wants her affection. Once Sarah Ruth sees the tattoo, he believes, she will have to love him. It is a picture of God, after all, and, "She can't say she don't like the looks of God."[22] As for his own response to God's "looks," when Parker sees the silent, still face of the Byzantine image, he turns white.

After a day and two multi-hour tattoo sessions, Parker returns home. The door is jammed shut. Sarah Ruth refuses to open it, answering each of his pleas with the question: "Who's there?" She refuses his thrice-given answer, "O. E." He turns as if someone behind him might answer her, then sees a tree flame with light on the horizon, and falls against the door as if speared. Then he answers, "Obadiah." At this confession of the name he has long suppressed, light enters him, turning his soul into an arabesque of colors, "a garden of trees and birds and beasts."[23] And he completes the confession: "Obadiah Elihue." He gives up, for this moment at least, concealing his name.

Sarah Ruth's anger is unquenched. In fury, she opens the door to him. She is a volcano of invective, which Parker interrupts to insist she look at his back. Unmoved, she lays into him for getting another tattoo. His anguished insistence that it is a picture of God only makes matters worse. She screams: "Idolatry! Enflaming yourself with idols under every green tree! I can put up with lies and vanity but I don't want no idolater in this house!" She beats him with a broom until large welts form on the face of his Christ tattoo. He is outside now, and she looks at him mercilessly, her ruthless eyes denying her own given name. "There he was—who called himself Obadiah Elihue—leaning against the tree, crying like a baby."[24] So ends her iconoclastic violence.

The Promise of the Image: Awakening to the Search

Images inspire both Parker and Binx to undertake their ambiguous searches. Parker first knows his life as anything other than purely ordinary when he encounters the circus man's rippling tattoos of flora and fauna. They are, for him, a flash of paradise—a fleeting sight of a time when God walked with humans and the abiding presence of the divine remained unbroken by sin and death. Through the paradisal images, Parker glimpses a world beyond what is visible to him, even a divine presence formerly unimagined by him. His ordinary self and world has been touched by the divine.

Though it is not exactly an image in the conventional sense that initiates it, Binx's quest begins when the ordinary appears to him as something other than flatly ordinary. Just after he receives an injury in the Korean War, he spies a dung beetle, which inaugurates the search for the first time. He forgets about his search until years later, when he looks at a pile of belongings on his dresser. Once as "invisible as his own hand," they become "unfamiliar and full of clues," and here the search begins anew. In seeing what was formerly invisible in its ordinariness as unfamiliar and full of possibility, Binx finds that his search itself has become possible.[25] His ordinary world appears to him as if pointing beyond itself; something more than the ordinary is present to it.

As the search progresses, images—movies, really—energize it. They dramatize the vertical search in their storylines, for they show a person "coming to himself in a strange place."[26] Like Binx, the movie hero begins by seeing the ordinary as strange and unfamiliar. The content of movies, in this way, reflects the content of the search. It is not just movies' content that mirrors the search. Their form does, too. To watch a movie is to go into a dark theater and have the projecting light draw the beholder's consciousness into a strange place and time. The once-invisible moving images become suddenly visible on the screen, as the moviegoer sees a world, however familiar, presented as unfamiliar—larger, more luminous, and in those ways, more visible.

When he is not at the movies, Binx often pursues the kind of reality movies create as a denser, more vivid version of reality. He describes the way movies "certify" existence.[27] They render the places that appear in them more real than they otherwise are. They elevate the people who encounter movie stars to a heightened reality that temporarily dispels everydayness.[28] Movies are not the objects of the vertical search, but they and their aura approximate for Binx the search's object. Binx, then, is a moviegoer because he is a seeker, because the moving image resembles a more vital, more legible reality that it therefore seems to promise.

The Betrayal of the Image: Illusion, Object, Idol

O'Connor and Percy do not simply celebrate the image in their stories. Images also take on a darker role in their narratives, for the image that inspires the search also troubles it. In O'Connor's story, Parker misunderstands the splendor of the images he saw on the tattooed man. For years, he strives to recreate the splendor by filling every inch of his body with tattoos, only to be constantly disappointed with the results. They give him a temporary lift that withers away. Again and again he is dissatisfied. His dissatisfaction is inevitable, for he pursues images qua objects rather than qua images. He does not, that is, see and venerate them as signs; he collects them like things, talismans that might magically conjure the experience he once had of the tattooed man.

As Parker's iconophilia fails to lead him out of his misery, so, too, does Sarah Ruth's iconoclasm fail to fulfill her own desires. Her drive to extirpate images from her faith undermines itself, as her very iconoclasm generates the story's final cruciform image. She so worries about idolatry that she forswears the institution of the church from which her anxiety about idols derives, and after breaking faith with her institution, she breaks faith with her anxiety. She makes the very thing she hates.

Sarah Ruth's hatred of images nests in a bed of antipathies toward the visible and the material world. Early in the story, Parker hopes to excite Sarah Ruth's physical attraction by showing off his tattoos. Later, he tries to elicit jealousy by pretending he works for a beautiful woman. In both cases, she remains unmoved by the visible. The only time the visible world moves her in the story, it is to fury, and then she beats her husband into an image of Christ crucified. Both Parker and Sarah Ruth are thwarted by images: Parker in his grasp at splendor and Sarah Ruth in her efforts at aniconic faith. Images vex the attempts to figure both the visible as if cocooned from the invisible and the invisible as if unmoored from the visible.

The Moviegoer gives some insight into why images disappoint these efforts. There is a character in the novel who, though quite unlike Sarah Ruth otherwise, resembles her insofar as he, too, aspires to aniconism. Binx describes him as a romantic. He is the perfect vertical searcher, a person so caught up in his idealized world that he cannot bear the messiness of actual life. He is the kind of person who can manage to say an ordinary word like "bus" only if he says it ironically. He is, in Binx's words, a moviegoer who does not go to the movies.[29] There is something of a symmetry here between Sarah Ruth, a Christian who does not go to church, and this moviegoer who does not go to the movies. What this romantic moviegoer makes plain, though, is that the desire to eschew images is a temptation the image itself can arouse. It is his love of the movies, Binx implies, that prevents the romantic from going to them. We have a clue here that movies can delude the search they also catalyze—they can incite desire for something that they themselves defy.

Binx is aware of this peril intrinsic to moviegoing. He describes it as the "danger of slipping clean out of space and time," for in seeing the moving image, a person sees "one copy of a film which might be shown anywhere and at any time."[30] As an image, the movie makes present what it is not. Movies present another world, another setting, other characters, other dialogue. There is a danger that this world the movies mediate will be so absorbing that it will overtake the visible, material world into which it is projected. *The Moviegoer* everywhere adverts to this danger, as Binx often finds his personality overtaken by the affects of movie stars like Rory Calhoun and Gregory Peck, and the romantic is caught up in a similar venture of living life like a movie.[31]

The danger is that the image might become more real than reality—an image that disowns its status as image. If, for Parker, the image becomes an object, for Binx the danger is that his image relationship will degenerate into one similar to the image relationship pornography names in Chapter 1: an illusion, both more and less real than an image. In *The Crossing of the Visible*, Jean-Luc Marion thematizes a similar danger as intrinsic to the televisual image. For Marion, the televisual image "has no original other than itself and itself alone" and so the image becomes the original.[32] Usurping the role of prototype, the image no longer points beyond itself. It absorbs the beholder into its own world, as if the image is the ultimate reality. In television, Marion insists, something "attains being . . . only insofar as it accepts not only being reduced to self-as-image but above all conforming this first image to the draconian laws of another image—the idol (of desire) of the viewer."[33] Nothing is if it is not seen, according to this logic, and so television establishes the regime of the visual, the tyranny of the image. The image displaces the prototype as the screen substitutes for the world by taking hold of desire itself. Marion's televisual image is an illusion that works against the logic of images, for it ceases to point to a prototype.[34]

In the *Moviegoer*, the ironic romantic gives himself over to a logic of illusion similar to what Marion describes. If an illusion is a way of relating to the image that spurns the visible, concrete world in which one encounters the image, then the romantic is well on his way to living life as illusion. After using the image to reject the visible realm, he then rejects the image by dismissing its visible reality as well. He is a moviegoer who doesn't go to the movies, as Binx says, an iconophile whose particular brand of iconophilia ends in an iconoclastic imagelessness.

Binx is not blind to the possibility that movies might tempt him into an image relationship of illusion. Alive to this danger, he tries not to surrender to it. He authors a strategy to combat the illusion tendency of film images. Intending to prevent the movie from swallowing up reality, Binx speaks with the ticket seller to learn about the theater and the people with whom he sees the movie.[35] That way, he might avoid becoming an Anybody Anywhere, or, as he also calls it, a ghost.[36] He wants to remain a Somebody concretely located in space and time, even as he gazes at the image that mediates an elsewhere in another time.

He pursues that goal by negating the image in a way that reminds him it is an image. Binx's conversations with the ticket seller restore the "is not" to the moving image, negating it so that it does not mediate a presence that overtakes, possesses perhaps, the material reality of Binx's existence. Whereas Marion commends film festivals and film shoots as locations that highlight the image status of films and combat illusion, Binx goes to pains to locate and name the world outside the image in order to maintain the image in its image status.[37]

In addition to becoming illusions, movies can go awry in two other, related ways. Though they begin with such promise—"a fellow coming to himself in a strange place"—they forsake that promise by ending with that same fellow mired in the everyday, living the life of a nice, very ordinary citizen. "In two weeks' time," Binx scoffs, "he is so sunk in everydayness that he might just as well be dead."[38] As the promise of the search is embodied in both the movies' subject and medium, so, too, is this danger mirrored in form as well in content. After two hours of awakening in the dark to the strange place of the movie's setting, the viewer goes back to her ordinary existence, perhaps sunk into the everyday. This is the second of the two problematic responses the moving image provokes, and it resonates with Parker's own promise-and-despair cycle of pursuing tattoo images. It is a contrasting case with the romantic, for whom the movies inspire a quest for the transcendent cut loose from the immanent. For the romantic, the movies work like illusions. But in this second case, the movies themselves substitute for the transcendent that the moviegoer desires. In figuring themselves as the end of the search, the movies reconcile the moviegoer to the immanent. They displace the transcendent from the seeker's horizon. In claiming transcendence for itself, the moving image becomes an idol—the second image danger. And this slides into the third image danger. In the way it refuses mediation to the invisible, an idol is a small remove from a talismanic object, an image danger fully realized in Parker's tattoos.

The journeys and transformations of Binx and Parker illumine three different degradations of the image: images that act as illusions, as idols, or as objects. And these three degradations suggest two directions in which the search fails, by tempting the seeker to eradicate the visible (illusion) or to exclude the invisible (in contrasting ways, idol and object). The vertical search spawns illusions as it dispenses with the world (though not the self), while the horizontal search issues idols and objects as it seeks nothing outside the visible, treating the visible as if it were total. These failed searches and resultant degradations of the image rely on a picture of the world in which beyondness comes over and against everydayness. They close the visible to the invisible, and so the everyday is either excluded or totalized. To put it in more philosophical terms: transcendence is ontologized against immanence. The vertical search seeks to jettison the everyday, to escape the ordinary into some immaterial realm. The horizontal search devotes itself to the material as the only reality. In both, the visible and the invisible are sealed off and alienated from one another.

The vertical and horizontal searches rely on structurally similar approaches to the world. Once the vertical search, with its wrongly ontologized transcendence, fails to banish images and visibility, Binx takes up its inverse, a wrongly ontologized immanence, in the horizontal search. Binx narrates his transition from vertical to horizontal search, in that same evening after he has been reading a fundamental book and watching *It Happened One Night*: "A memorable night. The only difficulty was that though the universe had been disposed of, I myself was left over . . . yet still obliged to draw one breath and then the next. But now I have undertaken a different kind of search, a horizontal search. . . . Before I wandered as a diversion. Now I wander seriously and sit and read as a diversion."[39] Anything that takes one away from the immediate, immanent world diverts from the search, because the horizontal search has abandoned the wholly transcendent for the wholly immanent. Once the vertical search has been abandoned, Binx's metaphysics demands this kind of move, because the transcendent is divorced from the immanent. The here and now is ripped away from the beyond.

Binx's horizontal search remains firmly within the everyday, a "little way" that parodies the Little Way of Thérèse of Lisieux, to whom Percy nods with a character named Thèrése (the inversion of the accented *e*'s intimating Binx's inversion of the little way). Thèrése even appears just after Binx introduces his little way, as if to highlight the connection. Thérèse of Lisieux's Little Way will be explicated shortly. Binx's little way is a simple-minded hedonism, and in it, the moving image is a diversion, a pleasure that makes life bearable.

Binx's little way is not the only form a life devoted to the immanent can take. His Aunt Emily's stoicism represents an alternative to his horizontal search. She, too, despairs of the vertical search, of securing the world's meaning by identifying transcendence. Her vision of life is tragic: the world crumbles around her. Once populated with Catos, it is now going to seed.[40] Aunt Emily's response to total immanence and the necessary tragedy it entails is to figure immanence as a kind of transcendence. "Man" is a tragic hero, who, though destined to go down, must live by his lights, as she says more than once.[41]

There is no coming salvation, no transcendent hope, but marshalling his inner strength, *man* can approximate divinity by living as if he is transcendent.

Both horizontal-seeking Binx and Aunt Emily live in reduced, wholly immanent worlds, though they position themselves differently in those worlds. Binx suffers from a chasm he continually opens between an inaccessible transcendence and an immanence he has ontologized against it. Aunt Emily tries to live into an immanence that figures itself as a kind of transcendence. It is *his lights*—his own light—by which a man transcends the crumbling world around him. Goodness is destined to be defeated, but a man must fight because, she claims, to do any less is to be less than a man. As for images, though her immanence figured as transcendence mirrors a temptation movies pose, Aunt Emily never goes to the movies in *The Moviegoer*. Why would she need to? She can see everything she needs to see to live in the world. She has her own lights and lives by those alone.

The vertical and horizontal—the transcendent and immanent—aspects of these searches and image relationships also echo O'Connor's characters of Sarah Ruth and Parker. Just as Sarah Ruth aspires to the invisibility that religion and images point to—and then renounces the scaffolding of religion and images—the vertical searcher aspires to the invisibility images present—minus the images themselves. From the other direction, as Parker reduces the splendor of images to their visibility, their immanent aspect, so the horizontal seeker assesses images as objects, as purely visible objects rather than windows to something beyond. To put this in terms of the picture theorists' conversation, on the one hand, Sarah Ruth embodies the degenerate Platonism the picture theorists worried about—one that reduces images to what they point to, and so makes them invisible. On the other hand, the attempt to reclaim images from this transcendence runs the risk of denying the element of transcendence to the image, similar to Parker's approach. One pursues images vertically, the other horizontally. The unsustainability of these searches is thus epitomized by the end of "Parker's Back" and by the collapse of the vertical into the horizontal search in *The Moviegoer*. And the unworkability of these searches is a symptom of the false anthropology they assume.

The Betrayal of the Human: Angels, Beasts, and Angel-Beasts

Percy frequently invokes birds and soldiers in *The Moviegoer* to characterize people, their fears, and their journeys. At one point when she is near despair, Binx's step-cousin Kate wishes that she could be a soldier in order to have a flesh and blood enemy. ("What a lark!" she sighs.[42]) Later, as she travels with Binx to Chicago, he worries about the great "genie-soul" of the city perching on his shoulder "like a buzzard" because he is leaving the place where he is rooted.[43] Kate's stepmother, Binx's Aunt Emily, is described as both bird and soldier. She was a bird in her earlier years when she believed in and sought transcendence, but as her stoic despair sets in, she is described as a soldier.[44] Though they can appear together and can even describe the same person, birds and soldiers speak to contrary ways of being in the world: as soldiers are grounded in physicality and materiality, birds soar into the airy heights above most flesh and blood. On the face of it, their pairing is mysterious. Yet it is not entirely anomalous in Percy's corpus.

While the bird and soldier images that fill so much of *The Moviegoer* do not return in later works, a version of this figuration appears in Percy's later novel *Love in the Ruins* (1971). Instead of birds, it uses angels, and instead of soldiers, beasts. *Angelism* in that work names the anthropological fallacy that elides the physicality of human nature. It is the human's struggle to live as a spirit and thus be more angelic than human. Perhaps it is not intuitive that the intensification of angelism coincides with great violence in *Love in the Ruins*—though this coupling of soaring and brutalizing is anticipated in *The Moviegoer*'s pairing of birds and soldiers. Even so, there is a profound logic to this connection. Because angelism abstracts the self, it obscures the fragility of the body in a way that facilitates violence against it. For similar reasons, angelism often comes joined with its antithesis, bestialism, in which one is governed by the instincts of her animal nature, divorced from reasoning, morality, and higher-order thought. To suffer from bestialism is to succumb wholly to one's appetites, especially the appetite for sex, alcohol, and other physical pleasures. Bestialism names a self who lives wholly according to literalized desires. If angelism is the self straining to transcend its physicality, bestialism is the self stooping to complete immanence to its physicality. Characters in *Love in the Ruins* often suffer from angelism-bestialism disorder in a way similar to Binx's alternation between a vertical and horizontal search.[45]

The relationship between angelism-bestialism and Binx's searches exceeds their similarly oscillating structures. Binx's vertical search actually tends toward this angelic (bird-like) view of the self. Like the vertical search, the angelic view of the self also produces a kind of iconoclasm, in the form of the moviegoer who does not go to the movies. Angelism aspires to be image free. This is a false invisibility, one that ignores the visible, material world—until the visible world inevitably reasserts itself, swinging the one suffering from angelism into bestialism, from a self soaring toward the transcendent to a self sealed off from the transcendent.

Angelism and bestialism equally, though antipodally, deny the duality of the self as spiritual and animal. These anthropological distortions mirror Christological ones—just as the anthropological union of soul and body serves as the most frequently invoked analogy for the human-divine union in Christ. The resemblances between angelism and bestialism and ancient Christian heresy are noteworthy. For example, angelism reduces humanity to its spiritual nature and so trumps the immanent with the transcendent; similarly, the divinity of the Monophysite Christ swallows his humanity. In bestialism's reduction to the material, it parallels Arianism's attenuation of Christ's divinity in favor of his humanity. The truly transcendent is considered, by Arians and bestial humans, out of immanent reach. Bestials are not even convinced it exists. And the entire angelism-bestialism phenomenon—for the two distortions can come together in one complex—strikingly approximates the heresy that most dominated Byzantine discussions of images: Nestorianism. The sickness of angelism-bestialism names a splitting of the spiritual and material aspects of the self, the soul and the body.

The danger of angelism-bestialism is hinted at in *It Happened One Night*, the movie that forms an important turning point for Binx. He moves from vertical to horizontal searching after watching this movie and solving the problem of the universe but then finding that he himself is left over. What is it about this romantic comedy that energizes the turn from the vertical to the horizontal search? One clue is found in the movie's powerful visual metaphor, a blanket ("the walls of Jericho") that separates the characters of Peter (played by Clark Gable) and Ellie (played by Claudette Colbert) as they change clothes and sleep, allowing them to maintain their sense of an unmarried couple's proper distance from one another. Drawing on the history of film censorship in the time of the movie's release, Stanley Cavell argues that the blanket is also like a movie screen, an image that both censors its object (withholding it from the audience) and also gives it to the audience in the movements on the screen.[46]

But at a climactic moment of the film, as the pair lie in their separated beds, Peter describes his vision of a woman he could marry. Moved by the vision, Ellie crosses to Peter's side of the blanket-wall to embrace him as that woman, and Peter fumbles, stupefied, telling her to go back to her side of the barrier. His dream comes to him as flesh and blood, and he does not know how to receive it. "Why can he not allow the woman of his dreams to enter his dream?" Cavell asks. "But just that must be the answer. What surprises him is her reality. To acknowledge her as this woman would be to acknowledge that she is 'somebody that's real, somebody that's alive,' flesh and blood, someone separate from his dream who therefore has, if she is to be in it, to enter it; and this feels to him to be a threat to the dream, and hence a threat to him."[47] Cavell interprets this moment as one in which the blanket figures the censoring of Peter's knowledge that there is a human on the other side of it. It identifies Peter's difficulty in connecting Ellie's body and soul, a separation that "does violence to" and "makes monsters of" others.[48] We make monsters because we are afraid of risking ourselves, our dreams, our loves on one who could reject them, threaten them, or make them true—transform them, that is, into reality instead of dreams. By the end of the movie, Peter risks his dream becoming flesh and receives his romantic reward. But the difficulty dramatized in *It Happened One Night*, of recognizing a dream when it comes to you in flesh and blood, of recognizing the soul that comes to you in this body, is repeated by Binx himself. He cannot hold spiritual and material, soul and body, dream and flesh, divinity and humanity, visible and invisible together. He abandons his airy transcendent for the earthy immanent, his vertical for the horizontal. In his separation of the two, he veers into angelism, then bestialism, then angelism-bestialism—what Cavell calls a monster.

Binx's angelism-bestialism ends in a howl, for "howling desire" is how Binx narrates what has happened to himself as he reaches the end of his horizontal and vertical searches. He rehearses a litany of despair that ends, "there is nothing to do but fall prey to desire." He repeats, "Nothing remains but desire, and desire comes howling down Elysian Fields like a mistral. My search has been abandoned."[49] The howl evokes both wind and wolves—the desire to which he is "prey" and that is "like a mistral." The howl figures the self made simultaneously beast and angel. It also conjures the hollow created by the distance between those selves. And Binx abandons himself to a howling desire: the togetherness of his animal and spiritual natures comes under pressure and begins to fray, opening a chasm through which the howl travels. His life with images has led him to this howl that is at once Arian, Monophysite, and Nestorian. Something has gone astray in his image gazing. Angelism, bestialism, and angelism-bestialism—these anthropological analogs to the old Byzantine heresies invoked in the iconomachy—indicate that something is wrong in his relationship both to images and to Christ. To discern what has gone wrong, one must also learn what the human is, if not an angel-beast.

Pilgrims of the Ordinary

The human is neither angel nor beast nor angel-beast. She is an animal-spiritual hybrid, whom Percy describes as a pilgrim. She is a wayfarer in trouble, as he writes, and trying to get out of it. Her journey takes her through a world whose essential character is elucidated by the sacraments: filled with ordinary things like water, bread, and oil, which are given the highest significance.[50] These sacraments illumine the pilgrimage as a journey through the ordinary that opens up to the extraordinary.

In his 1989 essay, "The Holiness of the Ordinary," Percy describes the pilgrim anthropology as "the best recipe for novel writing," and he was already drawing on this recipe almost three decades prior in The Moviegoer—his first novel—and quite explicitly.[51] By the end of *The Moviegoer*, Binx no longer prattles on about searches. He now narrates his life as a "dark pilgrimage."[52] The significance of this transition is at least partially signaled by the adjective. The darkness of the pilgrimage contrasts with the lights Aunt Emily lives by. It names for the reader the complicated perception of grace, which, by the end of the novel, comes as a "dim dazzling trick."[53]

The moves from search to pilgrimage and from lights to darkness speak to what it means for a spiritual-animal hybrid to seek a divine-human being—a God who became ordinary without ceasing to be God. Christ's ordinariness, as the anthropological analogy expresses, yields a surplus without yielding its place to that surplus. As the soul is not circumscribed by the body, neither is Christ's divine nature circumscribed by the human. Moreover, as the animality of humans cannot be removed so that they may live out a purely spiritual existence, neither can the humanity of Christ be circumvented to encounter his disincarnate divinity. The animality of humans and the humanity of Christ are something like Fra Angelico's pillar, declining to yield to us naked divinity.

Yet Angelico's pillar is not simply blocking us from Christ. It is also giving us Christ, who is a column. *Columna est Christus*, as 1 Timothy 3:15 claims in the Latin of the Vulgate. Like the flesh of the Word, the column both veils God and presents God. This in a sense is what is accomplished in the sacraments, which are so important to Percy and which point to the human's status as pilgrim. They give to and in the ordinary, visible world a Christ who is not an obvious departure from the ordinary.

It is worth noting that only two characters are mentioned as receiving sacraments in *The Moviegoer*. One is anonymous. The other is Binx's half-brother,

Lonnie, who receives extreme unction and fasts during Lent, despite his physical difficulties. He is distinct among his immediate family—Binx's mother's and stepfather's family—for treating the sacraments as anything other than (only) ordinary. He is also distinct among them because he is, as Binx claims, a moviegoer, like Binx. As a moviegoer, Lonnie, like Binx, is attentive to the image. In Lonnie's case, the moving image does not tempt him to become an angel or a beast—a bird or a soldier. It sustains him in his pilgrim life of the true Little Way of love.

The ambivalent role the moving image plays in *The Moviegoer* displays the complexity of images in this pilgrim life. They convey beyondness—they offer something additional to the world in which they appear—and insist on hereness. Like humans and like Christ, images have an amphibious character—a hybridity or duality in which they do not exist in between two natures but fully comprise both. They are present in and make present to *this* world, and in making present they also underscore the absence of that which they make present. They render visible and, in doing so, show us the invisible that remains unenvisagable to us. The "is" and "is not" form of images means that they encompass visibility and invisibility, presence and absence, immanence and transcendence. An image that attempts to deny the visible world becomes an illusion. An image that excludes the invisible by denying the invisibility of its own nature becomes an object; if it does this while claiming for itself the significance of the invisible, it becomes an idol. This is both why images can go so wrong—they can tempt us into one side of these polarities—and why they are so important—they speak to the hybrid nature of humanity and communicate the dual-natured Christ.

"Parker's Back" conveys the amphibiousness of images in the antagonistic characters of Parker, who chases immanence through images, and Sarah Ruth, who disdains images in favor of an unmediated transcendence. Parker's search begins when the tattooed man images paradise and awakens him to a sense of wonder, which he seeks to recapture through his own tattoos throughout the story. While the image communicates something invisible to Parker, he tries to replicate what it gives him by focusing only on its material reality, as if it were wholly visible to him, like an object. Near the end of the story he receives his invisible soul image (the arabesque of beasts and flowers), which recapitulates both the image of the tattooed man and his own Byzantine Christ tattoo, which later merges with his own suffering body to generate an image of Christ crucified. It is significant that the soul images appear only after he has sought and seen the Byzantine Christ with eyes that remind him of the icepick eyes of his iconoclastic, transcendence-oriented wife, Sarah Ruth. This is not an image that sides with transcendence against immanence, or immanence against transcendence, as contemporary image theorists sometimes do. Only once his wholly immanence-oriented iconophilia has incorporated something of transcendence-oriented iconoclasm does he receive the world-opening image he seeks. Only once his relationship to the image shifts from the visible closed in on itself to the visible that is negated does that image open onto the invisible.

Aside from icepick eyes, what exactly does this iconoclasm internal to iconophilia, this negation internal to presence, look like?

Apophaticism: An Iconoclasm of Fidelity

Comprised of both the visible and the invisible, images are always in danger of teetering toward visibility or invisibility and so becoming objects, idols, or illusions—all terms that name false image relationships. How does one resist these dangers? Binx tries to prevent the degeneration of image into illusion by grounding the image in the material realities of the world. But what of the threats of objecthood and idolatry? Of the two, objecthood is the less complicated. There is nothing intrinsically wrong with an object as object. It simply signifies nothing beyond itself. It mediates no presence except its own and attempts no negation of itself. Though it is unfortunate when objecthood is the result of degrading an image, an object in and of itself need not pose a problem. An idol does. Like an object, an idol signifies nothing beyond itself. Unlike an object, it claims a presence beyond itself as its own. It negates nothing about itself and so refuses to be an image. Yet even while it points only to its own immanence, an idol paradoxically claims transcendence. An object has not achieved image-hood; an idol has betrayed it. For idols, then, we need iconoclasms of fidelity. These iconoclasms will also prove salutary for objects to the extent such objects aspire to an illusion of transcendence, inasmuch as they are talismanic, like Parker's tattoos.

In identifying iconoclasms of fidelity to restore the image, I diverge again from Marion. Worried though he is about the image-saturated age and the idolatry of the televisual image, Marion cannot commend iconoclasm as a response. For him, iconoclasm simply inverts the problem of the idol. If the idol wrongly prioritizes the visible, iconoclasm wrongly prioritizes the invisible. Iconoclasm therefore confirms the divorce between the two. In Percy's language, it can only lead to a howl. But this, of course, is to assume that iconoclasm always looks like the iconoclasm of Sarah Ruth or of the romantic, that iconoclasm is always an iconoclasm of temptation. I insist there are other forms of breaking and chastening images, and that these can be rehabilitative because they restore to imaging the negation that makes imaging possible. The first strategy of negation—one with which Marion might sympathize—is apophaticism, a negation aggressively deployed in *The Moviegoer*.

Searching, as Binx Bolling knows, frequently produces idols, what he will call "shit." In the critical address in which Binx abandons himself to howling desire, he claims that his only talent is "a good nose for merde" in this, "the very century of merde." He goes on to elaborate what qualifies as *merde*: "the great shithouse of scientific humanism where needs are satisfied, everyone becomes an anyone." Everydayness seems to have won, for "malaise has settled like a fallout."[54] Shit is the staunch immanence that parades as a new transcendence in scientific humanism and ultimately leads to an angelism that ends in malaise. It is the closure, or totalization, of the visible.

Binx's declaration of his shit-smelling talent immediately precedes his reception of grace. These two events are not unrelated. For, far from worthless, his capacity to smell shit is a gift that helps him identify divine work in the world. It is a kind of apophatic identifying of what is not God. To relate to something as an idol that pretends transcendence? Shit, not God. Yet to impugn idols by naming them as shit is not to condemn them to eternal separation from God nor to declare they lack capacity for meaning. The final scene before the epilogue communicates the way shit may be received as itself a medium of grace.

The novel's last scene takes place on Ash Wednesday. A man Percy names a "Negro" leaves a church. His "ambiguous sienna color and pied" forehead makes it "impossible to say" whether he has received ashes. The dark color of the man's skin and the darkness of the ashes make this moment an apt illustration of how Percy thinks about the workings of grace in the world. For the dark and pied forehead that may or may not be marked with the grace of penitence itself images what Percy calls the "dim dazzling trick of grace."[55] Has grace come through darkness on darkness? It is "impossible to say." The question can be answered only in hope.

It is fitting that the medium of possible grace is the ash of penitence. The ash of Ash Wednesday reminds the faithful that the shit of idolatry may become, through confession, the ash of grace. To assail the closed off visibility of an idol, to name it shit, is also to name a way it can be received anew, by being reincorporated into the ordinary in which grace comes to us. It is difficult to discern these idols-turned-shit-turned-ashes, because they are received within the ordinary. The difficulty of discerning such ash mirrors the difficulty of receiving Christ, by whom we also receive God in and as the ordinary. Percy's ash-touched Negro in this way figures the Christ who abides with us, visible dimly. It is no coincidence that the great image defender John of Damascus used similar language, describing images of invisible things as "provid[ing] in bodily form a *dim* understanding of what is depicted."[56] God's abiding in our world is dim to us, even if it is a dimness that is also dazzling.

Like the idols-turned-ashes, God, too, became dust, ash to dwell in our shit-sodden world. Christ is difficult to discern because he is like us in all ways except sin. Augustine writes of the difficulty this creates for the world in perceiving Christ, who "was plainly visible to the carnal eyes of the world, while manifest in the flesh; but [the world] saw not the Word that lay hid in the flesh: it saw the man, but it saw not God."[57] Pseudo-Dionysius describes the paradox of Christ's plainness and hiddenness, claiming, "the transcendent has put aside its own hiddenness and has revealed itself to us by becoming a human being. But he is hidden even after this revelation, or, if I may speak in a more divine fashion, is hidden even amid the revelation."[58] Christ appears to the world seemingly indistinguishable from the world, true God appearing as truly a human as any other human. Vladimir Lossky describes this "paradox of the Christian revelation" in terms of transcendence and immanence. He writes of how the God who is transcendent reveals himself as transcendent in the immanent. Such a paradox, Lossky claims, implies "the existence of an apophatic attitude," which he glosses as "a going beyond everything that has a connection with created finitude."[59]

Binx adopts an apophatic attitude when he names idols as shit, which is a way of distinguishing the transcendence that created finitude can claim from the radical transcendence of God. Even as Binx nears despair, his words, read through Lossky's paradox, suggest real hope. For Lossky claims that an apophatic attitude is a way of knowing God by eliminating all that is not God. It culminates in the impossibility that any human knowledge finally can contain God.[60] For Binx, this looks like rebutting false claims of transcendence—naming idols as shit—so that the rebuttal itself signifies the radical transcendence of God. Rejecting the false transcendence as not-God opens up immanence to point to a transcendence both within and beyond it. The idol becomes an image of God by indicating what God is not. The shit, in Binx's case, is reclaimed as ashes.

Confession: Another Iconoclasm of Fidelity

Binx ends his speech about *merde* by declaring that he has to find a girl. At that moment, a girl comes to save him. It is not *any* girl. It is a specific girl: Kate, his step-cousin, closest friend, and fiancée, who comes to him as a figure of grace.[61] And the way she mediates grace is both by the pledge to him her presence signifies at that moment and by what she does next. She confesses.

The significance of confessing is tipped by the novel's original title, *Confessions of a Moviegoer*. It is more obliquely indicated at the end of the novel, which returns to Søren Kierkegaard, who supplies the book's epigraph. In the epilogue, Jack (like O. E., Binx grows into his given name by the end of his story) explains why there is nothing more he wants to say about the search, and he alludes to the "great Danish philosopher" who offered "edifying discourses" because he had no authority to give sermons. "[I]t is not open to me even to be edifying, since the time is later than his [Kierkegaard's], much too late to edify or do much of anything except plant a foot in the right place as the opportunity presents itself—if indeed asskicking is properly distinguished from edification."[62] The first of Kierkegaard's edifying discourses to be translated into English was *Purity of Heart Is to Will One Thing: Spiritual Preparation for the Office of Confession* (1938). It is a discourse that prepares for confession. For himself, Binx does not exactly claim to edify. Asskicking—booting that which produces shit—is all Binx offers. And still, it is reasonable to think that connected as it can be to edification, asskicking, too, prepares for confession. The novel moves toward confession as its culminating moment; that is all there is to say now about the search.

There is a great building toward confession in the novel, and yet only one character ever describes her speech as confession: "I'll make you a little confession," Aunt Emily declares, in the speech that drives Binx to near-despair. Then she works up to a rousing defense of herself and her kind: "But one thing I am sure of, we live by our lights, we die by our lights, and whoever the high gods may be, we'll look them in the eye without apology."[63] What she has made, with her unapologetic god-eyeballing, is an anti-confession. She has shored up her self and returned to her inner lighthouse.

Kate is the next character to arrive on the scene after the anti-confession. She is Aunt Emily's countertype. Where Aunt Emily lives by her lights, Kate's eyes are always turning to discs, as if to protest false light. Shortly after she appears, she and Binx watch the Negro enter the church. He is ordinary, "more respectable than respectable" and "more middle-class than one could believe."[64] His gestures, moreover, indicate to Binx that church is routine for him. Binx watches him go in, and Kate begins confessing to Binx. She confesses her crippling fear. She confesses her neediness. She confesses that she lacks conviction she will ever really truly change. She begs him not to laugh at her.

Throughout her marvelous display of vulnerability and dependence, Kate cannot make a clean confession: her solemnity is "not-quite-pure." As impurity cuts through her solemnity, so her actions of self-harm unravel the edges of her confession. She picks at her thumb, tearing away little pieces of flesh. Unlike Peter in *It Happened One Night*, Jack knows how to receive a vision that has come to him as flesh and blood. He takes her hand, kisses the blood, and says, "But you must try not to hurt yourself so much." "I will try! I will!"[65] Kate's eager response draws her back to repentance. She offers in her confession a natural analog to the holy sacrament.

At just that moment, the ordinary Negro reappears from the church, perhaps marked with an ashen cross. He is an image of the "dim dazzling grace" that Jack has received through Kate and she through him. Why, Jack wonders, has the man come? "It is impossible to say why he is here. Is it part and parcel of the complex business of coming up in the world? Or is it because he believes that God himself is present here at the corner of Elysian Fields and Bon Enfants? Or is he here for both reasons: through some dim dazzling trick of grace, coming for the one and receiving the other as God's own importunate bonus? It is impossible to say."[66] It is difficult to discern a divine who comes to us in the ordinary, especially when that divine points beyond the visible to the invisible.

Parker, too, confesses near the end of his story. Sarah Ruth, the only person who knows Parker's first names and his shame about them, refuses to open the door until he identifies himself by them. After she dissents twice to open to "O. E.," he acknowledges himself by the name he has avoided his whole life, "Obadiah Elihue"—at last identifying himself with a lifelong source of shame. Instead of repressing his name to project a false (or at least incomplete) image of who he is, he claims his full name—and then receives grace. With Parker's confession, he breaks his self-image and his soul, once a "spider web of facts and lies," receives the invisible, splendorous arabesque he had been seeking in tattoos all his life. His soul opens in a new way to the invisible world.[67]

In apophatic naming of God, idols are broken so that they might image God. In confession, the self is broken, so that it, too, might resist closing in on the visible. It is broken as a false image and as a false beholder of images. For if what an idol names is a wrong relation to the beheld, then the self relating to what is beheld must also be addressed. Like a doctor setting a bone, confession breaks the self to bring it into line with the invisible God. Gregory of Nyssa describes the way the self is opened to the love of God as a wounding, a puncturing of our sin-sick selves that enables us to see Christ rightly.[68] A person, Gregory writes, must be wounded in love; then is the visible rightly related to the invisible. Confession names one kind of wounding, this breaking that orders the realm of images to the realm of the invisible. Confessing his name, Obadiah Elihue Parker images the paradisal arabesque in his soul; confessing her sickness, Kate opens new possibilities for healing and for deeper unity with Jack.

The Little Way That Transfigures the Everyday

These iconoclastic-iconophilic strategies of apophaticism and confession—iconoclasms of fidelity—aim not at forswearing the everyday in favor of some transcendent invisibility, nor at fencing off the everyday from transcendent visibility. They aim, as did Saint Thérèse of Lisieux's Little Way, at the transfiguration of the everyday. Where Binx's little way embraces little everyday physical pleasures as if they are the sum of life's meaning, Saint Thérèse's Little Way extends love to everyone she meets and everything she does in her everyday life. Imitating the Christ who became everyday, Thérèse meets Christ in the everyday by her little sacrifices of love in her routine and ordinary life. The Little Way is a path through the ordinary that recognizes and imitates a God who came to abide in the ordinary. For without scorning the ordinary, Christ orients it in a new way toward divine life. We meet this abiding Christ in images that negate the visible to open them to the invisible. We betray this abiding Christ through abandoning the visible, as pure iconoclasts do, including Sarah Ruth, the romantic, and Binx in his vertical search, as well as through attempts to close the visible in on itself, as certain kinds of iconophiles do—including Parker in most of his life and Binx in his horizontal search. Breaking the idols of these iconoclasts and iconophiles enables them to open to the invisible, to see and become divine images that mediate the presence of the Christ who abides in the ordinary without being reducible to the ordinary. This is not a form of breaking that destroys idols but that turns idols into images. It is a breaking that recognizes the world as an image of God and images as both transcendent and immanent, neither vitiating the other.

The Eucharist: Presence and the Centrality of the Invisible

The sacrament of confession prepares the supplicant for another sacrament. It is Walker Percy's paradigmatic example of how a sacrament confers holiness on ordinary things—the very one, in fact, that iconomachs used to dismiss images—the Eucharist.[69] The iconomachs insist that the Eucharist is the paradigmatic image. According to them, it reveals that images work by being consubstantial with the imaged. But this argument both underplays and overplays the role of negation in images. It underplays the role of negation because it insists that images must be so like the imaged that they are all consubstantial with it. The argument thus neglects how strongly the image can *not* be what it presents. While Christ is consubstantial with the Father, that strong form of identification is not necessary for all images, which are both *like* and *unlike* what they image.

If the iconomachs' description of the Eucharist underplays the negation, it also, for the Catholic Church of O'Connor and Percy, overplays it. While the Eucharist involves a deep form of likeness between sign and signified, one shared by no image except for Christ himself, the Eucharist also entails a deep change in the signifier that images do not. The theology of the Eucharist is not uniform across churches or times, but Thomas Aquinas articulates a version of Eucharistic theology importantly different from image theology. He describes the way the bread and wine become the body and blood of Christ by a negation unlike the negation of images. The way the Eucharist negates itself, unlike the way images do, involves a change in the signifier. The substance of the bread and wine does not just mediate the substance of Christ's body and blood; it becomes it. One is tempted to speak of displacement or erasure, but Thomas Aquinas, for one, refuses such language. He prefers instead to speak of *change*. The substance of the bread and wine are like air consumed by a fire. The air is no longer there but neither is it annihilated; it has become—been converted to—the fire.[70] And this deviates not only from images. It diverges from the incarnation as well. For Christ's consubstantiality with the Father does not come at the cost of his consubstantiality with humanity. As we have explored in this chapter, Christ is amphibious in the way that images are. Both negate by opening, not eradicating or, in the case of the Eucharist, consuming. In this way, Christ and images are importantly dissimilar with the Eucharist. As a sign of Christ, the Eucharist is sui generis. Strangely, though the bread and wine before consecration can be images of the body and blood of Christ, they become their own type of sign through consecration.

Even if the Eucharist does not model how all images must work, it is an important channel and sign of Christ's presence, and as such, it shares certain interesting features with images. One is this: though the bread and wine of the Eucharist *resemble* the flesh and blood of Christ, they do not look exactly like flesh and blood, nor do they look more like flesh and blood than ordinary bread and wine. One looking at the Eucharist does not physically see Christ's body. In this way, the Eucharist insists both on the importance of visibility and the ultimate invisibility of the presence it mediates. It is important that the bread and wine resemble flesh and blood, and it is also important that they cannot be visually confused with flesh and blood. Whereas Binx alternates between the invisible and the visible in ways that disjoin the universe and himself into a howl, the Eucharist points to a God who is visibly present in the world in a way that is ordered to the invisible *and* discernible in the visible. We might draw on Lossky to say that the Eucharist is like apophatic speaking in that it has silence (invisibility) built into its mode of making present.

While not an image, the Eucharist must be pivotal for how we approach images, for it points to the centrality of both the invisible and the ordinary. Paul Evdokimov draws on this affinity between image and Eucharist when he writes, "The veneration of the gospel book, the cross and the icon are united together with the liturgical mystery of the presence that the church proclaims from her Eucharistic heart: 'Our doctrine is in agreement with the eucharist and the eucharist confirms our doctrine,' according to St Irenaeus."[71] The iconomachs were right, then, to go to the Eucharist to confirm or contradict the legitimacy of icons. They were wrong in their insistence of Eucharist as the paradigmatic image. As a means of presence, the Eucharist shares with images important structural similarities—especially the important orientation toward the invisible. At the same time, it is not perfectly equivalent to images. Neither the type of presence the Eucharist bears (sacramental or real) nor its way of bearing that presence is identical to what is found in images. When the Eucharist is made essential to a theology of and practice around images, the image remains oriented to the invisible without discarding its visibility. When the Eucharist is distinguished from images, a diversity of presences within images is possible.

The Amphibious Image

Christ, humans, and images—they are all analogies for one another because they share an amphibious structure. That amphibious structure is constantly in danger of being misconstrued. As both human and divine, Christ can be misrepresented as human rather than divine (Arianism), as divine rather than human (Monophysitism), or as a disunified conjunction of human and divine (Nestorianism). As both animal and spiritual, humans can be misconceived as animal rather than spiritual (bestialism), as spiritual rather than animal (angelism), or as bipolar creatures who oscillate between the two (angelism-bestialism). These Christological and anthropological misunderstandings are frequently registered in our life with images. Images are hybrid in that they are visible-invisible and can be misunderstood in ways that include denying the invisible (idolatry or objecthood) or denying the visible (illusions). They can emphasize their transcendence at the expense of their immanence (a degenerate version of Platonism) or their immanence at the expense of their transcendence (a degenerate version of the picture theorists' correction). But images are both; they are amphibians, like the human and divine Christ.

They are linked, these three amphibians. The characters of "Parker's Back" and *The Moviegoer* who relate wrongly to images also relate wrongly to themselves as humans and to Christ. They find healing—however slight or murky that healing is—through employing strategies of negation. Parker incorporates the transcendence-seeking, icepick eyes of the Byzantine Christ and Sarah Ruth into his tattoo; and he identifies with his name that has caused him such shame. In negating the tattoo image, his desire for images, and his self-image, all of these open up to the invisible, to the divine in hopeful ways that do not leave behind the visible. Through Kate, Jack also learns to negate the self through confession, which proves a better strategy of negation than his attempts to prevent movies from becoming illusion. These negations mean that the visible opens onto the invisible; that the invisible remains central to what an image is—a lesson that the Eucharist reiterates each time it is celebrated.

Maria Orans: Revealing the Abiding Presence of the Hidden Christ

In the icon called the Virgin of the Sign, *Maria orans* stands with her hands out in prayer, dressed in the clothing typical for Eastern icons: head covering, long sleeves, draped dress. Overlying this clothing, a large circle opens in the middle of the image. Spanning the length of her torso, it exposes the Christ-babe her pregnant body nurtures. The image may seem, in one way, to be the inverse of Fra Angelico's altarpiece at Cortona. Where that painting introduced a pillar that blocked the divine from view, this icon pulls back the curtain of Mary's clothing and flesh to display the God made human. The contrast is too facile, though, for *Maria orans* does not simply displace hiddenness with revealedness. She reveals the Christ-babe *as* the hidden Christ—hidden, that is, in both the mother of Jesus and in the mother church.[72] Rowan Williams puts it well in a meditation on this icon, "But if we think of the essential hiddenness that the image reminds us of, we must not suppose that being aware of that presence will necessarily make it easier for us to pin down where it is."[73] We cannot pin down the center of Christ's presence in the church any more than Jack can confirm that the Negro received ashes. The Virgin of the Sign expresses the difficulty of discerning Christ in a world where Christ became human. It is an image about the mystery of imaging.

The Virgin of the Sign icon unites the three amphibians—the visible-invisible image, the animal-spirit human, and the human-divine Christ—to convey the mysteriousness of discerning Christ's presence. It is mysterious because, in Christ, God abides with those who are not God by becoming what is not God. God is discernible in and as not-God without being reducible to not-God. In the Virgin of the Sign, Christ is discernible in and as the body of Mary, the church, and humanity, without being exhausted by those realities. It is also, then, an image that alerts us to the dangers of images. As Williams writes, the church imaged in the Virgin of the Sign is "suspicious of idolatry, able to stay with the mysteriousness of Christ's presence rather than creating an accessible but false picture to hang on to."[74] This, finally, is why the iconomachs were right that iconoclasm is at times an important response to images: iconoclasm can be wielded to break images that are overly hasty identifications of the invisible God in the visible—what I have been calling idols. Iconoclasms of fidelity found, for example, in confession and in apophatic ways of naming God, make the mystery of the invisible God central to our relationship to images. Such iconoclasms negate the visible to make present the abiding Christ, so that we may better love the visible image of the invisible God.

FIGURE 3. Matthias Grünewald, Isenheim Altarpiece, 1512–16. Unterlinden Museum. Public domain (Wikimedia).

3 CRUCIFIED, DIED, AND WAS BURIED

Riven and Riving Presence

THE CRUCIFIED CHRIST painted on the Isenheim altar is famous, striking, and gruesome. As rendered by Matthias Grünewald, Christ's crucified body echoes the shape of the chalice at the foot of his cross. Nails driven through flexed hands fix Christ's strained arms in a wide V. A single stake fastens his right foot on his left, twining his legs together. His head hangs limply down, eyes closed, mouth agape. Blood drips thickly from his hands, his feet, his side, and his thorn-crowned head. He has become the cup he asked the Father to take from him, the cup he has told James and John he must drink. He offers himself on the altar as the chalice of salvation.

Grünewald's image stages Christ's union with what is dissimilar to him. The chalice-shaped body adverts to one union: Christ's union with the Eucharistic elements, which, despite their dissimilarity from Christ, nevertheless communicate his real presence to the faithful. The altarpiece displays another union. This second union is not announced in the shape of Christ's body but in the sores eating through his skin, wounds shared by the plague victims beholding the altarpiece. Stationed in the hospital chapel of a monastery devoted to those with skin afflictions, Grünewald's representation of Christ as skin-diseased stresses that despite Christ's dissimilarity from the faithful approaching him— *they* could not offer themselves for salvation—he resembles them in their affliction. In the Isenheim Christ, the suffering of flesh disease merges with the suffering of crucifixion. Just so is the Isenheim Christ present to the suffering of those beholding him. Christ's skin sores in this image reiterate God's presence to the darkest and bleakest parts of our world. They dramatize the logic of the cross: where God seems most absent, there God the crucified is supremely, uniquely present. On the cross, God is found in the difficulty of finding God.

The visual rhetoric of the Isenheim Altarpiece affirms a view of the image as the union of similar with dissimilar and visible with invisible. But the altarpiece also announces a still more startling claim. It is not just that on the cross, God makes Godself known through a visibility utterly dissimilar to God. It is that God is present to brokenness *as God*. The Isenheim Altarpiece, after all, is a picture of God in the midst of brokenness—not a picture of one who used to be God but now is broken. Like other images of cross and crucifix, the Isenheim Altarpiece claims that even in brokenness, God does not cease to be God, nor is God overcome by brokenness. God remains fully and unchangingly God all the way through brokenness. This is why the cross is such a profound source of hope: By remaining God even in brokenness, Christ on the cross images the breaking of brokenness.

Though it prefigures the resurrection, the breaking of brokenness the cross displays is not the same breaking that the resurrection gives us. (I take up that type of breaking in the next chapter.) Rather, the cross breaks brokenness by showing that brokenness—sin, violence, torture, death—cannot exclude God's presence. At one level, the cross announces an absence. It sounds an absence of health, vitality, power, and, in the case of Christ's wounds, an absence of flesh. Crucifixes, having a dead corpus, even declare an absence of life. Yet by these publications of absence, the cross makes, at another level, a powerful proclamation of presence. Churches, homes, and individuals fill their lives with crosses to mark the ubiquity of divine presence in the world. To put a cross on an altar, whether by painting one on it, like Grünewald's Christ, or setting one nearby, as Catholic canon law requires, identifies the cross with the proclamation of Christ's presence in the liturgy of the mass. The cross's status in the Eucharistic liturgy underscores the way divine absence is bound to divine presence. On the cross, where the negation of the Image would seem to go too far—to overtake and vitiate, rather than unlock, presence—that negation is itself negated. The negation of negation celebrates a new presence, whereby God is present even in death.

What kind of presence is this that the cross proclaims? It is God's riven and riving presence. Christ is riven: his body punctured with thorns, nails, a spear. He is riven when he is beaten, flogged, tortured, hung. At the same time, Christ on the cross also rives. He rives the power of sin, destroying its dominion over humanity. For Christ does not allow violence to make him violent, nor affliction to turn him from the path of perfect love. In the brokenness of his flesh, Christ breaks the brokenness of the world.

Christ's rivenness and rivingness come together. As they are bound to one another, so are Christ's impassibility and vulnerability. The strength of God's love is God's utter vulnerability to humanity, rejection, torture, and death. Humanity's attempt to destroy the Image reveals the love of God that cannot be destroyed, that persists even when the cost of that love is death. On the cross, God remains perfect love, determined neither by fear nor death, even as such love travels through, not around, death by torture. God's vulnerability on the cross means violence never becomes more decisive than love; love does not cease to be love because of violence. In this way, vulnerability is not opposed to the impassibility of God. It is impassibility's anterior side. God's naked, suffering, vulnerable body on the cross is the impassibility of love made visible. Breakingness comes with brokenness as the negation of the Image is negated. Here we arrive at the turning point of the chiasm.

An Absence That Proclaims a Presence

Working from around 1512 to 1516, Matthias Grünewald finished the Isenheim Altarpiece on the eve of the Reformation. The following year, Martin Luther published his *Ninety-Five Theses* and the year following that, he wrote his theses for the Heidelberg Disputation, where he first contrasted the theology of the cross with the theology of glory. The contrast is Luther's attempt to formulate where God is and where God is not, to mark where divine presence has been wrongly assimilated to worldly wisdom. In these efforts, Luther pits revelation, reality, and the cross against human perception, appearance, and glory to claim that God is revealed in the hiddenness of the cross. God's power is found in the cross's impotence, God's wisdom in its folly. Chasing flashes of humanly perceived glory will yield simply a human projection of God.

Luther's theology of the cross helped to galvanize an iconoclastic impulse latent in the church. In 1522, shortly after Luther left Wittenberg, a mob there committed the first significant acts of Protestant iconoclasm.[1] Luther himself neither endorsed nor condemned iconoclasm, as long as it was orderly, but Protestantism spread in tandem with iconoclastic acts and agendas. In their efforts to eradicate images, Protestant mobs defaced paintings, broke windows, and burned textiles. They also stripped altars, an act that points to the strangeness of much Reformation iconoclasm: it enacted what it criticized. Liturgically, the stripping of the altars is the last act of the Maundy Thursday service, as the host is taken from the tabernacle into a side chapel. The faithful process out of the main church, following the host, and then disperse as the service ends in the side chapel. The real presence of Christ in the host has, at that point, left the main church. The next services occur on Good Friday with the faithful entering into the anguish of God's death and the absence of Christ. No host is consecrated that day, nor until the light of Christ processes back into the sanctuary in the Easter vigil. In the stripping of the altars, the Holy Triduum has begun.

The Maundy Thursday and Good Friday liturgies express complex dynamics of divine presence and absence. Good Friday is exceedingly holy because God's death is an absence that proclaims the unceasingness of God's presence. The faithful worship on Good Friday because God is present even unto death. So when the iconoclasts stripped the altars, what divine absence did they proclaim? Were they preparing the church to encounter the cross of Christ? To enter a kind of Good Friday? It seems they wanted to claim that God's presence does not depend upon liturgical rituals or ecclesial images. As the Holy Triduum liturgy celebrates God's presence through proclaiming God's absence, so did the Reformation iconoclasts declare God's absence in these rituals and images in order to insist on the universal availability of God's presence. There was a sense, among these iconoclasts who believed themselves faithful to the Lord, that proclaiming a form of God's absence (God is not in this image) is a way of proclaiming God's presence (images are not needed for God to be present). The parodic liturgy of iconoclasm embodies a dynamic of divine presence and absence more similar to than different from what it mocks. As the Good Friday liturgy proclaims a divine presence that cannot be circumscribed by death, so did the Protestant iconoclasts proclaim a God who cannot be circumscribed by human artifice. As iconoclasm mimics aspects of the Good Friday liturgy, iconoclastic proclamations of divine absence can make way for asserting diverse forms of God's presence. Another way to put this is to say that Reformation iconoclasm—and to some extent all iconoclasm—is strangely intimate with the image logic of Grünewald.

The logic of Grünewald is also a logic of revelation in hiddenness. God is depicted in God's becoming what is profoundly dissimilar to God. God's life is revealed as it is ebbing away. This is an image that, in one historian's words, both saves and rejects appearances.[2] It is an image that is also an erasure, visualizing a paradox of hiddenness and revealedness similar to Luther's theology of the hidden God. (The number of Isenheim Altarpiece prints hung in Lutheran seminaries testifies to the popularity of that view.) Though compatible with Luther's theological conviction, the Isenheim Altarpiece speaks to a dynamic larger than his distinctive theology. It dramatizes a dynamic of negation and presence, breaking and revealing, iconoclasm and imaging exemplified in the cross of Christ across Christian traditions.

In the Catholic tradition, Jean-Luc Marion writes about crosses and images in terms Luther (or at least Grünewald) might find amenable. He describes the cross as eschewing the logic of images—a logic of resemblance—and announcing an iconic logic of visuality. Marion's language is dramatic: "Christ kills the image on the cross, because he crosses an abyss without measure between his appearance and his glory."[3] What Marion means by *image* here is what I call *spectacle*: something wholly identified with its appearance. The problem with the image-spectacle, for Marion, is that it is organized by a logic of similarity; it moves from one visible thing to another similar visible thing, such that one who is glorious appears in glory in her image. Prize athletes appear with laurels; empresses with crowns. The cross, Marion notes, does not work that way; for, as he describes it, the cross moves from visible to invisible; it is the stigmata of the invisible in the visible. Thus, on the cross, Christ is not known by visual spectacle but through recognition, as when the centurion recognizes on the cross the mark of the invisible God in the visible world. On the cross, the invisible God imprints on the visible, in Marion's words, as a wound. There is a sympathy here with Luther's hidden and revealed dynamic. Marion's eschewal of image-spectacle for the imprint of God on the cross could be a Catholic counterpart to Luther's affirmation of the presence of God, not in worldly glory but in the hiddenness of the cross.

Luther, Marion, and Grünewald press the significance of God's death on the cross. In various ways for all of them, the cross underscores the importance of dissimilarity, hiddenness, and absence for receiving the divine. It highlights the way God cannot be circumscribed by any feature of the world. Perhaps it is unsurprising, then, that the cross has an ambivalent history in relation to images. At some moments in the past, iconoclasts wielded the cross against images; at other times, iconoclasts targeted the cross as a uniquely pernicious image. The cross has energized the proliferation of images and marked the absence of them. And these contingencies of history point to a theological truth of the cross: as rivingness and rivenness come together in the cross, so, too, do iconoclasms and images. These two aspects of the cross—generating images and inciting iconoclasm—are both important roles that ought not to be sundered from one another. Although many times images perform faithfully, sometimes they perform like idols. Similarly, although iconoclasms can be unnecessary and undesirable—what I have been calling iconoclasms of temptation—iconoclasms can also be Christ-like. The cross calls for discerning iconoclasms of fidelity even as it affirms a wide variety of images as faithful to it.

This chapter sojourns with a variety of writers, saints, scenes, and poets—fellow pilgrims and moments both iconoclastic and iconophilic—to paint a vision of the cross that illumines a broad approach to cross-imaging (a strong iconophilia) that is inflected with an iconoclasm of fidelity (a weak iconoclasm). The vision is that of the cosmic cross, the cross that goes with the grain of the universe. The cross is ubiquitously both imaged and iconoclastic because it breaks brokenness itself. This revelatory moment is key. The cross, where the Image is broken, is God's central image in God's life with what is not God, the fulcrum of gathering and turning for images that present the divine. The image of the cross draws together—figuring or prefiguring—all other moments in God's life with the world.

I begin with scenes of iconoclasm.

A Pastiche of Iconoclastic Acts: The Cross as an Image of Iconoclasm

Basel, Switzerland, 1529. Gripped with Reformation fervor, a mob wrenches a crucifix from a church and hauls it into the market. They shout at it, mocking its impotence. "If you're God, then save yourself, but if you're man, then bleed."[4] In taunting the image, these iconoclasts echo jeers similar to those of the crowds in the crucifixion accounts of the gospels.[5] *If you're the Son of God, then come down from the cross.* And, *If you're Christ, then save yourself.*

Hildesheim, Germany, 1543. A tailor's guild drags a statue of Christ from the church of St Andreas into a bar. They order it to drink and then mock its inability to do so with lines from Christ's tormentors in the Passion plays. *Now how's he supposed to drink? Can't you see? He's been whipped, his blood is squirting out of him and he's holy and impotent, so he just can't do it.* Then they force the statue to "drink."[6]

Ulm, Germany, 1534. The mouth of another Christ statue is filled with something rather less pleasant than water.[7]

Central America, sixteenth century. It is the time of the Spanish conquest. Christopher Columbus's discovery has excited a young Dominican friar-to-be, who makes the long journey to the New World. His enthusiasm softens and then melts in horror as he witnesses his kinsfolk robbing the indigenous people of land, life, and freedom. Later, as a Dominican friar, Bartolomé de las Casas describes his church as complicit in the iconoclasm of crucifixion, declaring, "I leave, in the Indies, Jesus Christ, our God, scourged and afflicted and buffeted and crucified, not once but millions of times."[8] In part, the Spanish had come—las Casas had come—to convert a people they believed idolatrous. What las Casas witnesses while there is the idolatry of his own people, who worship gold and torture people. He decides his people did not bring Christ. They crucify him anew.

France, 2011. On Palm Sunday morning, four young adults enter an exhibition just after it opens. They come with hammers to attack what has become one of the Modern West's most familiar objects of iconoclasm: Andres Serrano's 1987 photograph of a plastic crucifix submerged in urine, *Immersion* (*Piss Christ*). One young adult threatens a guard with a hammer. Another smashes the protective Plexiglas and slashes the photograph. After the destruction, gallery director Eric Mézil reopens the museum to display the damage.[9] Moreover, the photograph itself is already an image of damage, according to Serrano. He conceived it as an iconoclastic gesture against the "billion-dollar Christ-for-profit industry."[10] What is it Mézil displays—a damaged image of an image of damage that has itself been damaged?

Some iconoclastic scenes in this pastiche are horrific; others redundant. Or they are both. They can be both because they concern the crucifix, itself an image of horrific iconoclasm—the breaking of the Image of the invisible God. In his descriptions of the conquest as crucifixion, las Casas saw both horror and a parodied repetition. In the abuse and murder of the indigenous people—which the Spanish justified by labeling the indigenous people idolaters—the Spanish broke the suffering ones identified with Christ in the world, and so repeated the breaking of the Image of God on the cross.

Iconoclasm repeats crucifixion. This claim is not new to las Casas, nor to descriptions of him. It is at least as old as the Byzantine iconomachy. One image conspicuously testifies to this claim. In the margins of a ninth-century psalter, a scene of crucifixion doubles as a scene of iconoclasm.[11] It features two Roman centurions, one offering up a sponge of vinegar on his spear, and the other hoisting a spear near Christ's bleeding body. Near them, an iconoclast dips an icon of Christ into a pot of vinegar, used by iconoclasts to take off paint. To erase an image of Christ, the image insists, is to crucify Christ again. In this way, an iconoclast creates a new image of the crucified God, even while erasing an existing image.

At one level, iconoclastic acts can image the crucifixion because iconoclasm produces images. Increasingly, iconoclasm is being studied as a phenomenon that both generates and destroys. A 2002 exhibit explored this phenomenon, under the title *Iconoclash*. Iconoclasm, the catalogue essays for the exhibition argue, does not just annihilate and eradicate. It also builds and creates. The term *iconoclash* names the destruction that is also a creation. Mézil exhibited iconoclash in his gallery when he opened it to show the violence against *Piss Christ*. Mia Mochizuki notes this type of phenomenon when she describes how supposed iconoclasts in fact generated a robust visual culture in the sixteenth-century Netherlands, one in which the word, said to supplant images, becomes itself an image.[12] Joseph Leo Koerner points to the many examples of iconoclash in Reformation iconoclasm, examples in which the residue of the attacked image becomes itself an image. In these acts, "image-breakers ... become image-makers."[13] Bruno Latour makes a similar point about iconoclasm broadly when he claims that "defacement" and "effacement" are coeval.[14] Iconoclasm does not (just) destroy an image; it creates images of destruction.

The way image-breaking makes an image mirrors the way making an image can also entail acts of destruction. Is the hammer raised by a sculptor breaking the rock or is it held by an iconoclast riving the statue? Acts of creating an image involve breaking; acts of breaking images make them. That is why breaking can be redundant. And it can be horrific to the extent the new image created by iconoclasm is a palimpsest of the violence and rivenness of iconoclasm.

The redundancy of iconoclasm is evident in the case of *Piss Christ*. Serrano sees the crucifix as being made complicit in a broken economic system, and so he attempts an iconoclastic gesture of protest against it. His submerging the crucifix in urine simply repeats the humiliation of Christ on the cross. (Does he, like las Casas, argue that the profiteers crucify Christ anew? Does he, like Grünewald, display Christ's presence to those suffering from a plague consuming bodies all around him?) Then the iconoclasts' attack on the photography displayed by the museum simply creates one more iteration of the broken Image. A torn photograph of the humiliation of a riven God.

This repetition of destruction was performed in Reformation iconoclasm against the crucifix, too. The defacement of crucifixes repeats the breakingness internal to the crucifix. It negates an image that already negates itself.[15] The image generated by iconoclasm—the mob dragging the crucifix into the street, for example, or the many decapitated crucifixes in Reformation England—simply reiterates the destruction intrinsic to the original image. Both the Reformation iconoclasm against the crucifix and the crucifixion itself are meant by the perpetrators as a breaking that unmasks an absence of power. It is, in a way, fitting that the Reformation iconoclasts repeated the taunts at the cross, for in both cases, an image is broken to show that it has no power, that it cannot prevent its own breaking, nor can it avenge its brokenness. The brokenness demonstrates its powerlessness. Iconoclasm, like crucifixion, creates a broken image that can witness to the image's own impotence, and the images of brokenness that iconoclasm creates echo images of the broken image. (And yet the very urgency to break an image insinuates the existence of a power that needs to be denied.) In brief, as an image of violence meant to prove impotence, the crucifix is an image of horrific iconoclasm.

The issue goes deeper still, for it is not just that the crucifix is an image of iconoclasm. If the crucifix only imaged iconoclasm, it would leave us the puzzle of why so many of the faithful are so often caught up in iconoclastic programs and agendas. Why would Christ's faithful want to be aligned with Christ's crucifiers? Of course, they do not. But the crucifix not only images iconoclasm; it also demands it. Rivenness and rivingness come together on the cross. It is no accident that the iconoclastic outbreaks in the church often center on the cross.

The togetherness of rivenness and rivingness is Scriptural and can be found particularly in the writings of the Apostle Paul. For Paul, the cross is, on the one hand, an image that displays Christ. In passages such as Galatians 3:1, Paul refers to himself as an image of Christ crucified. He claims that before the eyes of the Galatians, Christ was "publicly exhibited as crucified." Here, Paul describes the cross as an image that presents God by presenting himself as broken. He becomes a cruciform image by his assimilation to Christ. This is the cross of the pastiche of images described above, one that emerges as image from a type of breaking. On the other hand, the cross, for Paul, is also iconoclastic—folly and a stumbling block rather than worldly wisdom (1 Corinthians 1:23, 22), the destruction of human artifice that contrasts with the presence of God. In Galatians, as he discusses sin, Paul writes: "But if I build up again the very things that I once tore down, then I demonstrate that I am a transgressor. For through the law I died to the law, so that I might live to God. I have been crucified with Christ; it is no longer I who live but Christ who lives in me" (Galatians

2:18–20). The cross takes on an iconoclastic logic insofar as it aids in tearing down rather than building up. It is the destruction of sinful artifice, that by which Paul dies to himself that Christ might live in him. Here, the cross calls for iconoclasm against whatever does not conform to the cruciform Christ—much as the cross is figured in the diptych of iconoclastic acts, as discussed below.

Diptych of Iconoclastic Acts: Cross Against Image

Constantinople, eighth and ninth centuries. The most public battle of Byzantine iconoclasm is waged at Chalke Gate, the main entrance to the imperial palace in Constantinople. As the iconomachs and the iconodules trade power, each group marks its ascendancy with a symbol at that gate. The iconomachs place a cross there; the iconodules an image of Christ. Leo III and Constantine V erect a cross; Empress Irene installs an icon, known as *Christ Chalkites*.[16] In 815, when the iconomachs temporarily regain power, Leo V replaces *Christ Chalkites* with another cross—and five acrostic poems adjacent to it. One reads:

> Clearly Moses destroyed the leaders by this figure [*tupos*],
> Prevailing over the enemy. Now the cross, the glory of the faithful,
> Has stemmed the mighty current of deceit.
> For the soulless artificial form inscribed here,
> Devised as a hidden weapon by an illicit impulse,
> Has been completely taken away.
> For it is appropriate to discern Christ in this way.[17]

Christ Chalkites is named in this poem as "the soulless artificial form" that contrasts with the *tupos* of the cross, which breaks the tide of deceit. The cross, according to this acrostic, offers an appropriate—rather than artificial, deceitful, soulless—way to discern Christ. As Marion points out, the iconomachs' logic of the cross articulates within a logic of resemblance; it assumes that the image is simply a bad (artificial, deceitful, soulless) copy.[18] But this cross does not just destroy deceitful artifice. It also (for Moses) destroys "the leaders" who are "the enemy." More specifically, it destroys Amalek, defeated in battle when Moses raises his arms, turning his body into the shape of the cross. The cross, according to this poem, breaks both image and person. As at Chalke Gate, so elsewhere throughout Byzantium: iconomachs replace images of Christ with the cross, performing the cross's defeat of the deceitful artifice of images. For Byzantine iconomachs, the cross wars with images.

London, seventeenth century. A different story about cross and image is told in London in the middle of the 1600s. One of the city's most famous monuments has been under attack for decades. Previously featured in processions, horse races, jousts, and coronations, Cheapside Cross is large (twelve meters high) and celebrated. The attacks begin late in the sixteenth century, as reformers push to replace the Greek cross atop the monument with an obelisk.[19] Iconoclastic fervor heats up during the English Civil War, and unofficial assaults on Cheapside Cross increase. At last the order comes from London's Common Council to remove it. On May 2, 1643, Cheapside Cross is demolished.

Like that of *Christ Chalkites*, the fate of Cheapside Cross symbolizes a larger program of iconoclasm. In the same decade it was removed, the English legislature forbids crosses and crucifixes as emblems of superstition and idolatry.[20] To these iconoclasts, the cross does not war with images. It is itself an image—or, as William Fuller had written earlier to Queen Elizabeth, in protest of the cross she kept in her chapel, it is "that foul idol, the cross."[21] Over on the continent, Ulrich Zwingli feeds such anxiety over crosses by insisting he has never seen a cross that had not been turned into an idol.[22] In this new era of iconoclasm, the cross does not defeat idols. It is one more idol to be defeated.

For reformers, the abundant cross images are idols because they compete with the true cross. Scottish Puritan William Mure expresses this position in his 1629 poem "True Crucifix for True Catholics." He paints an opposition between the true crucifix of the Scriptural Christ hanging on the Scriptural cross and all attempted images of this crucifix. We "look" on Christ by "search[ing] the Scriptures, which of Him record,/ And crucified before our eyes afford."[23] References to eyes, looking, and seeing abound in the poem. Rather than describing physical sight, these references elaborate what Mure calls "faith's piercing eye."[24] Scripture is the location of the "true portrait" that is "wonderfully expressed."[25] Mure calls his reader to the cross:

> *See, now through tears, how He himself presents*
> Nailing unto his Cross Thy oblishments,
> Cancelling those indictments which did tie
> God's wrath in justice Thee to underlie,
> Resolving more by sinning, to abstain.[26]

Here Mure calls the reader to use faith's eye to see, without making, the cross of Christ. (Does he, in this call, create a literary image of the cross? Or merely point, literarily, to the Scriptural one?) The only cross images Mure encourages his reader to create are the ones generated by imitating Christ "in our life."[27] All other crosses are "vain inventions,"[28] "feigned shapes" and "fancied crosses"[29] produced by a "frantic freedom."[30] The made crucifix, for Mure, is a dangerous idol. As he writes in a side note, "The Popish crucifix does but mock and not express the sufferings of Christ."[31] In Mure's logic—a logic reminiscent of the *Piss Christ* iconoclasts—to attack a material crucifix is to attack the mockery of the cross and thus to reaffirm the "true crucifix." Where Byzantine iconomachs replace images with crosses, Reformation iconoclasts replace crosses with the true cross. In both cases, the cross energizes Christian iconoclasm, and in the Reformation, the cross seems to have fomented an iconoclastic energy that has grown, targeting even images of itself.

The Dynamic of Iconoclasm

Perhaps this movement from Byzantine iconoclasm to Reformation iconoclasm exemplifies the *dunamis* (dynamic, power) of iconoclasm identified by James Simpson.[32] Tracing iconoclasm in the Anglo-American tradition, Simpson identifies the endlessly emerging forms of iconoclasm. The new forms of iconoclasm target objects the iconoclasts of previous ages considered safe. Iconoclasm's energy grows as it devours new objects, moving to immaterial targets as it wearies of material ones.

Simpson's story of an ever-expanding, ceaselessly adapting iconoclasm resonates with this diptych of Byzantine and Reformation scenes of iconoclasm. Byzantine iconomachs wield the cross to discount images of Christ. Reformation iconoclasts commend the "true cross" of history and Scripture to reject material crosses. In the rhetoric of this cross-centered iconoclasm, the (true) cross is a divine act that contrasts with human acts of making—which in the Byzantine acrostic poem, are artificial and deceitful, and in the Reformation poem by Mure are vain, feigned, fancied, artificial. The cross, in such rhetoric, is a divine act that exposes the poverty in all human aspirations. It burns away the dross of human falsity.

The cross, though, is not just something God does. It is something that humans do, too. Humans crucify God. Taken (like *Piss Christ*) as blasphemous by religious authorities and threatening by political ones, Christ is broken so that the threat of Christ might be broken. In this way, the breaking of Christ on the cross is similar to the iconoclasm that nearly all regimes throughout history practiced— eliminating those images that testify to a power that threatens their own. Read as a human act, the cross is a horrific instance of iconoclasm. Christ is the Image riven at the hands of humans, who attempt to break the one who is God.

The agency at the cross is complex, for Christ's suffering at the hands of humans is not flatly passive. Christ suffers rivenness in order to rive it. Christ on the cross breaks brokenness itself. The cross is God's refusal to let violence be determinative. For, on the cross, Christ reveals God to be love all the way down. Christ shows that love is not so shallowly rooted in the universe that it can be pulled out by trial and torture. This is a love so deeply embedded in the fabric of the cosmos that even death cannot alter it. To break the One who is Love Itself simply discloses the depths of that Love that moves the universe. One might say that on the cross, Christ is the rock of love, and the power of death is the wave that breaks against the rock. For Christ to break brokenness means that Christ is present even to rivenness itself. Read as an activity of Christ, the cross is a hopeful act of iconoclasm. It is important to hold the cross as image and as iconoclastic act together. As will become apparent, attempts at pure iconoclasm degenerate into parodies of iconophilia, while attempts at unlimited iconophilia flirt with violence and idolatry.

Receiving and Refusing Images of the Broken Image

The way images emerge from breaking images echoes the way crucifixes emerge from breaking crucifixes, which itself echoes the way the Image of God discloses God in the breaking that is the cross. Iconoclasm and its emergent images mediate the riving and riven image of Christ. The love of Christ cannot be eradicated. What does that mean for the roles of images and iconoclasm today? What does it mean that we are called to participate in this Image? How do we think about images of this Image?

To answer these questions, I turn next to an argument about Christ imaging from the Mennonite theologian John Howard Yoder, whom I take to be a strong iconoclast—one whose anxiety about images leads him to iconoclasms of temptation. His argument will take us into both material images of Christ and images of Christ in saints' lives, two highly significant genres of images for iconoclasm. They are significant because of their role in debates over images. The later Byzantine iconoclasts, rather than claiming the Eucharist as the one true image, as the earlier Byzantine iconoclasts did, claimed saints' lives for that honor, even as they continued to justify material crosses as *tupoi* rather than images.[33] For their part, Reformation iconoclasts went on to question many of the trappings associated with saints and also denounced material crosses as idols. Yoder, as we shall see, went a step further still.

Yoder exemplifies both Simpson's argument that iconoclasm expands across the centuries and the significance of the cross to that expansion. In his essay "Liberating Images," Yoder, not unlike the Byzantine iconoclasts, calls for a renewal of what he names Mosaic iconoclasm, so that Christians will not assimilate Christ to the thought of each new age.[34] This is another concern with the deceptions of human artifice, but the artifice here is not a material image. It is an imitation of Christ in a human life—what Byzantine iconoclasts claimed as the true image over and against material images. Yoder wants to distinguish *which* imitations of Christ are the true ones. He spells out true and false imitations in various writings, most famously in *The Politics of Jesus*. To imitate Christ, he claims there, is to imitate Christ on the one point of *vulnerable enemy love*, "the one realm in which the concept of imitation holds."[35] He polemicizes against involuntary suffering, as occurs with illness and accidents—the cross is not just any kind of suffering, he claims—and against "naïve, outward (Franciscan) imitation," such as barefoot itinerancy and poverty. Franciscans imitate Christ "slavishly" or "externally"; it is not true imitation but "rigid mimicry."[36] In Marion's language, we might say that for Yoder, Franciscan imitation of Christ unfolds within a mimetic logic of resemblance, moving from visible to visible; it is a logic counter to the cross itself and so, for Yoder, must be false.

Wrongly claimed *imitationes* and false images must, for Yoder, be broken. In his broad skepticism about saints' lives, he diverges from the Byzantine iconoclasts who, in their second wave of influence, claimed saints' lives as the true images over and against icons. In that skepticism, he is more similar to the Reformation iconoclasts. Indeed, Yoder stakes out a Mure-like position of contrasting the true cross with false crosses. Where Mure identifies the true cross as the Scriptural, historical, or spiritual cross, Yoder takes this position further. Not all claims at imaging the cross in a human life should be entertained. In fact, all claims that are not centered on vulnerable enemy love must be upended. This is the "one point" that authorizes Christ imaging for Yoder. From Mure to Yoder, iconoclasm has morphed into another stage.

Authorizing Yoder's iconoclasm is a set of contrasts: voluntary against involuntary imitation, vulnerable enemy love against Franciscan outward mimicry, and concrete action against inward experience. The contrasting pairs are too porous to justify the iconoclasm Yoder promotes. They exist in complex, connective relationships with one another from which they cannot easily be extricated. What Yoder sees as false imitations can open up into, prepare for, and express vulnerable enemy love, such that his distinction between true and false imaging becomes more obscure. Two medieval lives illustrate how this occurs: those of Margery Kempe in England (c. 1373–1440) and Margaret Ebner in Germany (1291–1351). They challenge Yoder's iconoclasm by testifying to a breadth of the possibilities of Christly imitation displayed in the porousness of Franciscan imitation to vulnerable enemy love (Kempe), involuntary to voluntary suffering (Ebner), and inward experience to concrete action (both). The expansiveness of their imitations, moreover, links cross images and Christly imitation such that it pressures a reformulation of iconoclastic concerns.

What the lives of these women display, then, is the way vulnerable enemy love of the cross cannot be sundered from the "outward" forms of saints' lives, nor from the images of Christ crucified that the saints venerate. Kempe and Ebner repair Yoder, but they are not undamaged themselves. What Yoder calls "vulnerable enemy love" and some liberationist theologians call "revolutionary love" remains, as the lives of Kempe and Ebner show, an important lodestar for rehabilitating a relationship to images that has become violent and idolatrous. While Yoder is right to point to vulnerable enemy love as a criterion, he is misguided in how he wields it. It functions negatively or weakly, not positively. Images that reject such love must be rejected, but Yoder's "true images" of vulnerable enemy love do not authorize iconoclasm against "external" images. These "true images" illumine the relative truth of other images rather than spotlighting those images' inadequacy or falseness. They display the way Christ crucified breaks brokenness to bear his riven and riving presence even to that which would separate us from God.

MARGERY KEMPE: MYSTICAL IMITATION AND "NAÏVE, OUTWARD (FRANCISCAN) IMITATION"

Not quite halfway through her book, Margery Kempe records her loud cry, "The Passion of Christ slays me."[37] She utters the cry as an explanation for her uncontrollable sobbing that breaks out at representations—verbal or visual—of Christ's suffering.[38] Her screams and tears display herself as slain, proposing a connection elaborated throughout her book between herself and the slain Lamb of God. Kempe's weeping is a gift that causes her both suffering and ecstasy. By it, her life merges with Christ's.

Kempe's gift of weeping is elicited and disciplined by representations of cross and crucifix. In her world, crosses and crucifixes were unregulated and abundant, for she lived prior to the polarizing politics of the cross that plagued England a century after her death.[39] For Kempe, material crosses and crucifixes are self-evidently central to Christian worship—though they are not *just* about worship. What she displays, over and over again in her book, is the connection between imitations of Christ in material like wood and imitations of Christ in a human life. To love the crucifix rightly, for Kempe, is to become cruciform.

One encounter she describes with an image of Christ takes place on Good Friday—the date itself redolent of cruciformity—as the priests and worshipful are "devoutly representing the lamentable death and doleful burying of our Lord Jesus Christ." Beholding this representation, Kempe's heart is suddenly "occupied" by "the mind of our Lady's sorrows, which she suffered when she beheld his precious body hanging on the Cross and afterward buried before her sight." Narrating Kempe's experiences of God in the third person, the book describes how the "poor creature" is drawn into Mary's sorrows, and her ghostly (spiritual) sight of Christ's Passion "wound[s] her with pity and compassion" such that she "[spread] her arms abroad, said with a loud voice, 'I die, I die.'"[40] She weeps with Mary and dies with Christ.

Kempe's double identification with both Mary and Christ is a theme throughout her book. Seeing a representation of Christ's suffering, she enters through *her* bodily sight to *Mary's* bodily sight, which becomes *her* ghostly sight, which is made manifest in her bodily imitation of a crucifix. Kempe enters *Mary's* sorrows and *Christ's* suffering. Bodily sight does not compete with spiritual sight, as the two do for William Mure; the two interpenetrate one another as they effect Kempe's transformation.[41]

The first time bodily sight, ghostly sight, and weeping are linked for Kempe is on her pilgrimage to the Holy Land. It is there that her gift of tears changes, for it is, as Kempe claims, "the first cry that ever she cried in any contemplation."[42] She is walking the stations of the cross, and a Franciscan friar—one of those Yoder deems guilty of "naïve, outward" imitation—lifts up a cross and leads the pilgrims through descriptions of Christ's suffering. Kempe's weeping intensifies "as though she had seen our Lord with her bodily eye suffering his Passion," yet it was "by contemplation" that she saw him. Then, at Calvary, she is slain. She describes it dramatically:

> And when they came up onto the Mount of Calvary, she fell down so that she might not stand or kneel but wallowed and twisted with her body, spreading her arms abroad, and cried with a loud voice as though her heart should have burst

asunder, for in the city of her soul she saw verily and freshly how our Lord was crucified. Before her face she heard and saw in her ghostly sight the mourning of our Lady, of Saint John and Mary Magdalene, and of many others who loved our Lord. And she had so great compassion and so great pain to see our Lord's pain that she might not keep herself from crying and roaring though she should have died from it.[43]

Spreading her arms and twisting her body, she is a mimesis of Christ crucified. Crying, mourning, and roaring, she is *not* Christ crucified; she is one who mourns Christ crucified, more akin to Mother Mary, Saint John, or Mary Magdalene. In her double image of Christ and mourner of Christ, she images the riven presence of Christ to rivenness. In other words, her double-image displays what Christ the Image is: himself and so united to more than himself. The Christ who sustains the universe displays the character of the universe as love, which can then be imaged in the mourners "who loved our Lord."

It is at this point—during her pilgrimage to the Holy Land, while walking the stations of the cross, specifically at Calvary—that Kempe describes weeping in a new way, where "[s]he had such very contemplation in the sight of her soul."[44] This weeping comes to her as gift that is liturgically and geographically cruciform. It comes in response to a cruciform object that her own body imitates, even as she proclaims herself as not Christ in her mourning. Further, this weeping is not a one-time experience. It inaugurates a new era of tears that lasts for many years.[45] It is loud, bewildering crying that leaves her weak, and it is newly catalyzed by hearing the Lord's Passion, seeing the crucifix, or seeing a person or beast beaten. Seeing or hearing such events, Kempe claims "she thought she saw our Lord being beaten or wounded just as she saw in the man or in the beast."[46] Her love of the cross and her conformity to Christ crucified sensitizes her to the suffering of all creatures, and she makes a nuisance of herself as her form of (nonviolent) intervention into the suffering victims of violence. Her astonishingly loud weeping during the beating of a beast or human is not unlike the strategies of more modern protesters, forcing attention to injustice by making themselves conspicuous, even irritating. What may seem to Yoder an "external imitation" is critically connected to her vulnerable enemy love.

Sites of human and non-human animal suffering, for Kempe, image Christ crucified. In them Kempe sees "our Lord being beaten or wounded." They do not image Christ crucified, though, apart from Kempe herself pointing to

Christ crucified. They image Christ crucified to her because she images Christ crucified to others. She becomes such an imitation of Christ crucified that she longs to kiss lepers, to be near them as Christ was near them and love them as Christ did.[47] For Kempe, vulnerable, nonviolent love is an outworking of her love for and identification with Christ on the cross, an identification brought about by her relation to the physical image of the cross and pilgrimage to and through the Franciscans' stations of the cross. As she becomes a sign of Christ crucified, her bodily sight opens up to ghostly sight such that she can discern rightly the signs of Christ crucified in the world around her. The images of the world open to the Image, the signs of the world to the Signified, as her bodily sight opens up to ghostly sight.

In the elevation of "ghostly eyes" over bodily ones, Kempe's book might connote a Mure-like priority of memorial or mental images over material ones. Yet in her reaction of imitating the cross by stretching out her arms and seeing Christ everywhere, her text insists on the ubiquity of the cross. The result is a web of crosses related to one another, the material opening onto spiritual, which open onto the one cross of Christ. Instead of Yoder's confident distinction between naïve, outward Franciscan mimicry and the imitation of Christ's vulnerable enemy love, Kempe presents the reader with a Christ who pervades reality, principally the reality of suffering, such that *imago Christi* may appear to and as the one who weeps for Christ. Her "inner experience" of Christ's suffering, moreover, motivates and is recapitulated in her attention to non-human animal suffering and to other victims of violence. Yoder may not agree that intervention in the suffering of non-human animals constitutes vulnerable enemy love, but Kempe's narrative at least makes plain the way "mystical experience" might energize or reconstitute itself as concrete social action, including resistance to violence. Her love of physical and "external" crosses does not remain trapped in visible mimesis. Kempe's is a vision of *imitatio Christi* in which vulnerable enemy love is as inextricable from her gift of weeping and her walking the cross stations as ghostly sight is from its intertwining with bodily sight.

MARGARET EBNER: MYSTICAL IMITATION AND INVOLUNTARY SUFFERING

Margaret Ebner spent most of her life in the Dominican monastery of Maria Medingen in southern Germany. Her book *Revelations* is the major source of information about her life, and it focuses primarily on her illness and its transformation. She describes the way her illness (involuntary suffering) becomes

Christ-like as she learns to embrace her suffering as Christ's own. Her narrative, in other words, destabilizes the strong opposition between voluntary and involuntary suffering, even as it continues to query the line between inward experience and outward action.

Both Ebner's illness and her understanding of it transform over many years as she devotes herself to Christ's Passion. In the first few paragraphs of *Revelations*, Ebner describes herself as longing for health,[48] and by the end of that book, her longing has been redirected to intimacy with and even assimilation to Christ. Critical for such transformations was her veneration of crosses. She describes how she "kissed ardently and as frequently as possible" "every cross [she] came upon." She would press each cross against her heart, as she said, "so that I could not separate myself from it and remain alive." Her rhapsodizing of the cross continues as she describes carrying crosses, wearing crosses, pressing them against her, even sleeping with them.[49] As she seeks out every cross she can to kiss and to hold, Ebner finds that there is a large crucifix she cannot take down from her choir without the help of a sister, who, worrying about Ebner's frailty, refuses to assist her. Standing before the cross image in a dream, Ebner sees Jesus bend down from the cross; he lets her kiss his open heart, and she drinks the blood flowing from it.[50] In this Eucharistic image, Ebner is granted an intimacy greater than what she could manage in all her cross kissing and embracing. While pressing the cross against her heart grants her nearness to the Passion of Christ, the blood pouring from Christ's heart into her body mingles her body with Christ's body, her passion with Christ's Passion. In drinking Christ's blood, she is open, her body porous to Christ's suffering.[51]

Ebner's description of Christ's blood circulating into her own body immediately follows a section in which she describes her body conforming to Christ. Her suffering had, over the years, taken on a liturgical shape, intensifying during Lent and breaking into relief and joy on Easter. One Lent, after the death of a dear sister, she finds herself not simply enduring suffering but desiring suffering. Specifically, she says, she desired "that my whole body would be full of the signs of love of the holy cross, as many as were possible to be on mine, and that each one would be given to me with all its suffering and pain over my entire body."[52] In response to this prayer, she is granted a pain she describes as "severe and unceasing," and it brings her "immeasurable sorrow" such that she believes future happiness impossible for her.[53] Contrary to her expectations, a kind of happiness visits her again. Taking the Eucharist on Easter, she finds sweetness once more, and in this sweetness, she begins one of her trademark activities:

the unwilled and constant repetition of Christ's name: "Jesus Christus." Like Kempe's sobbing, Ebner's unwilled outcries and also periods of binding silence are sources of both suffering and grace to her. She responds to the sweet grace of her Easter outcrying by kissing crosses and ultimately receiving her visionary draught of the Crucified's blood. In turn, the adoration of images of the Crucified begins conforming her to the Crucified, turning her into an image herself.[54]

The pattern of Lenten suffering and Easter lightening continues throughout Ebner's *Revelations*. During one Holy Saturday, she is carried up to her little room, very sick and lying prone. She remains in this tomb-like state until she hears the *Gloria in Excelsis Deo* being sung at sunrise Mass on Easter. She is "flooded with power," and the conformity to Christ is explicit: "I had suffered with [Christ]; I should also happily rise with him now."[55] To the wonderment of her sisters, Ebner arrives in the choir at matins, happy and well, an image of resurrection.

Ebner's identification with salvific suffering, perhaps surprisingly, stops short of fetishizing suffering. The suffering of others occasions mourning, even angst, whether the suffering is human or non-human animal. Early in *Revelations*, Ebner describes her "heartfelt sorrow" at a sister telling a servant she is not worthy to serve her. In the same breath, she claims that she "could not bear the slaughtering of the cattle." Her response to these painful sights is to weep and then resolve to avoid afflicting such violence or harshness. She describes such tenderness as cultivated by giving her will over to God, for in understanding she "[can]not direct [herself]," she is "set at peace with all that God had created."[56] Out of that peace flows the compassion Ebner describes for fellow creatures. She communicates this compassion as anguish that a fellow creature would call another unworthy when God never said as much to Ebner, and that a fellow creature would be slaughtered when God never slaughtered Ebner for her misdeeds. Ebner's meditation on the cross conforms her to God's own suffering such that she can draw near and mourn the suffering of others.

As Ebner presses crosses against her heart, her body and life conform to the one broken in mercy, the one broken that all might cease from breaking others. Initially sorrowful about her own sickness, she learns to embrace it as a way to enter into the brokenness of Christ, to display Christ's brokenness for human healing. Putting herself in relation to the crucifix, Ebner, too, opens to the sufferings of others. United to the merciful suffering of Christ, who in mercy wills his own suffering rather than willing the suffering of his enemies, she becomes sensitive to the suffering of others inflicted by the mercilessness of fellow creatures.

Ebner's suffering refuses Yoder's distinction between involuntary illness and willed enemy love. She begins *Revelations* as a sick woman longing for health, but as her cross-kissing nurtures her love for Christ, Ebner wills the conformity of her own suffering to Christ's.[57] Her suffering becomes cruciform, witnessing to those in her monastery of the suffering of Christ for humanity. What she had not chosen she learns to embrace by saying with Christ, "Not my will but thine." Ebner's is a more complicated story about agency than Yoder's—one in which a person might find agency *in* suffering, even suffering that is unprovoked, such that she may display Christ's freedom within it. (In this way, her suffering is not so dissimilar from an initially reluctant martyr's.) Though the suffering is not strictly voluntary in that she did not will her illness, it is not by the end of her story *in*voluntary. She has learned to will the identification of her suffering with Christ, and her illness takes on a liturgical shape and bears Christic fruit. We might read Yoder's attempt to discount involuntary suffering as a failure to take seriously the nature of imaging as both like and unlike the imaged, and of us creatures as both like and unlike Christ. For, given our status as (only) creaturely, finite, and power limited, how like can we be to the one who is both creaturely and Creatorly, such that we could imitate the Son's perfect freedom in choosing obedience unto death? Unlike Christ, we, after all, are subject to the winds and the waves; not they to us. Our freedom is attenuated by our creatureliness, and such unlikeness is precisely what *image* denotes: our likeness to Christ will always emerge in the substratum of our unlikeness.

Vulnerable Enemy Love as Negative Condition

To reflect on Ebner and Kempe as imitations of Christ is not to insist they imitated Christ perfectly. At moments, their zeal for Christ's presence turns violent. For Kempe, that violence is the wish that her husband be slayed so that she may commit herself to holy celibacy. Though she had once enjoyed intercourse, after fifteen children, Kempe desired to live chastely, in greater intimacy with Christ. Her husband does not agree to a celibate marriage, but on a walk home one summer evening, as she is carrying some beer and he some bread, he asks her, "Margery, if there came a man with a sword and would smite off my head unless I should common naturally with you as I have done before, tell me the truth from your conscience—for you say you will not lie—whether you would suffer my head to be smote off or else suffer me to meddle with you again, as I did at one time?" Kempe confesses that she would indeed rather see him smote than have him meddle with her again, to which he mournfully replies, "You are no good wife."[58] Eventually they broker a deal in which she negotiates her chastity without taking her husband's life.

More troubling than Kempe's fantasy of violence-secured celibacy is a dark episode in Ebner's life. She writes of a woman who takes two unconsecrated hosts from a church where the Virgin Mary was known to be gracious. She attempts to sell the hosts but is caught. Ebner describes what happens next matter-of-factly. "When she was sentenced to death, a child was cut away from her. It was baptized and then they were burned."[59] The modern reader may look for her horror to be mirrored in the tenderhearted Ebner, who does indeed describe herself as "filled with sadness." She cannot bear to look near the place where it happened, nor can she speak or even hear about it. So much we might expect from a woman so sensitive to suffering. What she laments, however, is not the execution of the woman nor the death of her child. Her horror is directed wholly at the pregnant woman's dishonor of God. In fact, Ebner claims she "could not endure it if anyone felt sorry for her" because "anyone who had dishonored a dear friend could not expect mercy from the one who had been dishonored."[60] She tries to pray for the woman but cannot even desire to pray for her.

The questions about why a pregnant woman would venture so risky and desperate an act as stealing a host in a devout land are effaced in Ebner's narrative, which describes the violation of God's honor and the violence its restoration must entail. The pregnant woman corrupts the sacrament of the Eucharist, and such dishonoring is rectified (for Ebner, incompletely) when her baby is cut away from her that it may be baptized before it and she are burned. The brief narrative of violence turns on these sacraments. The rites of baptism and Eucharist are preserved as the woman and her baby are sacrificed.

It is moments like these that underscore the importance of keeping vulnerable enemy love in view.

Earlier, I argued that the lives of Kempe and Ebner indicate the inadequacy of Yoder's reduction of Christ imaging to vulnerable enemy love by showing its unsustainability as a singular criterion. Now, I want to offer a repair to Kempe and Ebner's approach to imitating Christ: Kempe and Ebner do not image Christ in these moments of violence in which they reject vulnerable enemy love. Vulnerable enemy love is central to discerning imitations of Christ, but not because there is one thing called vulnerable enemy love that alone imitates Christ. It is because no act that rejects vulnerable enemy love imitates Christ.

Though there is not a single condition, no lone criterion that can name how Christ imaging may appear, we do need to be vigilant for anti-Christ imaging. There are forms of imaging that point to worldly power rather than to Christ. There are images—more fittingly called idols—that attempt to obliterate the cross. Even cross images are not invulnerable to the temptation to idolatry. When they are identified with wealth, power, and war, cross images cease to point beyond themselves to Christ, for they deny their own logic of riving rivenness. They conceal their dependence on the imaged and present themselves as self-sufficient, as an end. At that point, cross images become idols. But this is difficult to discern. For, simply because one person (say, Constantine) has once identified a version of the cross with war, it is not the case that all crosses have become idols. Nor is it the case that a visual metaphor of military victory or kingship (in, say, *Christus Victor*) is violent prima facie. Images and idols always name relationships that are negotiated and renegotiated in particular places and times. Even Christ the ruler and judge can be an image of vulnerable enemy love. And if would-be idols can be venerated as faithful images, so, too, can would-be faithful images degenerate into idols. While Kempe's and Ebner's use of crosses to draw near and become like the Crucified insinuates that Mure was wrong that crosses and crucifixes are *necessarily* idols, he must be right that it is possible for them to become idols. *Idolatry* might help us diagnose what has gone wrong in Ebner's relationship to the Eucharist.

Vulnerable enemy love is important because it helps us discern when images become idols; when they draw attention to themselves rather than to Christ; when they augment their power by worldly violence rather than pointing to Christ's divestment of the same; when they insist on clanging speech rather than the "worldly silence" of Christ's cross.[61] These are images that attempt to resist their dependence upon Christ, that attempt to displace Christ by refusing to wait for Christ's eschatological consummation of all things. Smashing Christ images assimilated to worldly power is the weak iconoclasm—the iconoclasm of fidelity—that keeps images from the brink of idolatry. Yoder wields vulnerable enemy love as an iconoclasm of temptation, but it can be reclaimed to function more generatively, as an iconoclasm of fidelity.

As an iconoclasm of fidelity, the criterion of vulnerable enemy love, paradoxically, does more rather than less work. It is not just that there are some times when it is relevant—for example, when one is engaged in a certain political act—while in most ordinary life it is not. No, even in everyday life, even in every sexual encounter, vulnerable enemy love can be invoked to discern anti-

Christ imaging. Kempe and Ebner were guilty of violent thoughts and wishes, but what can we say about Yoder, that verbal champion of vulnerable enemy love, now notorious for stomach-turning violence against women? His own life and legacy have been suffused with a violence that the cross itself would rive. The criterion of vulnerable enemy love, wielded as an iconoclasm of fidelity rather than temptation, points to the anti-Christ imaging of Yoder's own life.

Weak Iconoclasm as an Iconoclasm of Fidelity

While resisting a strong Yoderian iconoclasm in which all images of Christ that are not based on vulnerable enemy love must be crushed in their claim to Christ imaging, I want to commend a weaker iconoclasm: all images of Christ in which vulnerable enemy love is rejected must themselves be rejected in their claims to Christ imaging. Vulnerable enemy love is still a way of disciplining *imitatio Christi*. It does so, though, by excluding cases like violent restoration of honor, not by excluding poverty, holy woundedness, itinerancy, and the like.[62]

The weak iconoclasm presumes a vision of sainthood in which Christ can be imaged through an inexhaustible range of images that refract diverse aspects of the God-human. This seemingly slight correction yields an entirely different world. There are endless possible imitations of Christ, including poverty and itinerancy, and unending numbers of crosses. For Kempe and Ebner, vulnerable enemy love is generated by their love for the cross of Christ, born with the crosses of Christ. The writings of Kempe and Ebner display the way vulnerable enemy love, even when it is incomplete, can come to us entwined with other forms of Christly imitation.

This is an expansive approach to imaging Christ, one that allows for a range of images of Christ, some true and some truer. Still the category of false images remains important, as does the iconoclastic urge to rive those images that would be idols. This approach of expansiveness with vigilance results from a sense of the abundance of Christ imaging. Such abundance not only accounts for the way inwardness appears with concrete social action, Franciscan imitation with vulnerable enemy love, and involuntary with voluntary suffering, it also makes Christological sense. There are Christological reasons to support an expansive approach to Christ imaging.

If, as Yoder famously claimed, the cruciform life goes "with the grain of the universe," might we learn to discern the universe's grain as imaging the cross?[63] There is at least one moment in Yoder's corpus in which he seems to bow to a vision of broad imitation. It is a lecture in which Yoder is describing what nourished late medieval pacifism. He says: "One medieval form of imitation of Jesus was the discipline of renouncing property.... This kind of imitation was naïve and symbolic, though not in a pejorative sense.... When I say this rejection is symbolic, I mean that it was not thought through in terms of social science or institutional theory. It fixed on outward expressions that represent the heart of what had happened.... These elements of Franciscan asceticism and imitation led to the rejection of violence."[64] Franciscan imitation, still described as "naïve" and "outward," receives more generous treatment here from Yoder. The two forms of *imitatio Christi* described—Franciscan and vulnerable enemy love—are genuinely connected. Franciscan poverty not only "led to the rejection of violence" but was itself a symbol (are we close to image?) of that rejection. This rejection of violence is not exactly the same as vulnerable enemy love, yet it is not entirely separate from it, either. So we might say that Franciscan asceticism, like involuntary suffering, is related to the rejection of violence and to vulnerable enemy love. The conceptual basis for the strict iconoclasm of Yoder is undone by the contrasts he invokes to sustain it.

Why would Yoder's contrasts undo themselves? We can answer this question at two related levels. First, we can return once again to Marion to claim that the cross itself embeds resistance to visually mimetic logic; it embodies, even in its "external," physical, material forms, the movement from visible to invisible. It pressures a likeness that is not strictly visible, thus connecting physical images of the cross to their invisible prototypes. Second and relatedly, the presence of God in Christ does not stand in contrast to the rest of the universe; it reveals the presence that sustains the entire universe. And that presence is not a violent presence. It does not vitiate the integrity of us, our neighbors, or our world. It makes such integrity possible. In other words, while Yoder is right that the cross images the love of Christ—a love that suffers death rather than turning violent, a love that can be rightly called vulnerable enemy love—he is not right about how that criterion (that prototype) should then be wielded. Yes, the cross is ordered toward love. But images can open obliquely onto that love such that the straightforward presence of vulnerable enemy love cannot be used as the sole criterion for Christ imaging. For the love of God is not an aberration in the universe; it is the very grain of the universe.

As in the sacraments, the cross is both unique and disclosive of all reality. It shows how reality is fundamentally ordered to God. That is why all kinds of attempts to imitate Christ can present Christ, and also why they lead to vibrant revelations of love. When the world resists this order to the God who is love, that resistance is violence, the brokenness that must be broken open to the love that sustains the world.

The Broken Center of the Cosmos

Though Yoder brandishes it as an iconoclasm of temptation, his criterion of vulnerable enemy love can be reclaimed in a more helpful direction, one which proposes a negative condition for the cross-world relationship: that in their violence, the violent of the world do not image the crucified Christ. In fact, the crucified Christ calls us to break such violence by entering into its midst to bear love to the violated. That is how we follow Christ in breaking brokenness. At the same time, the lives of Ebner and Kempe also show that the cross will not be limited to a single criterion. It exceeds any negative condition in its relation to the world. It even precedes and exceeds Christian history. The lives of Kempe and Ebner are concrete examples of a theology of the cross deeply embedded in Christianity: that of the cosmic cross.

To claim the cross is cosmic is to insist that the very cosmos is cruciform. It is to be unsurprised that the cross can be found in traditions outside Christianity. In the mid-twentieth century, crosses were found on the graves of first-century Jews who had died in the wake of the "abomination of desolation," when Herod placed a pagan idol in the Temple in Jerusalem; other crosses were found on the graves of those who died after the later destruction of the Temple. The crosses referred not, of course, to Christ—these were not Christian Jews—but to the *Tav* called for in Ezekiel 9:4: "Go through the city, through Jerusalem, and put a mark [*Tav*] upon the foreheads of the men who sigh and groan over all the abominations that are committed in it." Writing about this remarkable find, Joseph Ratzinger (later to become Pope Benedict XVI) identifies the cross-shaped *Tav* as an expression of humanity's longing for the presence of God. It designates those "suffering impotently yet at a distance from sin."[65] It is, at the same time, a sign of hope, marking a person for God's special protection even in the midst of suffering. It is iconoclastic (the protest against an idol in the Temple) and a lament for iconoclasm (mourning the destruction of the Temple) that signifies God's presence amidst such iconoclasm.

In addition to this Jewish tradition of the cross in the form of the *Tav*, there is a Greek one. Working out of the Pythagorean tradition that describes the intersecting orbits of the sun and the earth, Plato describes the sign of the cross

(*Chi*) as written into the cosmos itself. This sign for him signifies the "world soul," stretched across the universe. Christians like Justin Martyr and Irenaeus of Lyons identify the "world soul" as the Son, and so they show how a cross-shaped cosmos is radiant with the presence of the crucified Word. Irenaeus frames it this way: the crucified Christ is "the very Word of Almighty God, who penetrates our universe by an invisible presence. And for this reason he embraces the whole world, its breadth and length, its height and depth, for through the Word of God all things are guided into order. And the Son of God is crucified in them, since in the form of the Cross, he is imprinted upon all things."[66] The cross is everywhere, imprinted on all things, embracing all things. It signifies the love that moves the universe. Augustine makes this explicit in his own addition to this tradition. He interprets the height and breadth of Christ's embrace (Irenaeus's allusion to the love of Christ in Ephesians 3:18ff.) as referring to the form of Christ's love on the cross.[67] The cosmos is cruciform because the cosmos is formed by and in and for the love of God.

These traditions of the cross—impotent suffering for the divine, the divine imprint on the universe, and the form of God's endless love—express, in other terms, the way the cross is the riven and riving presence of Christ. The impulse to iconoclasm expressed by the reformers—the skepticism about images that abides in much of Protestantism today—can and should be grafted into the tradition of the cosmic cross. The cross breaks the brokenness, the violence of idolatry. It breaks brokenness to proclaim the ubiquity of God's love. It identifies the way God is present in a special way, a riven and riving way, to those suffering divine absence. It courses through the cosmos, which takes its shape, displaying the broken center of all things.

A Family Tree of Crosses

If the world is rife with crosses—if the very universe is cruciform—then William Mure cannot be our poet of the cross. There is no "true" cross (whether scriptural, historical, spiritual, or Yoderian) that delegitimizes all others. If not in Mure, then where can one find a vision for how the crosses of the world stand in relation to one another? One can find it, I submit, in the poetry of his near contemporary John Donne (1572–1631) and of our contemporary Christian Wiman (1966–).

In his poem "The Cross," Catholic-turned-Anglican priest John Donne critiques the suspicion of crosses and crucifixes in Reformation England. He begins by connecting the cross on which Christ died with images of that cross:

"Since Christ embraced the cross itself, dare I/His image, th' image of his cross deny?"[68] He goes on to insist that neither pulpit nor scandal nor law shall take the cross from him. "It shall not, for it cannot; for the loss/Of this cross were to me another cross."[69] Iconoclasm against crosses—like the denial of crosses—simply generates further crosses. Donne's visions here echo Koerner's descriptions of crosses emerging from iconoclastic acts. Donne underscores his point: "No cross is so extreme as to have none."[70]

It is not that crosses emerge just from attempts to break them. Crosses are everywhere. The iconoclastic program against them is doomed because crosses are embedded in the created world: swimming bodies, birds raising their wings, lines of longitude and latitude. These, Donne concedes, are inferior to "spiritual" crosses, which include crossing one's eyes, heart, and senses, so as to live into humility and virtue. Like a carver revealing an image hidden in stone, these spiritual crosses reveal the image of Christ hidden in a person. (There is an image-making here that involves both stone and sense breaking.) Swimming bodies and wing-raised birds are inferior to the cross of humility-marked virtue, yet they are also connected to it. Donne joins these spiritual crosses with material crosses and the cross of Christ in the last few lines:

> Cross no man else, but cross thyself in all.
> Then doth the cross of Christ work faithfully
> Within our hearts, when we love harmlessly
> That cross's pictures much, and with more care
> That cross's children, which our crosses are.[71]

The images of the cross work the cross into the life of the person who loves cross images "harmlessly." The cross's pictures, like all material and spiritual crosses, are children of *that* cross of Christ.

While Mure and Donne would agree, then, that there is a cross of Christ superior to its material representations, Mure sees competition and mockery whereas Donne sees preparation and continuity. For Donne, images of Christ's cross are part of a family tree of crosses. They are the cross's children, born from and pointing to the cross of Christ. The category of "spiritual cross" helps him to convey a link between loving the cross's pictures and orienting oneself more completely to Christ's cross, which bears the cross progeny found and cultivated throughout our world. In making his argument, Donne traces a cruciform shape to the world that finds its culmination in the cross of Christ. Where Mure distinguishes between crosses that are false and true, Donne sees crosses that are true and truer. The cross is fecund, bearing its cross children into the world that we might see the cross everywhere in the universe.

In Donne's poem, the very shape of the cross goes with the grain of the universe, as does the humility it entails. In Wiman's poem "Every Riven Thing," a cross-like rivenness is the way of the universe and God. Wiman connects the rivenness of the world to the presence of God, returning five times to the line, "God goes belonging to every riven thing he's made." Each time the line is made new, both by its punctuation and by the surrounding lines.[72] Wiman writes at one point, "every riven thing he's made/sing his being simply by being/the thing it is."[73] The singularity of each note in the symphony of being speaks of God. Even when these notes are broken, God is present to them, for God has "made/the things that bring him near,/made the mind that makes him go."[74] Even a thing sundered in itself cannot be sundered from God, for God is the Creator who holds that broken thing in existence.

Wiman's vision of a God who does not abandon his broken creation, who belongs to it, is consummated on the cross, where God stays with the universe even unto death. In an interview about his poem, Wiman says that he thinks of God as participating in, rather than healing, brokenness.[75] In and of itself, this statement does not sound especially hopeful, though perhaps we can understand the hopeful tone of the poem itself as suggesting a gloss on his contrast of participating and breaking: God's presence to brokenness *is* a form of healing. It names a love that is not defeated by brokenness, a love that retains its character as love, that is not distorted by suffering, and in this way foreshadows the resurrection. It is in brokenness that God breaks brokenness. For, this is a God who goes forth belonging to every riven thing, who goes forth *hopefully* from every riven thing, because this is a God who goes forth from the bread, in the love that rives rivenness, with the words, *This is my body, broken for you.* As those words are spoken in the liturgy, God unites with the elements so dissimilar to God in order to continue uniting with the broken of the world, by being broken. The God of the Eucharist is the God who goes forth from and to and by the riven.

The Broken Center of God

As Donne's poem describes, the cross is not just the shape of the cosmos. It names the form of God's relation to the world and the world's to God. Or, as Wiman's poem illumines, God's presence to rivenness evokes moments in God's life with the world other than the cross: especially, in "Every Riven Thing,"

God's relation to the world named by creation and resurrection. The cross is the broken (and breaking) center of the theological story of God. The cross images and gathers all other theological doctrines.

In his Great Catechetical Oration, Gregory of Nyssa argues for the orthodoxy of the incarnation by describing how it recapitulates creation.[76] As God unites with all humanity—and indeed all creation—as Creator, pervading and sustaining it, so God unites still more intimately with humanity in the incarnation. God's relationship to humanity in creation prefigures God's relationship to humanity in the incarnation. And the incarnation, as I argued in Chapter 1, prefigures the crucifixion: Before the scandal of the cross there is the scandal of the breast. Creation, incarnation, crucifixion—they are all images of the love that goes forth to difference. In the cross we see the depths of such love. For, such love is not limited by its opposite; it retains its character as love under even the greatest pressure. The crucifixion, like the iconoclasm-made images of the Reformation, displays its own powerlessness. The crucifixion is an act of iconoclasm that unmasks an absence of the Image's power. In that absence of power—that absence of *worldly* power—is the unbounded strength and presence of love displayed. In the midst of sin, violence, and death, love remains love, breaking their power and displaying its own strength in suffering weakness. This is the Pauline paradox of power made perfect in weakness. This is also why the cross is an image of the resurrection. In the cross, we see a love that is not determined by death; in the resurrection, we see love as conquering that death. And that is why, in the resurrection, we see an image of eschatological hope: the love that conquered Christ's death will conquer all death. Christ's resurrection is the first fruit of a general resurrection, so that the God who is love will be all in all. In the way the cross gives a love that remains love even under the greatest pressure, the cross foreshadows the love that will conquer all.

The cross is an image of suffering that is also an image of the defeat of suffering. So the cross is the pivot of our chiasm: it images the love that goes forth in difference (arriving to and abiding in it) and also the love that is neither bounded nor modified by difference (arriving to and abiding in love as love). The cross reveals the way all images of the divine must move from visible to invisible, without leaving behind the visible. It pressures a likeness beyond the formal or visual—a likeness that will be probed further in the next chapter. Here, at the cross, negation is itself negated to reveal the depths of God's love.

The cross is thus the central image in God's life with us.[77] It is the image that gathers all others to speak to the love that is the grain of the universe—the grain that is bread broken for we who are broken, the grain that breaks our brokenness by its own brokenness, the grain that is the riven and riving presence of Christ.

The Togetherness of Rivenness and Rivingness, Iconophilia and Iconoclasm

The cross is riven and riving: a central image and an iconoclastic impulse. To attempt to prise apart these facets of the cross is to risk parodying it. A cross that is purely iconoclastic cannot sustain its own iconoclasm. Liturgies of iconoclasm turn into parodies of iconophilia, as witnessed in the reformers who stripped the altars of churches. Attempts to preserve the true image, or what Mure called the "True Crucifix," inevitably generate further images, further crosses that are children of the true cross. The cross bears so many children into the world because it is the fertile grain of the universe. Attempts to deny this fecundity not only generate further crosses, they can also end in violence and horror, as with the conquesting Spaniards, whose attempts to end the idolatry of the indigenous Americans denied the humanity of these people in order to justify the Spaniards' violence against them. The Spaniards' battle against idolatry crucified Christ, in las Casas's words, "not once but thousands of times."[78] The cross—itself the broken Image—emerges from attempts to break images. The pure iconoclast cannot but be a degenerate iconophile—an idolater.

If pure iconoclasm is impossible and undesirable, so is an iconophilia undisciplined by any trepidation about images. As pure iconoclasm is an iconoclasm of temptation, so an iconophilia unmoored from the iconoclastic impulse expressed in the cross turns to violent idolatry. As seen in the worst moments described by Ebner and Kempe, an iconophilia absent the negations of iconoclasm can turn to violence, as the relationship between images and what they image is forgotten. Koerner describes the way images of Christ attempt to express this iconoclastic impulse themselves when he writes: "Long before the hammer strikes them, religious images are already self-defacing. Claiming their truth by dialectically repeating and repudiating the deception from which they escape, they are, each of them, engines of an 'iconoclash' that periodically destroys."[79] To love these images—images like Grünewald's Isenheim Altarpiece—is to love this dialectic of "repeating and repudiating" the deception the hammer seeks to expose. It is to love them in a way that allows one not to strike them, because one's love for them already acknowledges what the hammer would make plain. The true iconophile must be a kind of iconoclast.

The Riven and Riving Cristo Negro

> ... To every riven thing he's made
> there is given one shade
> shaped exactly to the thing itself:
> under the tree a darker tree;
> under the man the only man to see
>
> God goes belonging to every riven thing.[80]

Bartolomé de las Casas was around thirty when Grünewald's Isenheim Altarpiece, that masterpiece of the dialectics of divine presence and absence in the crucifix, was finished. He had just had an epiphany about the indigenous people of the West Indies—the first of several—and had freed his slaves, advocating before the Holy Roman Emperor for their rights. His victories were small scaled against the atrocities he witnessed. Still, his years in the West Indies, Guatemala, and Mexico left their mark. His claim that the scourged Indians presented the crucified Christ is witnessed in an image that appeared in multiple chapels throughout Central America, and most famously and originally in Esquipulas, Guatemala.[81] That image is El Cristo Negro, the black Christ.

For centuries, El Cristo Negro was known as Señor Crucificado de Esquipulas. Historians and anthropologists have known about this name change for decades, as they have also known that the statue's blackness caused unease among some church members, notably those in the church hierarchy.[82] What historians did not know, until the last twenty years, was why the name of the statue changed. In 1998, a restoration effort revealed that the name changed because the color did. El Cristo Negro was not made as a black statue. Like most images of Christ in Colonial Latin America, it began fair—olive-skinned, in this case. Its hue resembled the Spanish conquistadors and missionaries who converted the darker women and men of Esquipulas. The beloved statue darkened as the faithful from Esquipulas and beyond prayed before it, lighting as they did an herb incense heavy with resin, causing thick smoke. The smoke clung to the Christ, as did the grease from pilgrim hands, the dust from years of display, and other pilgrim relics, including hair and threads. Over many years, this pious residue darkened the crucified Christ to black. Under the tree, a darker tree.

El Cristo Negro became a prophetic witness to Las Casas's lament that the scourged Christ was present in the dark indigenous people of Latin America, for the statue makes manifest what Las Casas had seen years earlier: the suffering

Christ can be found not in the Spanish slave masters but in the darker, scourged indigenous slaves. Gustavo Gutiérrez writes about a similar black statue, one he encountered in José María Argueda's novel *Deep Rivers*, and he interprets it together with las Casas's description of Christ in the indigenous people of Latin America as he writes, "The resemblance of the crucified Jesus and the Amerindian servant reminds us that the poor of Latin America (and elsewhere in the world) are 'a crucified people.'"[83] Breaking the bodies of the indigenous people staged them as Christ crucified, and the conquistadors as crucifiers of Christ. In El Cristo Negro, Christ crucified testifies against the iconoclasm targeting black bodies, an iconoclasm that itself masks the idolatry of gold.

In El Cristo Negro, we see both the riving and riven presence of Christ crucified. We see the broken Christ, the Christ who was crucified by the Romans, the Christ who declares solidarity with the darker peoples scourged by the conquesting Spaniards. El Cristo Negro, like Grünewald's Christ, declares solidarity with and presence to the broken. We also see in El Cristo Negro the breaking Christ who breaks brokenness itself. We see the Christ who takes a statue that is an emblem of both iconoclasm and idolatry, and rives its riven history to be present in even the world's gravest suffering. This is a Christ who invites us to participate in his iconoclasm—his breaking of brokenness—that we might more fully enter into his images of brokenness, his presence of a love that goes all the way through brokenness, going forth from every riven thing.

FIGURE 4. Vladislav Andrejev, *Icon of the Myrrh-bearing Women*, 2010. Used with permission.

4 ROSE AGAIN ON THE THIRD DAY
Abiding Presence

IN THE MAIN CURRENT of the Byzantine iconographic tradition, there is no image of the resurrection moment.[1] Instead, this tradition follows the silence of Scripture, and so the resurrection is celebrated through two icons developed centuries apart: Christ's descent to the dead and the myrrh-bearing women at the tomb. These icons mark the time just before and after the resurrection. No image depicts the time between them. The resurrection moment remains imageless, and in this way it keeps faith with what the fourth-century bishop Epiphanius calls "the great silence" that "reigns . . . on earth."[2]

But if this diptych nods to silence, it also speaks to the breaking of it. In the icon of the myrrh-bearing women, Christ's empty linens lie on a slab that is both the grave and the *kapporet*. Derived from the Hebrew word that means "to cover" or "to make expiation," the *kapporet* is the throne of mercy, rimmed by two cherubim on the Ark of the Covenant. It is the place for Yahweh to appear.[3] In this resurrection icon, sometimes one, sometimes two, angels attend the *kapporet*-grave, revealing that Yahweh has uncovered the divine face, appearing as the Christ who has made expiation. Through the resurrection, the Ark of the Covenant—an image of God's invisibility and transcendence—has become an image of God's visibility. This icon testifies that the resurrection inaugurates a new presence of Christ.

Twentieth-century Russian theologian Paul Evdokimov claims that the icon of the myrrh-bearing women discloses how iconic imaging works. It reveals the divine presence in icons by which Yahweh appears on and speaks from the throne of mercy.⁴ In this image of the myrrh-bearing women, we see what all icons do and how God is present to them. We see the resurrection as a divine mercy that gives us a new kind of speech and a new kind of imaging. From the silence of the empty tomb, from the angel-ringed invisibility of the *kapporet*, a plenitude of speech and images pours forth. Rising from the grave to new life, the one called Word and Image comes to us again, bringing new words and images that participate in this new life. Thus is the great silence broken.

Vladislav Andrejev's version of this icon connects this moment with Christ's first arrival. In his rendering, three myrrh-bearers approach the empty clothes on the grave as the three Magi approached the swaddled babe. In the resurrection, Christ begins a new form of abiding, similar to but not identical with the abiding Christ began as a babe. The resurrection in Andrejev's icon also evokes the feast of the epiphany; it is framed as a new showing forth of the God who dwells among us. God is newly known in the Christ who rises from the dead. In rising to new life, the Word and Image births a new divine presence into the world. And yet Christ's presence in the icon remains mysterious, elusive even. The figure of Christ himself is, as is usual for this icon, absent in Andrejev's image, his prior presence only alluded to by the empty burial shroud. The myrrh-bearing women's first experience of this new presence of Christ—the first description of resurrection in Scripture—is one of absence. This icon that is supposed to be paradigmatic of all iconic imaging presses the question: how can the Risen Lord be sought and seen? What does it mean to see him in the icon, which, like the empty tomb, is also an absence that proclaims presence?

The Risen Image Who Looked Like a Gardener

One of the myrrh-bearers is Mary Magdalene, who, in the Gospel of John, weeps at the empty tomb. Two angels ask her why she weeps. Too grieved to be startled, she does not need the traditional angelic greeting to humans, "Fear not." Wrapped in sorrow, she responds, "They have taken away my Lord, and I do not know where they have laid him." She turns. There is Jesus, but Mary does not know him, even when he speaks to repeat the angels' question. She supposes him the gardener, and pleads with him to tell her where they have taken her Lord. He says her name, "Mary." She turns again, knowing him now. "Rabbouni!" He begins his next words with a warning, "Do not touch me." As countless painters and theologians know this moment: *Noli me tangere*.

The Word speaks, "Mary." He is known first by this word and only after by his appearance. There is a great mystery here in Christ's encounter with the Magdalene. Why does Jesus prohibit the touch of his dear friend? Why does Mary not recognize hers? Before the resurrection, people failed to know Jesus as God; now his close friend fails to know him as Jesus. Most of Jesus's friends will repeat Mary's error, as Jesus mysteriously appears among them and just as mysteriously becomes, in some moment of that appearing, familiar. Newly risen, the Image of the invisible God images newly.

The Paradox of Resurrection Imaging

There is a paradox in resurrection imaging. The diptych of resurrection icons keeps a silence about the resurrection and yet interprets the resurrection as paradigmatic for iconic imaging. Joseph Ratzinger,[5] a great admirer of Evdokimov, points to a similar paradox. He claims that there is no portrait of the Risen Lord, nor any icon of the resurrection—and also that all sacred images are images of the resurrection.[6] In the same vein, Hans Urs von Balthasar describes the resurrection as a garland of images around "an inaccessible midpoint which alone has the magnetic force to arrange [the garland]."[7] These descriptions of the resurrection communicate the way it defies imaging and attracts new possibilities; it exceeds visibility and also models a new visibility for icons. Inaccessible and silent itself, the resurrection insists on an imagelessness that invites iconoclasm; as known by and paradigmatic of images, it embodies a profligate image-love that streams forth in the generation of new images.

If this sounds similar to my argument about the incarnation in Chapter 2, it is because the resurrection fulfills and completes the incarnation. In the resurrection, the abiding presence of Christ saturates the cosmos, from the underworld to the high heavens. As the cantor sings of the resurrection moment in the Exsultet of the Easter Vigil: *O vere beata nox, in qua terrenis cælestia, humanis divina iunguntur.* "O truly blessed night, when things of heaven are wed to those of earth, and divine to the human." The wedding of the divine to the human and the earthly to the heavenly means that our earthly, human life—already both a visible and invisible existence—enters into a new relationship with the invisible. In the crucifixion, the Image crosses a measureless abyss (to paraphrase Marion) between his appearance and his glory, thus killing any logic of resemblance for divine imaging. The risen Christ has passed through this abyss and comes through it unrecognizable to his friends. What does Love look like on the other side of torture and death?

The journey through death to new life pressures a new visibility. It is a visibility born in the mystery of the wedding of heaven to earth, bubbling up from the spring of divine mercy on that truly blessed night. From the unfathomable depths of that font, a new tradition of images flows forth, bearing new visibility. This new visibility is one to which we must be adequated. As the resurrected Christ both is and is not visibly recognizable, so the likeness these new images bear both is and is not visible. The iconodules call this likeness *hypostatic*. And like the resurrected Christ himself, hypostatic likeness is given as mercy and received as mercy.

Hypostatic likeness is a weighty form of likeness that designates a profound unity between image and prototype. It identifies an important way that the resurrected Christ continues to abide, one that will be integral to this chapter. While Chapter 2 explored how the theology of the incarnation of Christ sustains and authorizes a theology of imaging, this chapter explores how a theology of the resurrection warrants the honor given to particular types of images—and then teaches us to see all the world as image. Where the second chapter explored images of the divine at a general level, this chapter attends to specific imaging traditions intimate with the resurrection and explores how they open the world to us. These traditions include icons, of course, and also images made without human hands (*acheiropoieta*) and those beings whom Christ, in Matthew 25:31–46, calls "the least of these." In that Gospel passage, Christ calls his listeners to show mercy to the least of these and identifies with them in a likeness the Cappadocian theologians—Gregory of Nyssa, Gregory of Nazianzus, and Basil of Caesarea—call *prosoponic*.

These forms of resurrection imaging resist two types of imaging dangers: tokenism, on the one hand, and idolatry or spectacle, on the other. A token is something one sees *through* to its signified. To relate to an image as a token is to overlook its visibility and deny that it bears presence. A token hurries the gaze through the visible world, pointing beyond itself to the invisible. An idol, in contrast, not only claims presence; it circumscribes the divine presence it claims. Often idols are also spectacles, which are hyper-visible, claiming that there is nothing invisible left of the signified. In a spectacle, everything is reduced to the visible. Images and icons become tokens when we surrender to iconoclasms of temptation. Idols and spectacles persist when we fail to practice iconoclasms of fidelity—iconoclasms that entail fighting the urge to cling to images that should instead help us to ascend in love to Love and descend in mercy to the miserable. To practice an iconoclasm of fidelity is to receive the abiding presence of the resurrected Christ by avoiding and breaking resurrection spectacles and idols—by ascending and descending in imitation of the Image who is love and mercy.

By mercy, the world is transfigured. In the resurrection, God's mercy brought life even to the darkest places of death. Tokens, idols, and spectacles, on the one hand, fall short of this transfiguration because they polarize the visible and invisible. Images of the resurrection, on the other hand, speak to the newly transfigured world of the resurrection, where a strangely deep invisibility abides, transfiguring the visible. Heaven, after all, has been wed to earth in the resurrection. At the same time, that deep invisibility yields a still greater revelation. Earth can give us heaven. For the resurrection means that life is present everywhere, transfiguring even death, and that means more, not less, is revealed by the visible world.

We must prepare to perceive this new reality. Seeing rightly means entering into the right image relationship with both Lord and world, a relationship of love-driven ascent and descent that weaves together icons and poverty, seeing and loving, visibility and invisibility. As the wedding of heaven to earth, as the vindication of God's merciful love, the resurrection orders the world to a new, invisible reality that saturates and transfigures the visible. It gives us new images, endows old images with new significance, and requires new forms of fidelity. We begin with the likenesses of resurrection images.

Icons, the Least of These, and the Presences They Bear

Icons and the least of these are like Christ in different ways, but the difference between their forms of likeness is subtle. The two types of likeness are named by the Greek terms *prosopon* and *hypostasis*. So similar are these likenesses that they can both be translated as "likeness of person." Not only do the hypostatic likeness of icons and the prosoponic likeness of the least of these overlap in their range of potential meanings, they also share a similar structure. In both cases, the likeness of person justifies the honor given to the image passing through to the prototype; it names a unity of image and prototype that answers charges of idolatry. Still, as similar as these two likenesses are, they are not identical.

To help distinguish the shades of difference between *prosopon* and *hypostasis*, we must briefly dip into the murky etymological histories of *hypostasis*, *prosopon*, and *ousia*, three terms with imbricating meanings, distinguished over decades of debate. Early in Christianity, *ousia* was used synonymously with *hypostasis*, which was used synonymously with *prosopon*. The fourth century was crucial for their distinction. So were the Cappadocian Fathers. They used *ousia* to express the oneness of God. The worship given Christ is not idolatry because Christ is *homoousios*—of one substance—with the Father. *Ousia* names the oneness of Christ and the Father that makes the adoration of Christ true worship rather than an idolatrous gesture. The work of the term *hypostasis* is different. Where *ousia* designates the oneness of the Trinity, *hypostasis* comes to name the three-ness of it. While the Son is like the Father because the Son is *homoousios* with the Father, the Son is also unlike the Father. *Hypostasis* identifies this unlikeness. The Son and the Father have distinct *hypostases*—different individual subsistence or personhood.

Like *hypostasis*, *prosopon* can also denote person, though these two words' ranges of meanings do not entirely coincide. Where *hypostasis* tends toward meaning "substance," *prosopon* can mean "face," "mask," "role," "appearance," "countenance," and "character." For a time, early in Christianity's history, *hypostasis* and *prosopon* were used interchangeably, even in synods and councils, and even by the Cappadocians themselves. But as the Trinitarian debates raged in the fourth century, *prosopon* fell out of favor, largely because of its associations with third-century theologian Sabellius. Condemning the word *hypostasis*, Sabellius preferred the word *prosopon* to designate the Trinitarian members—the Father, Son, and Spirit—as three modes or roles God assumes. As the Cappadocian Father Basil increasingly battled this modalist theology, he declared that Sabellius minimized the threeness of the Trinity. Trinitarian members are not just roles or masks God wears; that statement seems to suggest the threeness is illusory. For Basil, the reality of threeness means each member has a singular subsistence, a distinct personhood. As the Trinitarian debates wore on, *prosopon* came to reek of its modalist association with Sabellius. So after years of using *prosopon* and *hypostasis* interchangeably, Basil began eschewing *prosopon* in his Trinitarian theology. He began to prefer *hypostasis*.[8] That, however, was not the end of Basil's use of *prosopon*.[9]

At the same time that Basil stopped using *prosopon* in his Trinitarian formulations, he found another use for the word in some sermons he delivered during a great famine in Cappadocia.[10] In those sermons, the concept of *prosopon* helped him redress the suffering in his see while simultaneously resolving an interpretive issue in a popular Scriptural passage: Matthew 25:31–46. In that passage, Christ imagines an eschatological scene in which he comes again in glory to separate the sheep from the goats. He invites the sheep into the kingdom by saying that when he was hungry, they fed him; when a stranger, they welcomed him; when naked, they clothed him; when sick, they cared for him; and when imprisoned, they visited him. The righteous do not remember seeing and tending a hungry, sick, imprisoned, strange, naked Lord. And so he tells them: inasmuch as you have done it to one of the least of these brothers (and sisters), you have done it unto me. The converse is true for the unrighteous. By failing to honor the least of these, they have failed to honor Christ. The honor or dishonor given to the least of these passes on to Christ. Why would that be? Worship of Christ and the Father is one because they are *homoousios*, as Basil persuasively argued in his Trinitarian debates. But why is honoring the least of these united to honoring Christ?

One answer is given by John Chrysostom, who preached on this text more than anyone else in antiquity. He focuses on the word *brothers* to restrict the meaning of the passage to baptized Christians and claims that the oneness the afflicted bear with Christ is the oneness they gain in baptism.[11] Honor passes from the afflicted to Christ because they are united to him in baptism. The Cappadocians take a different route. They identify Christ's union with the least of these as a union, not qua baptism but qua affliction—an interpretation more attuned to the weight of the passage, which falls not on brothers but on various forms of affliction. (And further: did Christ mean to restrict ministry to the Christian least of these? Surely not, especially given the inclusion of the "stranger" in his elaboration of the least of these and the number of stories and parables, like that of the Good Samaritan, about mercy given to those outside one's community or clan.)

For the Cappadocians, to honor the afflicted is to honor Christ because the poor are prosoponically like Christ. Preaching on Matthew 25, Basil claims that God takes up the cause of the afflicted "in his own person [*prosopon*]," for God "loves honor."[12] Basil's younger brother Gregory of Nyssa elaborates on the same passage to claim that the poor "bear the countenance [*prosopon*] of the Savior." As if to emphasize the point, he repeats it: "The Lord in His goodness has given them His own countenance [*prosopon*]."[13]

The Cappadocians drew on the range of meanings for *prosopon* that connote something like the self-presentation or self-expression of an individual. As the *prosopon* of the painter includes her brush,[14] so does the *prosopon* of the Lord include the afflicted. The Cappadocians' use of *prosopon* is in this way like that of the Apostle Paul: "For it is the God who said, 'Let light shine out of darkness,' who has shone in our hearts to give the light of the knowledge of the glory of God in the face [*prosopon*] of Jesus Christ" (1 Corinthians 4:6). For the Cappadocians, the least of these also shine to give the light of the knowledge of the glory of God. They are images of Christ, prosoponically like their prototype, such that they mediate Christ's presence to us and mediate our gifts to him. There is an analogy here in the Cappadocian logic: to worship Christ is to worship the Father because they share one *ousia*, and to feed the hungry is to feed Christ because Christ shares with them his very *prosopon*.

Centuries after the first articulation of likeness of *ousia* and of *prosopon*, theologians began to develop the likeness of *hypostasis*. It becomes important to Christian theology as the Byzantine iconomachy reached a fever pitch. In their fight against the veneration of icons, Byzantine iconomachs hurled many accusations against the iconodules, and like the claims of their Reformation-era and present-day heirs, their most severe and energizing charge was idolatry. To venerate an icon, they claimed, is to give to an image what should be given to God alone. The mature iconodulic thought of the eighth and ninth centuries drew on the logic of likeness already organic to Christianity in defending icons. Iconodules identified a unity of image and prototype such that honor given the image passes through to the prototype. As worship given Christ honors the Father, as to feed the hungry is to feed Christ, so to venerate the icon is to venerate the prototype.[15] It is not that the image is worshiped alongside or instead of the prototype (idolatry), but that the reverence given the image is one with the reverence given the prototype (iconodulia). In the case of the icon, the type of unity it bears with the prototype is found at the level of *hypostasis* rather than *ousia* or *prosopon*. What is important about an icon, then, is not that it looks like the person depicted. Its likeness is not the formal resemblance of a photograph. The icon is like the prototype because the prototype is gracious to us, because the divine shows mercy to us in the image. The *hypostasis* of Christ (or the saint depicted) mercifully appropriates the likeness of the icon, and so identifies with it, becoming uniquely present to it.

Hypostatic likeness is possible only because of the resurrection, because Christ lives to appropriate and be present to the figure of the icon. (It is similar with the saints, who have entered eternal life and so appear to us in a paradoxical relationship to time.) Though the resurrection does not originate it in the same way, prosoponic likeness also has an intimate relationship with the resurrection, one which will be unpacked later. For now, I want to note both the intimacy of these likenesses and also their differences from one another. *Prosopon* and *hypostasis* are sometimes used interchangeably today (often by iconographers), but throughout this chapter I use them as the later Cappadocians did, in order to invoke their distinct ranges of meaning. *Hypostasis* notes an individual person and the likeness icons bear; *prosopon* designates the self-presentation or self-expression of an individual (the face, the painter's brush) and the likeness the least of these convey.

One feature hypostatic and prosoponic likeness share is their complex relation to visibility and invisibility. In the case of icons, such complexity is made conspicuous by the twentieth-century Russian Orthodox theologians Paul Evdokimov, Leonid Ouspensky, Pavel Florensky, and Vladimir Lossky, who take up the mantle of the Byzantine iconodules to explain and defend icons to the modern world. They claim for icons a visibility that cannot, on the one hand, reduce to tokenism. It is not that icons are simply visible pictures that point to an invisible reality, or that they merely betoken a presence located elsewhere. This would amount to a denial that the icons themselves bear presence. Neither is it the case, on the other hand, that they reduce to idolatry. Icons do not make the invisible visible, nor do they circumscribe or otherwise exhaust the presence of the divine—which would paradoxically render the divine absent to us.[16] To give a fuller account of this relationship between visible and invisible, presence and absence, is to delve further into the hypostatic likeness icons bear.

The Visible and the Invisible in Icons: Hypostatic Likeness

Descriptions of icons are rife with paradox. They are absences that proclaim presences; they are visible and draw the beholder into the invisible. Breaking the surface of these paradoxes takes one into the deep waters of systematic theology, into the doctrines of the incarnation and resurrection. Eighth- and ninth-century Byzantine iconodule Nikephoros draws on the language of *kenosis* to describe the way divine figures are both present to and importantly absent from the icon. They are *inscribed*, not *circumscribed*, in the icon. Though kenosis is associated with incarnational language, Nikephoros takes this language to refer to the resurrection, and David Jasper elaborates the connection, writing that Christ's "very absence acknowledged through the image, is the sign of his resurrection."[17] Christ cannot be contained by death nor circumscribed in the iconographic line. That the icon inscribes, rather than circumscribes, means that it is not a representation of the invisible but, as Jasper explains, a threshold that renders visible the invisible *as the unenvisagable*, as that which cannot be fully captured or rendered.[18] For in the resurrection, Christ's absence is rendered as a new kind of presence, as Christ's invisibility is rendered as the unenvisagable.

The word often used to name the presence and visibility of the divine in icons—the inscription that is not circumscription—is *transfiguration*. The iconic body, the iconodules aver, is transfigured to reveal the divine. As an alternative to both tokenism (the denial of divine presence) and idolatry (the circumscription of it), transfiguration helps to articulate the hypostatic likeness of icon to prototype. What Christ "enhypostasizes" (that is, appropriates to his person) is his depiction, not the wood and paint.[19] Likewise for the saint, she appropriates the figure, not the substance of wood or color.[20] It is not the case, then, that the wood and paint of the icon become consubstantial with Christ or saint, nor is it true that the icon functions merely as a mnemonic, to aid in remembering the saint while one prays. The icon bears the transfigured presence of the divine. In Lossky's evocative phrase, "divinity become manifest in the saints," and this manifestation is repeated in the icon.[21]

Manifest can bear the sense of either visibility or presence, and in the case of icon and saint, the two meanings are inseparable, though they may be distinguished. Icons are often described in terms of how they make the divine visible. The icon offers a heavenly vision (or "an image of a heavenly vision") even while it is not *itself* this vision. It is an "outline of a vision," a "grid" through which Christ shines.[22] It is Christophanic, but only through participation in Christ.[23] Visibility and presence cannot be separated in the icon, for the divine visibility the icon offers is possible only because Christ has condescended to be present to the icon. As Theodore the Studite writes, divinity is present to the icon by "relative participation."[24] Visibility is always indexed to this participation of presence.

The integral connection of visibility and presence for the icon echoes and is derived from the connection of the same for the saint. The saints resist conformity to this world and have "resurrected their minds," so that they "bear witness to the invisible as they bear witness to themselves by their holy countenances."[25] Because the saint participates in the resurrected life of Christ, the icon of the saint displays the coinherence of this world and the next.[26] This is the heavenly vision offered by the icon. It offers this vision without collapsing these worlds, without rendering the invisible as visible. Thus, Ouspensky can write that holiness is actually visible in, rather than inferred from, the icon, while adding the qualification that such visibility is not the reduction of holiness to what can be seen. It is the opening of an entrance into the world that cannot be seen.[27] In Jasper's language, the icon renders the invisible as the unenvisagable.

In bearing witness to the next world, the icon makes the presence of that world visible to the current one. At the same time, it also *makes the next world more present* to the current one. Icons are often called windows, which captures the way they make the divine visible to us, but inasmuch as a window offers a view of only what is always already there, the analogy can mislead us about how icons also make the divine present to us. Other common analogies for the icon as threshold, border, or entrance perhaps describe this presence better. For hypostatic likeness identifies an *ontological* connection between the world of the image and that of the prototype. The ontological connection between the worlds is one the icon witnesses to (indicating what the resurrection *has* accomplished) and uniquely performs (suggesting what the resurrection *will* accomplish). To deny the ontological connection between image and prototype is to deny that honor passes through from image to prototype. It is to render iconodulia "criminal idolatry." To claim the icon as a token is, given the practices of veneration that surround it, also (paradoxically) to make it a dangerous idol.

To the extent that icons exist on the border of the visible and the invisible, they are always poised to be either more than themselves, becoming identified with the heavenly vision, or less than themselves, failing to open the beholder up to the world beyond and so being "merely a board with some paint on it."[28] The icon itself is not the heavenly vision, though, nor is it merely a board.[29] The analogies given—a grid for shining, an opening for entering, a threshold for crossing, an outline for offering a vision—highlight the performative quality of iconicity. An icon is always *for*. An icon performs its iconicity by opening onto the invisible world, the world beyond. If it fails to do this—if the beholder disallows it to do this—it is merely wood and paint. The icon is thus constantly in danger of becoming either token or idol.

Though it can become a token, the icon is not made to be such, for it is not made as an arbitrary sign of the divine. It does not betoken a presence that lies elsewhere, in some separate realm that one might encounter one day. At the same time, the icon has no reality of its own. It contains nothing in itself. It gains its iconicity through participation in the one who is Wholly Other.[30] It is not meant to be an idol because it does not materially localize Christ's presence. It is not consubstantial with the person it depicts, and to behave as if it were "encloses a presence in the wooden board. It would be to make an idol and make the person represented absent."[31] An icon is made to be neither token nor idol, yet is in constant danger of degenerating into either one or the other. An icon is only an icon because its iconicity is performed, because it can act like a threshold, an entrance, an opening. To refuse such performance by treating the icon as either token or as idol is ultimately to collapse the icon into flat absence. The unity named by hypostatic likeness means that the icon is more than a token, for it really makes present and visible the kingdom to come; and it also means the icon is less than (which is also more than) an idol, for it does not contain the kingdom nor reduce it to what can be seen. The icon is itself gripped by the kingdom, which becomes present and visible to the icon through the persons of Christ and the saints, in whom the kingdom is already manifest.[32]

It is the ontological connection, the hypostatic likeness, the suturing to the invisible that makes the icon what it is. To relate to the icon qua icon is to perceive the invisible in the visible, the *hypostasis* in the countenance, the living saint in the image. The invisible is not reduced to the visible; neither does the visible simply signify the invisible. Hypostatic likeness names an invisible that is present to, manifest in, the visible. In language the iconodulic tradition continually returns to, the invisible transfigures the visible in the icon. As Evdokimov is quick to point out, transfiguration refers not just to something that happens to the object. Transfiguration names a form of perception that requires active participation on the part of the beholder. The disciples can see the transfiguration only to the extent that their sight is transfigured, for to see the transfigured Christ is to be transfigured.[33] Such a claim, of course, presses the question of how a person is transfigured. Before addressing that question, we first turn to the other form of resurrection-intimate likeness: prosoponic likeness.

The Visible and the Invisible in the Least of These: Prosoponic Likeness

While centuries of iconodules have elaborated hypostatic likeness, prosoponic likeness lacks this deep philosophical tradition. Our main sources for probing prosoponic likeness are the clues left by Matthew 25:31–46 and those who preached on it. And in these sources, some affinities with hypostatic likeness assert themselves. As the risen Christ can be present to the icon through his hypostatic likeness to it, so Christ can be present to the least of these through his prosoponic likeness to them. And as an icon is misperceived when approached either as a token merely pointing to the invisible, or as an idol circumscribing the invisible, so the least of these are misperceived when they are overlooked (rendering them invisible) or reduced to their appearance (rendering them both hyper-visible and also invisible). The Cappadocians describe errors of both invisibility and hyper-visibility, displaying that to render an image a spectacle is to give it a hyper-visibility that collapses back into invisibility, just as idolizing icons renders the divine less present rather than more.[34]

In his homilies on Matthew 25:31–46, Gregory of Nyssa preaches in the second person, addressing the audience as those who are not hungry but who are nonetheless implicated in the suffering of those who are. We make the least of these invisible in our loud and bawdy banquets of excess, when we are so absorbed in our own greed we can neither hear nor see the needs of others, he says. We make the least of these invisible by forcing them to live like animals, hiding owl-like in the cracks of walls, foraging for food, drinking from springs, where they blend in with the background of natural life. We make them invisible because we simply cannot bear to look at them and come to terms with the horror of their lives. In these ways, we the satiated deny the visibility of the least of these.[35]

We also make them hyper-visible. Our refusal to come to terms with their visibility, our indifference to them, drives the afflicted to make themselves spectacles so that they may survive. Gregory of Nyssa excoriates his congregants for this sin:

> How do they arrive to make a parade of their infirmities and give the crowds the spectacle of their crippled bodies . . . ? [P]ressed by hunger, they come to throw themselves at the feet of the public and implore the first to appear. . . . To bargain for food, they carry their distress and show their ulcers by way of a beggar's palm. . . . What then? Is one not sinning against the natural law by reducing this person's suffering to theatrical phases, treating the disease with a speech and remembering it with a ballad?[36]

The afflicted ones are backed into "advertis[ing] their horror" to persuade the satiated to spare some of their excess. They make themselves into "atrocious spectacles"—a perverse and desperate form of entertainment to urge the satiated to attend their needs.[37] Such spectacalizing circumscribes the afflicted's suffering to the vision (and the subjectivity) of the satiated, rendering visible what is unenvisagable. It reduces the afflicted to a material visibility, shorn of the invisibility all humans bear as God-imagers and the afflicted bear as God's own face. Cut off from the invisible, images become idols; similarly severed, humans become spectacles. To see the afflicted as equivalent to their appearance is to fail to the see them at all. To see them rightly is to see them in relation to the invisible.

What does it mean to see the afflicted rightly, as prosoponically like Christ? Part of what makes this question difficult to answer is that Matthew 25 does not thematize the difference between the righteous and the unrighteous in terms of which group recognizes Christ rightly. *Both* the righteous *and* the unrighteous seem unaware, until Christ tells them, that what they have done unto the least of these, they have done unto Christ. The righteous seem just as surprised as the unrighteous to receive this knowledge. Yet Christ's prosoponic identification with the least of these can no longer be hidden, for the passage has given the secret away. Readers and auditors of these verses and of homilies on them know what the righteous and unrighteous in Christ's story did not.

Like the many other homilists speaking on this passage, the Cappadocians make use of the text's revelation of Christ's prosoponic likeness to urge their congregants to become righteous by knowing what the righteous in the story did not know. Gregory of Nazianzus, for example, preaches on this text by exhorting his auditors:

> If you believe me at all, then, servants and brothers and sisters and fellow heirs of Christ, let us take care of Christ while there is still time; let us minister to Christ's needs, let us give Christ nourishment, let us clothe Christ, let us gather Christ in, let us show Christ honor.... [L]et us give this gift to him through the needy, who today are cast down on the ground, so that when we all are released from this place, they may receive us into the eternal tabernacle, in Christ himself.[38]

Not only does Nazianzen urge his hearers to minister to the poor as a ministry to Christ, he urges them to do it *so that* the poor can receive them into the eternal blessedness that is Christ himself. Those who read the passage or hear it preached are exhorted to practice a form of righteousness that is in one important respect dissimilar from the righteousness of those in the passage itself. Those in the passage minister to the least of these as if the least of these are Christ without knowing this is what they are doing; we who read or hear Nazianzen's sermon are urged to minister to the poor as if they are Christ *because* they are (prosoponically like) Christ. What are we to do with this paradox? What does it mean that we are exhorted to imitate the righteous, who minister to Christ without knowing it, when hearing the story makes it impossible for us not to know it? How can we imitate them? Believing Christ's story, how can we fail to see the least of these as Christ? What kind of visibility (or presence) does the least of these bear?

At one level, we can answer that last question along with Sarah Coakley, who articulates seeing the resurrected Christ *as* serving the least of these. She does not thematize prosoponic likeness (though she does footnote Gregory of Nyssa's use of it) when she elaborates knowing Christ as serving the poor, as having "felt the indebtedness of the very gift of life that animates such service, and to have received the identity of Jesus back afresh in the process."[39] To serve the afflicted is to receive anew the Christ who was afflicted. At the same time that such service gives one Christ, it also prepares one to receive Christ further. It unblocks our capacity to know and respond, to enter into the dispossession by which we receive Christ.[40] She claims this way of understanding what it means to see the resurrected Christ as an important alternative to the "optimistic positivism" trumpeted by the "quest for the historical Jesus," in which one can see the presence or absence of Jesus by using the latest historical tools. It is not certain tools that allow one to see or not see Christ rightly. Christ is seen—and the afflicted are seen—rightly when the afflicted are served as if they are Christ. For it is in such service that one responds to the gift of life and receives further life, even life from death.

One might answer the paradox, then, in the spirit of Coakley by sidelining the explicit knowledge that distinguishes the people in the story from those of us outside it. "Seeing Christ" or "knowing Christ" is not explicit knowledge of Christ; it is behaving like Christ by behaving as if others are Christ, regardless of our explicit knowledge. This attenuates the difference between the righteousness those in the story practice and the righteousness those of us who hear the story are exhorted to practice, for explicit knowledge of Christ's presence to the poor is simply not the most important feature of this righteousness, nor is it the kind of visibility the least of these offer.

At another level—perhaps building on the first one—the Cappadocians describe the least of these as bearing a visibility that makes them singularly close to God. What does it mean that the afflicted bear the *prosopon* of Christ? "The poor," Gregory of Nyssa claims, are "the stewards of our hope, the doorkeepers of the kingdom" who permit the righteous but not the unrighteous into the kingdom of God. They defend the righteous and prosecute the unrighteous, not by speaking, Gregory explains, but simply "by being seen by the judge." That the least of these are part of God's own *prosopon* means that they make visible *to* God who is righteous and who is unrighteous, for "the deed done to them cries out to the one who fathoms the heart in a voice clearer than the herald's trumpet."[41] In this construal of the visibility borne by the afflicted, they are highly visible to Christ, such that what is done to them is especially noticeable to God. Prosoponic likeness speaks to God's special sensitivity to the afflicted and therefore to the deeds done to them. At this level of interpretation, the very act of telling and repeating the story helps the unrighteous into righteousness and the righteous into greater righteousness by helping them to see the least of these as God sees them, as imminently visible. Through telling this story, we learn to see the least of these as making visible to us the God who is mercy.

Still, the text asks us not just to see the least of these as especially noticeable. It presses us to see them as, in Gregory of Nyssa's words, "stewards of our hope." If our hope is resurrection to new life, then we begin to see here the great intimacy of prosoponic and hypostatic likeness. In the afflicted, the faithful see a prosoponic likeness to Christ that displays for them the hope that they, too, will be like Christ in the end, deified into the likeness of Christ's *hypostasis*. The unity the least of these share with Christ witnesses to a different unity: the unity for which all hope in the eschaton. The afflicted doubly image the resurrection. They image the resurrection to the extent that their likeness and unity of veneration with Christ is disclosed, according to Matthew 25, in the general resurrection; and they image the unity with Christ made possible by Christ's resurrection from the dead—begun at baptism and consummated in the deification of the faithful. The fullness of this interpretation was not available to the people in Christ's story of the Last Judgment, for it was the pre-resurrected Jesus who told this story. But later auditors receive this story Jesus told together with the story of his resurrection. Jesus's story should thus prepare these auditors to see the afflicted as resurrection images of Christ. They can then rightly perceive prosoponic likeness as an image of hypostatic likeness.

One such auditor, Rowan Williams, finds still another way the least of these image the resurrection. They image the way, in Williams's words, we "must meet the crucified Christ again as a risen stranger."[42] As Mary met Christ as a stranger in the garden, as the disciples met him as a stranger on the road to Emmaus and the shores of the Galilean Sea, so we meet him as a stranger today. We meet the risen Christ as the least of these united to him in prosoponic likeness. In the resurrection, we receive Christ back from death. The Word of God comes back from the silence of the grave, the Image of the Father back from the invisibility of tomb. We receive again the one who is Word and Image. To receive him *as Christ*, we must, Williams says, first recognize him as the one who was crucified, the one whom we betrayed.[43] To receive the resurrected Christ is to acknowledge ourselves as betrayers. To perceive this image of God, to receive the prosoponic likeness of Christ in the afflicted, is to reckon with the least of these in their affliction—which is to receive our speech back as confession and absolution, to receive our images back purged in this way. To receive the resurrected Christ is therefore to receive the possibility of new life, a possibility witnessed to in the God-bearing countenance of the least of these. In the afflicted, we meet Christ crucified, alive in a new way. As in icons, this transfiguration—the afflicted as Christophanic—is one we can perceive only by entering our own transfiguration. And this idea, that to see the resurrected Christ is to begin to change, is surely embodied in the Scriptural accounts of the resurrection appearances.

For, after the resurrection, Christ appears as a stranger whom his friends must learn to receive as familiar. The resurrected Christ is both visible to them and not visible to them, not until they recognize him in the breaking of the bread, the catching of the fish, or the calling of a name. There are striking resemblances between the resurrection appearances and, on the one hand, the appearance of the least of these—whose Christological identity is also mistaken—and, on the other hand, iconic presence, in which the person of Christ, in Evdokimov's words, shows "different aspects of himself."[44] But if the likenesses of icons and the least of these, hypostatic and prosoponic likeness, resemble one another as they witness to resurrection, so, too, does the *making* of each likeness. In their making, that is, these likenesses find further resemblance with one another even as they also further witness to the resurrection.

Spirit-Made Likenesses

If icons and the least of these are kin in their hypostatic and prosoponic likenesses—as yielding a visible that opens onto the invisible, as transfigured images perceived by transfigured sight, as images of the resurrection that testify to the resurrection—they are also kin in the making of each likeness. Both likenesses are Spirit-given, not made with human hands (acheiropoietic). The likenesses come from an invisible presence that rests on the image, transfiguring it. They are likenesses given to us to heal our infirmity; the *acheiropoieta* are gifts of God's mercy.

That icons bear an acheiropoietic likeness is perhaps the less obviously true claim, though it is essential to icon theology. The distinction is this: whereas humans make the icon, the Spirit makes the likeness. It is not that the making of the icon is unimportant—quite the contrary. Writing an icon is a prescribed process in which great attention is given to the materials used, the order of painting, and the training of the iconographer. And the icon is supposed to, in some sense, look like the saint; the pattern for the icon attempts to convey the history of the saint, her death, her vocation, and her character traits.[45] Yet this is not what makes an icon hypostatically like Christ.

In some Russian Orthodox churches, the icon becomes hypostatically like Christ or the saint in a ceremony of blessing. Invoked by a gesture of epiclesis in the blessing of the icons, the Spirit transfigures the body depicted in it by the "heavenly face of the [saint],"[46] thereby identifying the iconic image with the *hypostasis* of the saint. In other traditions, because the icon is already bathed in the prayers of the iconographer, there is no need for a further ceremony invoking the Spirit. For icons that are not handmade—reproductions that will have an ecclesial use—there is sometimes a tradition of leaving the image in the altar for forty days as a way of petitioning and waiting for the Lord's presence to come to the icon.[47] In any case, what matters is not that the artist "correctly" depicts Christ or the saint but that Christ or the saint appropriates the depiction, agreeing to make the depiction true by the Spirit. Thus, the same Spirit who deifies the faithful by uniting them to the *hypostasis* of Christ also identifies the iconic body with the *hypostasis* of Christ or the saint. Through such identification, the Spirit makes Christ or the saint present to the icon.[48]

Something of this complexity of valuing human and divine agency is seen in the stories and significance of a particular acheiropoietic image, the Holy Face, a miraculous image of the face of Christ. Its origin is given in several legends. Often, it is associated with the mandylion of Edessa, a piece of linen Christ reputedly pressed on his face and sent to King Agbar of Edessa, who commissioned a portrait from the impression on the cloth. This image is central to the iconographic tradition. On the day commemorating the Triumph of Orthodoxy, when the iconodules finally won the day in the great Byzantine iconomachy, the icon of Christ that is venerated is the icon of the Holy Face. This icon is venerated because, like all *acheiropoieta*, it shows what Lossky calls the "dogmatic principle of iconography."[49] The Holy Face makes apparent the Spirit's work in icons: as God made the image of the Holy Face, so God makes the likeness that makes all icons *icons*. And the Holy Face is important to iconography in another way as well. Even though "correctly" depicting the prototype is not what yields hypostatic likeness, the Holy Face became the model for icons of Christ. The Holy Face icon witnesses to the Spirit as the ultimate maker of likeness. It is the Spirit who transfigures the icon so that its visibility becomes an entrance into the invisible.

Evdokimov goes still further in his claims about the Holy Face. He argues that the Holy Face shows us something about how to look rightly at the world, not just at the icon. He writes, "This image teaches us that there is nothing that is made uniquely by man's hands, that everything visible is always a miracle and that we must *believe* and therefore *see* with and through the eyes of the Dove if we hope to penetrate into the mysterious heart of that miracle."[50] It is an astounding claim, one that puts *acheiropoieta* at the heart of all visibility. This acheiropoietic image shows how all the world opens up, like an image, from visible to invisible, when seen as the work of divine hands. The whole world can be seen as an image, with Spirit-given likeness that opens up to divine prototype. The world is like an icon given Spirit-made likeness to the divine. The icon's hypostatic likeness speaks to the *acheiropoieta*, which are entirely Spirit-made.

Like hypostatic likeness, so, too, prosoponic likeness is Spirit-given. Even so, it is not identical to hypostatic likeness, which has the Spirit's work in deification as its model. Prosoponic likeness does not require that the least of these have been incorporated into Christ's very *hypostasis*, to be united with him in everlasting glory. The least of these may or may not have that kind of likeness as well, but they do not have it by virtue of their status as the least of these. Prosoponic likeness signifies, instead, that God has chosen to share the divine face with the least of these, whether or not they are members of the body of Christ. And the Spirit, as the one who draws humans into the divine life, rests on the most vulnerable of society, giving them the face of God, making them God's own *prosopon*. The Spirit who brings life out of death identifies the ones our world has afflicted unto death with the One who is the giver of life.

Both the icon as a new site of Christ's presence in the world and the least of these in which Christ must be newly known hearken to resurrection, another new site of Christ's presence in the world in which Christ must be newly known. The Spirit who renders the *hypostasis* of Christ present to the iconic body and the *prosopon* of God present to the least of these also raises Jesus Christ from the dead. Just as the presence of Christ in the icon and the least of these must be newly recognized, so Christ had to be newly received and recognized in his resurrection appearances.

Making Christ present, whether in icons, the afflicted, gardens, roads, or seasides, is not human work. While human hands carve the wood, paint the icon, and invoke the Holy Spirit, human hands do not make the likeness. In the case of the afflicted, the human does not make herself prosoponically like Christ; it is a likeness given by the mercy of God to cultivate mercy. Hypostatic and prosoponic likeness are both acheiropoietic. It is no mere coincidence that both happen to be acheiropoietic and intimate with the resurrection. Hypostatic and prosoponic likeness are acheiropoietic because they echo the resurrection to which they witness. For the resurrected Christ is the originary acheiropoietic image. He calls himself such. *Destroy this temple and in three days I will make a new one, acheiropoietic, not made by human hands*, Christ commands in Scripture.[51] And Christ's resurrected body is given new life by the Spirit (Romans 8:11), as hypostatic and prosoponic likeness are Spirit-made. Hypostatic and prosoponic likeness are braided together with *acheiropoieta*, flowing from the acheiropoietic image of Christ's resurrected body.

How do we rightly receive the *acheiropoieta*—the acheiropoietic Temple and the acheiropoietic likenesses that witness to it? To address this question, we turn to reflect on three specific cases of our third class of resurrection images: acheiropoietic images.

Acheiropoietic Images

Do not touch me, Christ tells Mary in the garden. This prohibition of human touch sounds again in the exclusion of human touch from the making of that mysterious class of images, the *acheiropoieta*. The Holy Face, with its legend of Edessa, is among the most famous acheiropoietic images. We do not have the mandylion itself, but the image lives on in the iconographic tradition it helped to justify. The most famous *acheiropoieta* we do have today—the Virgin of Guadalupe and the Shroud of Turin—are contested images. Forensic evidence for both has been hotly debated. A third important *achieropoieton*, the Veil of Veronica, does not exist even as relic. It exists in stories and images of it, some intertwined with the mandylion of Edessa. The Catholic Church has remained agnostic on the historicity of these images, even as the images have attracted major cults of piety. The Shroud of Turin has spawned its own field of study, called *sindonology*. The Virgin of Guadalupe has been heralded as the Patroness of the Americas—the only image to be given such a high status. The Veil of Veronica is commemorated in the sixth station of the cross. These images are eloquently expressive of the Christian faith, and attending to these acheiropoietic images can yield insight into acheiropoietic likenesses: what it means that the Spirit makes them, and how we are to receive them.

THE SHROUD OF TURIN

Perhaps the most famous of the *acheiropoieta* today is the Shroud of Turin. The most recent chapter in its long story began May 28, 1898. It was then, in the tomb-like seclusion of a darkroom and bathed in blood-red light, that Secondo Pia watched as the image of a calm, crucified man developed, revivified across the centuries. The negative of the plate shows the likeness of the corpse more strikingly than the Shroud itself. Is it an image of the very body of Christ? For some time, this moment of technological probing—so often an iconoclastic moment of exposing and debunking—instead witnessed to the sacredness of the Shroud.

One hundred years later, debate continued over the authenticity of the Shroud as Pope John Paul II celebrated the anniversary of the photograph, calling the Shroud "an image of God's love as well as of human sin" and "an icon of the suffering of the innocent in every age."[52] The next two popes also picked up on the power of love and portrayal of sin together, connecting the Shroud explicitly to the hope Christ brings. Pope Benedict XVI describes the Shroud as "an icon written in blood," and claimed it "acts as a 'photographic' document with both a 'positive' and a 'negative.'"[53] The positive and negative are the death of God and the love of God, which are together in this image, displaying that "the darkest mystery of faith is at the same time the most luminous sign of a never-ending hope."[54]

The togetherness of darkness and luminosity speaks to the hope of the resurrection, which Pope Francis claims for the Shroud. In the tortured face, he sees "all those faces of men and women marred by a life which does not respect their dignity" and at the same time "the power of the Risen One who overcomes all things."[55] The last three popes, then, have interpreted the Shroud of Turin as an image of hope for the way it displays Christ's presence in (and so figures the overcoming of) pain and suffering. The image identifies Christ with those afflicted by the world. The very image itself, in fact, exists on the shroud used to cover the Christ who was naked in death. In this way, it is an image both of his affliction and the merciful tending given to him in his affliction.

THE VIRGIN OF GUADALUPE

The story of the Virgin of Guadalupe begins in 1531 with Juan Diego, a poor Aztec man, walking by the hill of Tepeyac. He hears sweet music, and a radiant young woman appears to him. It is the Virgin Mary as an Aztec woman, who tells him she wishes a chapel built in Tepeyac. Juan Diego tries to realize her wish by visiting the bishop of Mexico City, but the bishop instructs him to come back later. Again the Virgin appears to Juan Diego, who tries to defer her request by insisting that she choose someone of greater status to petition the bishop. Instead, she offers him a sign to present to the bishop: unseasonable and non-native roses growing on the hill of Tepeyac. Juan Diego gathers the flowers into his tilma (cape), and when he opens the tilma to show the bishop, the flowers roll away to reveal the acheiropoietic image of the Virgin of Guadalupe.[56]

At this sign, the bishop assents, and the chapel in Tepeyac is erected for the Mother of God. The chapel is today surrounded by multiple buildings to honor the image, including a basilica where the tilma still hangs. Millions of pilgrims have come to celebrate the image, which became, in 1945, the Patroness of the Americas, given to and by the poor man canonized in 2002 amid ongoing doubts of his historicity. When John Paul II beatified Juan Diego in 1990, he said of him: "In the likeness of ancient biblical personages, who were collective representations of all the people, we can say that Juan Diego represents all the natives who welcomed the Gospel of Jesus, thanks to the maternal assistance of Mary, always inseparable from the manifestation of her Son and the planting of the Church, as was her presence among the apostles on the day of Pentecost."[57]

In John Paul II's speech, Juan Diego is both a collective representation (a symbol) of a people and an individual person (a figure) who is beatified. As a symbol, Juan Diego represents not just his own Aztecs but all the indigenous people of the Americas who welcomed Christ with the aid of his Mother. As a figure, he offers the gift that enables this welcoming. The story narrates the way that the people of the Americas and especially Mexico, by finding their way to Mary by way of Juan Diego, found their way into the embrace of Jesus.

In this manner, the acheiropoietic image of the Virgin of Guadalupe testifies to the least of these as doorkeepers to the kingdom. It makes present the eschatological vision of Matthew 25:31–46 and the meditation on it by Basil, Gregory of Nazianzus, and Gregory of Nyssa: that the witness of the least of these determines whether we enter the heavenly kingdom. The least of these are the doorkeepers of life with God. Juan Diego's story is an earthly image of this doorkeeping role. He is without earthly power or wealth, and still Juan Diego nevertheless ushers millions into the church with his gift of the acheiropoietic image the Virgin gave to him. And Mary herself comes as one of the least of these, as an indigenous girl rather than a powerful queen. To receive this image, the authorities of the church (the bishop) had to yield to the authority of the least of these. The miraculous image then testifies to the heavenly doorkeeping role that the least of these play by virtue of their prosoponic likeness to Christ. When Mary imprints her image on Juan Diego's tilma, she testifies to Christ's identification with the least of these. The Mother of God appears on the cloak of the least of these; she gives her likeness to one of these, pointing to the way Christ has given his own face, his *prosopon*, to the afflicted.[58]

In the acheiropoietic Virgin of Guadalupe, the church welcomes a gift from the least of these (in the narratival interpretation of the story) and the Aztec people welcome Mary's Christ as one of their own (in the symbolic interpretation of the story). It is an image that sounds the significance of the least of these. To receive the Virgin of Guadalupe as an image of Christ's mother is to receive the least of these as doorkeepers of the divine, for they both give the image to the church and are figured in the image. The Virgin of Guadalupe reminds the faithful of the promise of Matthew 25; the divine life continues to abide in the least of these. God bears new life in the world through the afflicted. The Virgin of Guadalupe testifies to the least of these as sites of resurrection life.

The Virgin of Guadalupe, then, witnesses to the resurrection life inaugurated by Christ as she also testifies that hospitality to the least of these ushers a person into such life. Pope Francis has claimed Guadalupe as an image of hospitality, of an embrace of human life in all its stages and places. In Guadalupe, we see the embrace of the one who was a stranger. The Virgin of Guadalupe herself comes as a stranger by whom Americans are transformed into resurrection likeness to her Son.[59] The Virgin of Guadalupe's hypostatic likeness, Juan Diego's prosoponic likeness—these can invite our own eschatological hypostatic likeness to Christ.

THE VEIL OF VERONICA

Moved by the suffering of Jesus as he carries his cross to Golgotha, a woman— we call her Veronica—breaks into the violence of the soldiers and offers her cloth so that Jesus may wipe his face. This small but courageous act of kindness yields what some call the first acheiropoietic image of Christ.[60] His face imprints on the cloth in a moment remembered as the sixth station of the cross and endlessly reproduced in images of the Veil of Veronica—the *vera eikon* or true image. The scriptural meditation often given for this station is Matthew 25:40, Whatever you have done for the least of these you have also done for me.[61]

The claim of this pairing of Scripture and station is that Veronica reaches out to a man in pain and relieves the suffering of our Lord, who gifts her with his image. The way Veronica's mercy to the least of these redounds to Christ is now true of all acts of mercy. Her act reveals to us how mercy works. Christ is honored when we love the afflicted one carrying a cross. When we wipe the *prosopon* of the afflicted, we mop the *prosopon* of Christ. And then when Veronica's hands tend the face of the man with the cross, God's hands make the miraculous image of Christ's *prosopon* on her veil. God gives her—and the entire church—the gift of Christ's likeness.

Verbally walking through the stations of the cross on Good Friday, Joseph Ratzinger came to the sixth: "At first, Veronica saw only a buffeted and pain-filled face. Yet her act of love impressed the true image of Jesus on her heart: on his human face, bloodied and bruised, she saw the face of God and his goodness, which accompanies us even in our deepest sorrows. Only with the heart can we see Jesus. Only love purifies us and gives us the ability to see. Only love enables us to recognize the God who is love itself."[62]

In showing mercy to the one in pain, Veronica received an acheiropoietic image of Christ on her heart. In showing love, she sees the God who is love itself. The acheiropoietic image of the veil speaks to her ability to receive such an image of God. In the miraculous image on her veil, Veronica sees that the least of these whom she serves is the Christ. It is her love, according to Ratzinger, that imparts the true (invisible) image and enables her to see (images visible and invisible) rightly. Through tending the least of these who bear the prosoponic likeness of Christ, she receives the acheiropoietic image of Christ on her heart, that she may see Christ and see as Christ sees, drawing her nearer the hypostatic likeness of Christ.

Ascent and Descent in Love

What will the resurrected Christ's words to us be in our recognition? His words to Mary in the garden are *Noli me tangere*: Do not touch me, for I have not yet ascended to my Father. It is not that Mary's hands would pollute this Image made without human hands. Christ speaks in this encounter not about a touch of corruption but a touch of possession. Now is not the moment to seize, he tells her. Now is the time to prepare to ascend. As interpreters often render Jesus's command: Stop clinging to me.

Mary is tempted to cling to the resurrected Christ, as Peter was to the transfigured Christ. On Mount Tabor, Jesus does not bother to respond to Peter's eager offer to make three dwelling places, for him, Moses, and Elijah. There is no need, for after Peter's interjection, the Father booms his approval of the Son, and the disciples fall down in fear (in Matthew's account) and keep silent (in Luke's). There is no more mention of dwelling on Tabor. With Jesus, the disciples descend the mountain and continue their ministry: meeting in the very next story a man begging for his son's healing, "Lord, have mercy..." (Matthew 17:15), and sending laborers out into the harvest to proclaim the coming kingdom (Luke 10:2).

How do we understand this impulse of Jesus's intimates to cling and dwell when they should prepare to ascend and descend? Could it be that we in our avarice and fear can make an idol even out of Christ? At the very least, we render Christ an occasion for idolatry, clinging to moments of glory, trying to keep, to circumscribe, to idolize what we should instead follow. But clinging is not, according to Christ, how to receive him. There is an iconoclastic moment in receiving Christ's abiding presence. The locked gaze must be broken lest it become idolatrous. It must descend in mercy so that it can ascend in love.

Joseph Ratzinger describes a modern version of this iconoclastic moment. He gives his own exhortation to resist clinging when we should ascend and descend. Connecting the appearance of the icon to the appearance of the incarnate Christ, Ratzinger claims that "to reduce the visible appearance of Christ to a 'historical Jesus' belonging to the past misses the point of his visible appearance, misses the point of the incarnation." That point is to draw us into the life of God. Describing divine descent and human ascent, Ratzinger continues: "The Incarnation is aimed at man's transformation through the Cross and to the new corporeality of the Resurrection. God seeks us where we are, not so that we stay there, but so that we may come to be where he is."[63] Christ does not come to reduce divine presence to what can be measured and weighed. Christ comes so that through the empty tomb he can birth the world into new life, an eternal life beyond our standards of history and materiality. Or to put it another way, Christ did not come to earth that we might trap him there by nailing him to our very trees. Christ came that despite our nails we might learn to ascend with him. And such ascent is not leaving behind the earth, its trees, and its humans. It is an ascent that requires a descent down the Mount of Transfiguration to the people Jesus loves. For what is ascent to Christ but a descent in merciful love?

The abiding Christ summons us to iconoclasms of fidelity—iconoclasms of breaking our gaze and grasp to descend and ascend rather than stay and cling. And this iconoclasm of fidelity is echoed in the realm of icons. The icon, too, calls us to descend and ascend rather than lock onto its appearance. For there is an iconoclastic aspect to receiving the icon as well. The icon images the divine for the beholder in the moment its natural likeness is transcended so that its hypostatic likeness may be received. In a sense, then, the image is affirmed just when it is also negated.

To claim that the icon is affirmed through negation is another way to express Saint Dorotheus's oft-quoted saying that icons require a "fast for the eyes." Glossing Dorotheus's saying, Ouspensky writes that through fasting, icons open the "door to interiority" and provide a "path to follow" so that we might "enter the narrow gate."[64] For Ratzinger, we fast with our eyes through ascetic discipline and liturgical training, which purify the senses. Then, with our purified senses, we contemplate the icon which may "awaken new senses in us [and] teach us a new kind of seeing, which perceives the invisible in the visible."[65] Sight is denied so it may see more, so that it may learn to open up to the invisible. This is a sight that grows from and flowers into "interior vision."[66] It delivers us from "that closure of the senses that perceives only the externals, the material surface of things."[67] Through the fast for the eyes, our senses open up to "their widest capacity" so that we "see Christ rightly" and "say with Thomas: 'My Lord and my God!'"[68] Our senses open like a plant in bloom and we, like Thomas, like Mary, become the self that can recognize Christ.

When we fast with our eyes, we receive the icon as a gift of Christ. The icon arises from and gives rise to contemplation. Through the gift of contemplative sight, the icon teaches us to receive the world as image. Or as Ratzinger writes, "The whole problem of knowledge in the modern world is present [in icons]."[69] By giving us the presence of hypostatic likeness, rather than naturalistic representation, the icon leads away from a fixation on the visible to an encounter with the invisible in the visible. In a similar way, the whole world can be perceived as an image of its divine Creator when the invisible is received through the visible. When there is an interior opening up of the senses, we can "perceive the reflection of divine glory in creation."[70] The icon teaches us to see

God when we see the world. In the icon rests the whole problem of knowledge in the modern world because it poses the question of whether material reality exhausts the image—and therefore the world. The icon is paradigmatically what the world is to a lesser extent, and to learn to receive the icon rightly is to learn to see the world as image. It is to know rightly.

If the icon is paradigmatic for knowledge, then deformation of our relations to icons might speak to larger distortions in how and what we know. Evdokimov worries that a diminished response to icons—a prayer-less response, a contemplation-less sight—indicates a graver failure of our knowledge. It suggests that we have exchanged that which ever-opens up, ever-deepens, leading, perhaps to a meeting with the transcendent—a "reality pulsating with life"—for knowledge ordered to mastery.[71] By reducing the world to visibility, by circumscribing it to the domain of the visible, one submits the world to one's own powers. Such submission is not an ascent in love; it is a subjugation for power. When we deny the mystery of the world and its objects, we attempt to place them under our feet, to submit them to our standards. Iconoclasms of fidelity break us and images open so that we resist the will to dominate.

If to encounter objects sheared of their mystery speaks to one mistake, another is to react "in despair" by seeking the mystery detached from objects.[72] This is iconoclasm run amok, undisciplined by the resurrection of Christ. The invisibility to which the icon invites us is not a mystical invisibility, unmoored from visibility. Invisibility is, rather, always tethered to visibility, framed by it. To claim otherwise—to try to turn images into tokens—is to deny our humanity. Evdokimov sees this as a mistake that mirrors the docetists' attempt to seek the divinity of Christ detached from his humanity, which can be nothing but "a phantasmagoric game of bodiless shadows."[73]

The togetherness of mystery and object is realized Christologically in the ascent that is a descent in love. To seek the divine apart from the least of these is to deny God's own face. To attempt to receive an icon as merely a symbol rather than the presence of God is to exchange the possibility of transfiguration for a "game of bodiless shadows." At the same time, to receive an icon—to receive the world—as if exhausted by its objecthood, is to attempt subjugation of power. This subjugation denies the hypostatic likeness of icons and the prosoponic likeness of the least of these. It also rejects the witness of the acheiropoieta.

For *acheiropoieta* witness to the way God condescends to be visible and present to God's people as a mercy to them. The Shroud of Turin, the Virgin of Guadalupe, and Veronica's Veil are all received through an ascent in love to

God that is a descent by the love that is mercy to the people of God. Christ descends to us that we may ascend to him; we are called to imitate this movement. To receive acheiropoietic images rightly is to receive them as Christ's mercies, and to receive mercy is to be transformed so as to become merciful, like Christ. The Holy Spirit transfigures the merciful to be like the Merciful One. In this way, these acheiropoietic images elucidate for us what icons are: images of the divine, made sites of divine presence by God's merciful gift of likeness. To receive this likeness, the senses of the beholder, like the figure of the icon, must be transfigured.[74] The beholder is transfigured by the Holy Spirit as she ascends like the Christ who mercifully descends to us in the incarnation.

And this, too, is the witness of the least of these: that we receive the divine by serving those who bear no obvious trace of divine glory. We see the hungry, the thirsty, the stranger, the sick, and the imprisoned, and the honor we give them redounds to Christ. To ascend in divine love is to descend like Christ in mercy. The visible world is shot through with the invisible, and through the visible God transfigures us so that we may see Christ and ascend to participate in divine life.

Rebirth from the Tomb

In Chapter 2, on the incarnation, I reflected on confession as an act of iconoclasm—of breaking the self like a bone to re-set it, so that the self can discern Christ rightly. In the resurrected Christ, confession and absolution come to us together. God gives us resurrection images as a mercy to us, so that in them we might see God's mercy and become like the Merciful One. To receive Christ is to confess our falseness, to know that we have become this falseness, and to accept the possibility of a new way of being, the way of mercy. It is to recognize both the strangeness of Christ and the strangeness of this new way of being to which we have been called. The resurrection is thus image creating, iconopoietic. It gives us speech again; it offers us a new way of being, and it does so through painfully presenting the betrayal that it also breaks through. In the resurrection, we receive the selves that were lost. They are not the selves we thought we knew. The darkness of what we have become and the luminosity of what we may become; these come to us together, as Benedict XVI saw them together in the Shroud.

By the mercy of the resurrection, we enter more thoroughly into both the visible and the invisible. Always the visible has existed in, with, and by the invisible. In the incarnation, the Invisible One came to us as a visible presence, entering into and transforming the world both visible and invisible. In the resurrection, we are invited into that incarnational presence—not just to draw near it but also *to become it*. We humans are given a specific form for entering into that invisibility: the resurrected body of Christ. Through the empty tomb, we can be reborn into the new corporeality of the resurrection and witness the rebirth of a world where Christ will be all in all. Christ's resurrection opens in the old world a void—rupture, in-breaking—through which ascent to the new becomes possible.

As we are given a new form for entering the invisible, we receive a new form of imaging the invisible: hypostatic imaging. Because of the resurrection, the *hypostasis* of Christ and the saints can assume the likeness of an icon. Honor given the visible image passes through to the invisible prototype. This is the structure of hypostatic imaging, echoed also in prosoponic imaging, when honor given the least of these passes through to Christ. Both prosoponic and hypostatic imaging speak to a communion of visible and invisible and a likeness that is made by the Spirit—two important features of these images that acheiropoietic images dramatize. In these acheiropoietic images, God not only allows for an image of the divine. God also makes the image without any human agency, just as in hypostatic and prosoponic likeness God alone makes the likeness.

These God-made images and likenesses in turn invite us into the acheiropoietic resurrected body of Christ, another God-made image. In the resurrection, God does a new thing and begins a new kind of imaging. In this way, the resurrection is image-making. It births new images, in the image of the Acheiropoietic New Image. Such image birthing can also be iconoclastic. In the priority of invisibility; in the displacement of the old by the new; in the destruction of old self-image by new; in all these ways, the image-making of resurrection is both iconoclastic and iconophilic. It requires practicing iconoclasms of fidelity and resisting iconoclasms of temptation.[75]

Perhaps all this is simply another way to say that Christ rises in the great silence that reigns on the earth late on Holy Saturday and then breaks the great silence with the resurrection appearances on Sunday. In the resurrection, the Word breaks God's silence, speaking a new world into existence as God spoke the first world into existence. From the silence of Holy Saturday, the resurrection produces new speech and new images. From the invisible moment of resurrection, God gives us a new visibility. It is a visibility we must not cling to—turning icons into idols. Instead, we must learn to descend in order to ascend with and through this new visibility, like Christ himself. For God has come to us to draw us into the new world, speaking out of the divine images, erupting into our old world, making all things new.

A New *Maria Orans*: *Our Lady of Ferguson*

By images, the Image renews our old world. How might our own image-making participate in this renewal? In the summer of 2016, iconographer Mark Dukes created an image that expresses hope for participating in the re-creation of the world. Following the 2014 shooting of unarmed black teenager Michael Brown, Dukes wrote a new version of *Maria orans*. He called the icon *Our Lady of Ferguson*. In it, Mary is dressed in her traditional red and blue garments. Her face bears the same tender sadness it always seems to bear in icons. But she also looks different. She is a black woman, and the child in her womb is shown in silhouette, hands raised, in a position that echoes both his mother's *orans* position and the "hands up, don't shoot" protest slogan. Just above his heart are the cross hairs of a gun. He could be any child vulnerable to violence, any endangered son of a sorrowing mother. But he is not any son. His red heart, the one part of him in color, is encircled by thorns and emitting rays of holiness. This is Jesus, himself a victim of violence, whose sacred heart speaks to his merciful love for the whole world. The traditional letters identifying Christ (IC XC) affirm the figure's identity: this is a Christ who wholly identifies with the afflicted of the world. He is one of the least of these.

Our Lady of Ferguson is not just an icon of lament, though; the image also projects hope. Visually, the intensity of the gold and the framing of that sacred heart speak to that hope beyond violence. While the viewer is implicated in the gaze of the gun—it is *we* who have crucified Christ—Christ's glowing heart also proclaims that violence does not have the final word. Even we can receive God's mercy, and in that reception, we can cease from persecuting the least of these, who bear the prosoponic likeness of Christ. Receiving ourselves as the ones who have betrayed Christ, we receive Christ through the least of these. We can realize the hope of the resurrection, of a mercy that transfigures violence, even now, in our life with the vulnerable ones.

This resurrection hope is reiterated in the image genre as well. Mary can be present to the icon as the *orans* because Christ's resurrection means she can appropriate her likeness to be hypostatically present to the image. By mercy, Mary's and Christ's, *Our Lady* is present to us. Through their descent in love, we, too, can ascend by descending in love. *Our Lady of Ferguson* invites us into God's mercy by her own merciful prayers. Uniting in one image these three forms of resurrection imaging—hypostatic, prosoponic, and acheiropoietic—*Our Lady of Ferguson* shows forth the divine mercy in the world, visibly testifying to the presence of the invisible to us, reminding us that the visible is being transfigured by the invisible, that mercy has triumphed over death.

FIGURE 5. Nicolas Poussin, *The Adoration of the Golden Calf*, 1633–34. Source: The National Gallery, London. Author's photo.

5 WILL COME AGAIN IN GLORY
Arriving Presence

THE BRIGHT AND GARLANDED statue of the bull dominates the upper half of Nicolas Poussin's 1633–34 painting *The Adoration of the Golden Calf*. Mounted on a pedestal high above the action, the golden calf commands the space in a stillness that contrasts with the corybantic dancing of the humans below it. With their branches stretched toward the heavens, the trees also contrast with the humans, whose arms point toward created things, gesturing at the calf or reaching out to one another in revelry and veneration. Much less visible than either the calf or the dance, in the upper left corner of the painting, Moses comes darkly down the mountain, his stone tablet raised in fury. Those familiar with the story know what happens next. Moses will smash the stone in anger at the unfaithfulness of God's people.

Poussin's painting takes as its subject the paradigmatic scene of idolatry in the Christian and Jewish traditions. Yet *The Adoration of the Golden Calf* does not simply condemn images as idols. As a gorgeous painting that signals the seductions of art, as a visual warning about idolatry, and as an image that endorses forms of iconoclasm—it affirms both iconoclastic and iconophilic impulses. *Adoration* is the work of neither a guileless iconophobe nor a naïve iconophile. It is the work of an image lover who looks at images with one wary eye, a Catholic living in the wake of the Reformation and Counter-Reformation. There is a profound, subtle ambivalence about images in this work of early modernity.

The early modern context of Poussin's *Adoration* indicates that the questions in Moses's time live on in mutated forms, posing new forms of image ambivalence. Invoking Israel's wait for God at Sinai to speak to the church's ongoing wait for Christ's return in modernity, the painting raises questions about how these times are connected and what that connection can illumine about the role of images today. Moses brings the people of God "out of the camp to meet God." At the foot of Mount Sinai "they took their stand" and waited for the divine presence Moses promised, becoming impatient when Moses is delayed (Exodus 19:17; 32:1). What does the difficulty of waiting for divinity to arrive in the time of Moses expose about that difficulty in the time of modernity? Why, in this new age, should one reflect on how the Israelites were led astray by making an image? As the church anticipates the return of Christ, what possibilities do images offer? What dangers do they threaten? What does Poussin's image commend to us in our efforts to resist enthrallment to golden calves?

The question of resisting golden calves raises the subject of iconoclasm. It is time, in this final chapter, to turn our focus directly to that issue, to treat iconoclasm as the primary theme. Throughout this book, I have put to work the phrases "iconoclasms of temptation" and "iconoclasms of fidelity." Here I reflect on discerning these phenomena in our current world as part of detecting the Christ who arrives again within it. What kind of iconoclasm does faithfulness to this returning Image, this arriving presence, demand? What kind of iconoclasm tempts us away from faithfulness? These questions return me to two major motifs of this book: the entanglement of image-making with image-breaking and the decisive role of desire for right relationships to images.

Desire is a major category of the first chapter, but the work it does here is new. In Chapter 1, I argued that literal desire is broken open to the non-literal and that the divine desire of and for Christ cannot be excised from literal desires—even though those very desires risk betraying divine desire, literalizing desire by closing it off from further objects or meanings. In the case of the image, the product of such betrayal is an *illusion*. Here I want to pursue the ways that non-literal desire, too, can betray divine desire. No less than literal desires, non-literal desires can become diminished versions of themselves. They, too, need to be opened to what is beyond themselves, or they risk not illusion so much as *idolatry*. Idolatry names a desire that is stuck, that terminates before it reaches God, sometimes because it mistakes God for an object in the world. An idol is restored to its rightful status as an image when the non-literal desire for it is negated, allowing that desire to find its depth as desire.

It is not just, then, that literal desire must be negated so that it opens to the non-literal. Non-literal desire must also be negated to open to the divine.

All desire—even desire as such—finds its final meaning in Christ. In the way that Chapter 4 completed Chapter 2 by arguing that all the visible world can open up to the invisible, this chapter completes the first one by arguing that all desires can open to Christ's desire. Faithfulness to the arriving presence of Christ requires desiring images rightly, which means that as literal desire must be broken open to the non-literal, so, too, must non-literal desire be broken open to Christ.

Crucial to breaking open the desires images elicit is practicing iconoclasms of fidelity. Yet these are difficult to distinguish from iconoclasms of temptation. This chapter focuses on the difference between these iconoclasms, on how they express and train our desires, and how they render us more and less faithful to the Christ who will come again in glory. Moses, the people of God's most famous iconoclast, is key to this task.

The Golden Calf: An Image of Anxiety and Desire

For the gospel writers, Sinai foreshadows Tabor, that Mount of Transfiguration so important for iconographers. On Sinai, Moses ascends into the cloud of divine presence and his veiled face shines like the sun. On Tabor, Moses is present once again, this time with Christ, whose face glows unveiled. Tabor signals that in Christ God abides in a new way. Tabor magnifies the incarnation and prefigures the resurrection. Given that Tabor hails a new reality of divine presence in the world, why would a painter return to the scene at Sinai? Have not Sinai and its nearby idolatries been eclipsed by the reality of Christ?

The Adoration of the Golden Calf does not attempt to argue that modernity's situation is the same as Moses's. Instead, Poussin's painting signals that there is perhaps a new idolatry in the wake of Christ, one that consists not in making golden calves—and certainly cannot be in painting them—but in some other way of refusing to wait for divine presence. As the church waits for a new presence of God, when Christ will be all in all, it returns with Poussin to a version of Sinai. The people remember how and how not to wait for the divine to arrive.

The church's time of waiting grows late. Poussin paints in a time in which the image has become especially vexing. Often we moderns worry about images because they are human-made or false. At times, we even agonize that they are false *because* they are human-made. We also worry about images because they seem more ubiquitous than ever before. This leads to a situation that Marion traced decades ago in *The Crossing of the Visible*, in which images substitute themselves for reality. As described in Chapter 2, these reality-displacing images do not open up to the imaged; they obscure it, blocking it from us. Unlike iconic vision, which opens ever-up to the invisible, the "tyrannical" images of our day substitute the visible for the invisible, separating the two.[1] As we explored in Chapter 2, iconoclasm, for Marion, simply reverses this situation rather than correcting it, privileging the invisible at the expense of the visible and continuing their separation.

Marion concludes his lament of modern image tyranny by commending prayer and liturgy. In prayer and liturgy one bathes in the "pool of Shiloh" that heals the blindness that comes from obsession with "the incessant stream of static images that wall up our eyes on themselves."[2] Presumably, such bathing gives us a kind of immunity from what Marion calls "static" images, so that we can live with these images without being harmed by them. In this chapter, I pursue this possibility that static images (these golden calves) may become for us dynamic when restored by certain iconoclasms. Iconoclasm and idolatry, I argue, are not two horns of an image dilemma we have to wedge our way through, nor are they dangers to immunize ourselves from. Idolatry does name a sickness, but iconoclasm can be a cure.

To make the case for certain therapeutic forms of iconoclasm, I cast the scene of the golden calf at Sinai as this chapter's interpretive touchstone and Poussin as a privileged interpreter of this scene. Around this center, I constellate picture theorist W.J.T. Mitchell, philosopher Bruno Latour, phenomenologist Jean-Luc Marion, and fourth-century bishop Gregory of Nyssa. I begin, before engaging any of these thinkers further, by describing what I take to be the two major families of iconoclasms that dominate modernity, the Baconian and the Wittgensteinian. Neither can be straightforwardly identified as an iconoclasm of fidelity or iconoclasm of temptation, but they do help us to learn, in more indirect ways, how to discern these two iconoclasms in the world.

Modernity's Two Major Families of Iconoclasms

The modern age is suffused with anxiety about images.[3] It is charged with worry about falling captive to idols and preoccupied with achieving liberation from that captivity. The idols that bedevil us now are not only—perhaps, for Modern Westerners, not even primarily—material images. They are mental images, false pictures that may deceive and so enslave us. Modern Westerners characteristically respond to distress over mental idols with two types of iconoclasm, two ways of negating an image that does not seem to negate itself. I call these responses Baconian iconoclasm and Wittgensteinian iconoclasm.

The phenomenon I designate as Baconian iconoclasm is unmistakably expressed by Francis Bacon, though it is certainly not unique to him.[4] Bacon simply thematizes mental idolatry and its ensnarements oftener and earlier than most. He famously identifies four classes of idols and introduces science as the way to defeat them. For Bacon, real (scientific) knowledge destroys idols of the mind.[5] His is a straightforwardly iconoclastic program. Through science, one learns that the object of one's knowledge is not really what one once thought it was but is instead some other thing science has revealed it to be. The movement of Baconian iconoclasm runs "not *x* but *y*." It is the logic of a displacement narrative, of unmasking, and it is deployed by many of the major thinkers of modernity. *You think this is about virtue but really it is about power. You think this is about philanthropy but really it is about sex. You think this is love but really it is evolutionary biology.* These are statements of Baconian iconoclasm. In them, the iconoclast claims the power of knowledge over and against the naïve believer.[6]

The other family of iconoclasm is the Wittgensteinian. Where Bacon describes bewitchment by idols of the mind, Wittgenstein worries that "a *picture* held us captive."[7] Describing this worry as Wittgenstein's iconophobia, W.J.T. Mitchell points to specific instances of Wittgenstein's aversion to discursive hypericons, like the *camera obscura, tabula rasa,* and Platonic cave.[8] Yet perhaps the most interesting example of a captivating image that worries Wittgenstein is the one that opens the *Philosophical Investigations*: Augustine's scene of language acquisition in the *Confessions*. After describing it, Wittgenstein's next move is crucial: it is not to displace this picture with another but to resituate it by offering a series of images for how language can work otherwise. He does not attempt to eradicate Augustine's image, nor aspire to freedom from pictures of language acquisition. Instead, as Wittgenstein says, he offers his readers an album of sketches with which to surround the picture.[9] By attending to the plurality of language and its uses, Wittgenstein drafts multiple images of language and so loosens the grip Augustine's picture of language holds on the imagination. Wittgenstein's iconoclasm negates the image, not usually by *dis*placing it with another, but by *em*placing it in an album of images.[10] In this way, this present volume is itself a project of Wittgensteinian iconoclasm, which takes the guiding picture for the image crises of our times—iconoclastic Islam versus iconophilic Christianity and the Modern West—and surrounds it with pictures of how iconoclasm is internal to Christianity and the Modern West. It, too, is an album of sketches that attempts to loosen the grip a certain picture has on our imagination.

It might sound as if I am preparing to identify Wittgensteinian iconoclasm with iconoclasms of fidelity and Baconian iconoclasm with iconoclasms of temptation. But I am not so artless as to attempt to displace a displacement narrative. I do think there is an important place for Baconian iconoclasm—even an important place in discerning the arriving presence of Christ. Such iconoclasm is performed, after all, in Jesus's narration of the Great Judgment in Matthew 25: *You think you are sheep, but really you are goats*. Of course, there is an equally important Wittgensteinian iconoclastic moment here: *You thought you were doing unto the least of these but also you were doing unto me*. Neither brand of iconoclasm can be excised from Christ's own account of the Last Judgment. Baconian iconoclasm can be an important response to sin and deception. It is a way of responding to a false image as false.

Wittgensteinian iconoclasm attends to images differently. Where Baconian iconoclasm responds to the falseness of an image, Wittgensteinian iconoclasm responds principally to the truthfulness of it.[11] Where Baconian iconoclasm says "not x but y," Wittgensteinian iconoclasm says "x and also y" or "x and more importantly y." It reframes any x that takes itself as able to reframe all y's—without proposing to offer the frame that ends all efforts at reframing. And I want this Wittgensteinian logic also to describe, at a meta level, what I want to say regarding the eschatological significance of these two forms of iconoclasm: Baconian iconoclasm *and more importantly* Wittgensteinian iconoclasm. Wittgensteinian iconoclasm can be a therapy for Baconian iconoclasm, one that helps to temper its tendencies to seek a controlling mastery narrative.

Both Baconian and Wittgensteinian iconoclasms can be iconoclasms of fidelity or iconoclasms of temptation. Both can help us to love images rightly. However, Wittgensteinian iconoclasm gives the form for most iconoclasms of fidelity, while the form of Baconian iconoclasm tends toward an iconoclasm of temptation. The reason for this difference, as we shall see, has everything to do with the way these iconoclasms express, perform, and nurture desire. What do these iconoclasms *want*?

W.J.T. Mitchell and the Desires of the Golden Calf

The question of what iconoclasms want winks at W.J.T. Mitchell, who famously titled one of his books *What Do Pictures Want?*[12]—a question that inaugurates his iconology, his way, that is, of analyzing images. He introduces it by juxtaposing two advertising campaigns from the 1990s: Andre Agassi's famous declaration for Canon cameras that image is everything, and Sprite's riposte, a few years later, that image is nothing (for thirst is everything). Mitchell discusses these contradictory claims as symptomatic of Modern Westerners' double consciousness with respect to images. We behave as if they are alive while claiming that they are not.[13] We act as though images can seduce, command, and persuade, while insisting they have no agency. We then deny our duplicity by projecting the commitment to the aliveness of images onto some Other, locating animism in childhood, or far-off cultures, or distant times, while claiming for ourselves a rationalism that knows these images not to be alive. At the same time, we build entire industries around the power of the image and fiercely contest its legislative circumscriptions and circulations.[14] Thus, we insist images have no vitality and act as though they do. Mitchell proposes that we hold both sides of this paradox together by asking about *desire*. Desire attributes to the image both a kind of life and power, on the one hand, and a lack of it, on the other.[15]

Mitchell puts the question of desire to Poussin's *The Adoration of the Golden Calf*. What does the *Golden Calf* want? To ask about an image's desire, Mitchell claims, is to put the image in dialogue with others who can help it to "recollect" its desires.[16] For Poussin's painting, Mitchell chooses the anachronistic, yet illuminating, interlocutors, Friedrich Nietzsche and William Blake. He also engages his friend and University of Chicago colleague Richard Neer, who serves as a counter-model for Mitchell. Neer interprets *The Adoration of the Golden Calf* against the "visual prominence" of the foregrounded scene of idolatry in order to argue that the primary subject of the painting is the hiddenness of the divine—"a God known only through traces and allusions."[17] That the viewer's eye is drawn to the dancing and the calf implicates the viewer in the idolatry represented in the painting. The painting thereby discloses the viewer's own propensity to idolatry and so strengthens her resolve to imitate Moses in the shadows, resisting the temptation to identify God with objects in the world. Shadows, it turns out, are all we have. The full revelation of God comes only in the general resurrection.[18] The viewer's experience of this painting exposes her idolatries and offers a way beyond them. Thus, for Poussin, as Neer puts it, "[A]esthetic contemplation is spiritual exercise."[19]

According to Neer, then, gazing at Poussin helps us become better beholders of the divine by holding at bay our desire to see the divine. It is, we might say, a sophisticated version of Baconian iconoclasm, one in which the desire of idolatry is tutored toward a more virtuous desire. It is Neer's attempt to stage a Baconian iconoclasm that is also an iconoclasm of fidelity, by offering aesthetic contemplation as a strategy to sublimate the idolatrous desire to see the divine. *The Adoration of the Golden Calf* offers not just a different object for the viewer's idolatrous desires—the painting as a scene of idolatry rather than the idol itself. It also helps to impart a salutary form of desire, aesthetic contemplation, which holds the floodgates against the tidal wave of idolatrous desire. (At least until the resurrection.)

This is not the interpretation that Mitchell wants to offer—and it is interesting how Mitchell treats his counter-model. He does not expose its deficiency to stage his own interpretation. Instead, he refers to Neer's interpretation as "unimpeachable art history," and then claims he is about to offer an interpretation from iconology.[20] In this way, he performs for us Wittgensteinian iconoclasm, rather than the Baconian iconoclasm that undergirds so much academic critique. Loosening the grip Neer's interpretation might have on being thought *the* correct interpretation, Mitchell offers another image. To do iconology, to help the painting (not *Poussin* but the *painting*) recollect its desires, Mitchell turns to Nietzsche and Blake.

Mitchell chooses interlocutors who are interested in idolatry and iconoclasm and can therefore help to illumine the painting's own desires about images. He meditates on Nietzsche's famous declaration in *Twilight of the Idols* that he wants, not to smash the idols, but to sound them, as with a tuning fork—an act Mitchell describes as joyful and musical. This image of sounding rather than smashing idols will be important for Mitchell. The Nietzschean figure who interests him most, though, is Zarathustra, who, though also joyful, does engage in some smashing. Energized by jubilant desire rather than grim duty, Zarathustra breaks the tablets of the law, which consist of "thou shalt not desire" written by the "never gay" and "pious killjoys."[21]

While Zarathustra's tablet breaking is iconoclastic, it is not a purely destructive act. It releases desire from its suppressions and writes a new morality, one that threatens the social order and takes as its lodestar *Thou shalt desire*. Such creative activity constitutes the real social threat, far more than simple destruction. In response, the ones Nietzsche calls the Pharisees and "the goods" determine to crucify those who make their own virtue. Nietzsche wants to reject the rejection of the crucified creator and unleash the desire that the Pharisees wanted to suppress.

According to Mitchell, William Blake anticipates Nietzsche's creative iconoclasm. Mitchell finds Blake's engraving of Los and Jehovah, an illustration for Blake's poem *Milton*, interpretable as an act of either creation or destruction. Perhaps Los is molding Jehovah out of mud, or perhaps Los is pulling down an idolatrous statue of Jehovah.[22] Either way it is a demotion of the God Blake sometimes calls Urizen and sometimes Nobodaddy, that "silent and invisible" "Father of jealousy" who hides himself in clouds.[23] In his reaction to the expression of humanity's sexual desire, Nobodaddy "farted & belchd & coughd" and articulated his own desires in the rhyme, "I love hanging & drawing & quartering/Every bit as well as war & slaughtering."[24] Nobodaddy, like Nietzsche's "good" Pharisees, is another anti-desire power. Like those same good Pharisees, he reacts to human desire by literally killing—and then he consigns the humans to hell. Nobodaddy is the absent God who intervenes in human affairs only to quash desires and ambitions.[25]

These figures of Zarathustra and Nobodaddy migrate into Mitchell's reading of Poussin's *Golden Calf* as they help the painting articulate its desires. Mitchell offers this possible interpretation of the painting: "But up in the dark clouds is the angry patriarch, breaking the tablets of the law. Nietzsche's pious killjoy and Blake's Nobodaddy converge in Poussin's Moses."[26] Moses's iconoclasm here renders him a figure of anti-desire. He comes to quash the joyful expression of desire with an angry assertion of the primacy of written law.

Or perhaps not. This might not be the definitive reading of the painting, for perhaps Moses is not Nobodaddy but Zarathustra. The calf is, after all, the gorgeous center of the painting, beautifully intact (not smashed) and celebrated by the dancers with pleasure and festivity. So it might be that Poussin is, like Nietzsche, "*sounding* the idol with a . . . tuning fork, or (more precisely) a paintbrush."[27] Mitchell wonders, "What if that was Zarathustra up on the mountain, smashing the law and joining in the fun? What if the dark clouds are Blake's Nobodaddy 'farting and belching and coughing' in his cave on the mountaintop? Could it be that Poussin was (like Blake's Milton) a true poet-painter, and of the devil's party without knowing it?"[28] This Moses is an iconoclast *for* desire rather than against desire, breaking the thou-shalt-nots that would enslave humans and destroy their *eros*. Moses-Zarathustra's iconoclasm is an act of liberation.[29]

In a compressed space, Mitchell runs the reader through a gamut of possible interpretations of *The Adoration of the Golden Calf*: from Neer's interpretation of it as an education of one's desire away from idolatry, to Mitchell's penultimate interpretation of it as anti-desire and anti-image, to his final interpretation of it as pro-desire and anti-law. The effect of Mitchell's string of interpretations is a profound sense of the multivalence of the painting and the wide range of possibilities for interpreting its desires. He does not displace one interpretation with another and then another, as if playing king interpreter of Mount Sinai. Each reading is left intact as he surrounds it with more interpretations.

We have an example here of Wittgensteinian iconoclasm that respects the significance of prior images while relaxing the grip they have on the imagination and so drawing the beholder into the complexity of the painting as a profound piece of irony. What does it mean that *Adoration of the Golden Calf* is an *image* about the dangers of images, that it is a visual analog of Socrates decrying the written word in Plato's written words?[30] This image that warns of the temptation images pose surely epitomizes both the value of images (images are important sources of moral training) and their threat (images are occasions for betraying God). *Adoration* seems to raise the possibility of multiple interpretations.

Mitchell's strategy for reading this complex painting entails asking about the desire *of* the painting, which leads to an interpretation of desire *in* the painting in a way that seems to proliferate *images of* the painting. There is an intimacy here of desire and image proliferation. While Neer's interpretation of Poussin as promoting a sophisticated Baconian iconoclasm moves toward the tamping down of desire, sublimating and redirecting it, Mitchell proliferates interpretations to affirm desire. He generates something like Wittgenstein's album of sketches as he advocates the unleashing of desire over and against the pious killjoys. There is something about this Wittgensteinian iconoclasm, in its cascade of picture after picture, that affirms and strengthens desire.

As vital as desire is to Mitchell, the question of what pictures want is, in some sense, a metaphorical one—a hermeneutical question with no ontological agenda. When asked if he really believes that images have desires, Mitchell responds he does not, but that he cannot ignore that we behave as if we do.[31] Still, for Mitchell, images can, in language he borrows from advertising executives, "have legs" to take us into territory their creators could not have expected. In the words of the Israelites pleading with Aaron for an image, images can "go before us" and so help us find ways of going on.[32] An image can lead our desire to places we did not foresee. There is a sense in which images are other than their makers, and so can release presences other than those of their makers. When we are overly captivated by an image—a situation Poussin could name as idolatry—further images, further interpretations can release us from our thrall without squelching desire. We can take this as Mitchell's intervention in the contest between Baconian and Wittgensteinian iconoclasms. According to Mitchell's iconology, Baconian iconoclasm treats idolatrous desire by sublimating it; Wittgensteinian by releasing it to further images. Bruno Latour's writings offer their own intervention in the discussion of Baconian and Wittgensteinian iconoclasms, one which figures Baconian iconoclasm as less than successful in its sublimation. Together with Marion, Latour helps us thematize why Baconian iconoclasm is often an iconoclasm of temptation—and under what circumstances it can become an iconoclasm of fidelity.

Bruno Latour and the Desires of Iconoclasm

The Israelites have been waiting so long at the foot of Sinai for Moses to return. How do they worship during this time of anticipation? Reading his audience into the story, Bruno Latour wonders, "[W]hat have we been asked to do? It is so easy to be mistaken and begin molding the golden calf."[33] Latour, too, turns to the golden calf to interpret our life with images. He glosses the Scriptural scene rather than Poussin's painting, interpreting his golden calf material as creatively as Mitchell does his. Where Mitchell invokes Nietzsche's revision of *Thou shalt not* into *Thou shalt desire*, Latour emends the injunction against graven images. It forbids, not making images, but freeze-framing them. *Thou shalt not freeze-frame the image.*

We can see, through that emendation, why it is "so easy to be mistaken and begin molding the golden calf." For Latour, to mold the golden calf refers, not to an act of making—gathering the gold, casting the form, and sculpting the details. How could one mistakenly do that? No, to mold the golden calf refers to the way one can slip into a wrong image relationship, a relationship Latour calls freeze-framing. How *do* we live with images while we wait in faithfulness to the divine? How do we nurture desire for the divine, without displacing desire onto what is supposed to nurture it? How do we avoid freeze-framing the image? It is easy, as Latour writes, to be mistaken, to begin molding golden calves.

To combat freeze-framing an image, for Latour, requires practicing one type of iconoclasm. It is one among the five types of iconoclasm he identifies, and the only one he commends. He refers to those who combat freeze-frames as Type Bs. Type Bs "wreak havoc on images, break down customs and habits, scandalize worshippers, and trigger horrified screams of Blasphemer!"—but they do not aspire to eradicate images altogether. For Type B iconoclasts do not reject imaging as such; they reject fascination with a single image that is extracted from a current of images and deemed sufficient in itself—"as if all movement had stopped."[34] Such frozen fascination with an image is warped desire and contrasts, for Latour, with true iconophilia. Loving an image well means receiving it in a flow of mediations, together with many other images. Such iconophilia is thus guarded by Type B iconoclasm, which resists the perverted desire of the freeze-frame. Thou shalt desire the image, for Latour, requires that thou shalt not freeze-frame it.

Though they are cloaked in Latour's vivid and idiosyncratic language, the themes Latour explores should be familiar. What Latour calls freeze-framing is not so distant from what I have called idolatry. As the idol closes the visible off from the invisible, circumscribing a presence that does not admit of absence, so freeze-framing halts the image flow, causing an image to act like the final source of meaning. Both arrest desire. The freeze-frame acts like an idol.

If freeze-framing looks like idolatry, what does breaking the freeze-frame (Type B iconoclasm) look like? For Latour, it looks like dancing. He explains why. To break the freeze-frame is to break the viewer's habitual gaze in a way consonant with what Latour calls the "Christian regime of invisibility"— a regime that is not far away, not displaced from the ordinary world. In the Christian regime, the invisible is, according to Latour, *present* to the visible world, "the only one," as Latour writes, "which can be said to offer salvation."[35] The Christian leap of faith, then, does not hop toward a disembodied, transcendent invisible world. It aims, rather, at "jumping, dancing towards the present and the close." It leaps "to redirect attention away from indifference and habituation, to prepare oneself to be seized again by this presence that breaks the usual, habituated passage of time."[36] The leap is part of a dance that attunes one to the rich presences in the world by breaking the habitual gaze.

Poussin's painting might have associated dancing and idolatry, but for Latour, dancing religion is his metaphor for opposing freeze-framing religion. In his concern with the wrong leap of faith, Latour worries about an invisible divorced from the visible, a transcendent cut loose from the immanent, a non-literal sundered from the literal. He also worries about the opposite: a habituated gaze, fixated on the visible, immanent, literal—an indifferent gaze unprepared to be seized by divine presence. Dancing contrasts with both freeze-framing and other forms of iconoclasm, and its dynamism is mirrored in cascading rather than freezing images. The dance is a right leap of faith, a conversion, that "elongates the cascade of mediations one step further."[37]

Latour enjoins this image current by offering, among other stories, the description of Jesus chasing money-changers out of the Temple. Jesus overturns tables and seats; he drives out the money-changers. In the Gospel of John, he pours out coins, and he even makes a whip. It is perhaps Jesus's most overtly iconoclastic moment in Scripture. What Latour sees, though, is Jesus reinvigorating, not halting, the stream of mediations. Christ breaks the habitual gaze—perhaps one that has assimilated God to a monetary economy—and directs it toward "other, newer, fresher, more sacred images."[38] Latour reads this incident as a Type B iconoclasm that accords with the dynamism of humanity, with the way that we are always moving toward or away from some goal, we might say toward or away from the divine. Latour's Jesus attacks stultifying images intervening between people and the God they are supposed to mediate to those people. Latour's Jesus wants the frozen images to flow again. As Latour describes it, Jesus's outburst in the Temple is a moment of Wittgensteinian iconoclasm.

But *is* Temple-cleansing an image of Wittgensteinian iconoclasm? Interpreters of Scripture have long understood this event as substituting one image with a truer one: *Destroy this Temple and I will build it again in three days, acheiropoietic.*[39] Christ's body is the new image that displaces the old. Not *x* but *y*. Is this, in fact, more like Baconian iconoclasm than Wittgensteinian? Why would Latour not frame his Type B iconoclasm in a more Baconian vein, as substituting the real for the image of the real, or if not that, then the less tired image for the more tired one? Why would the Temple-cleansing be the elongation of an image stream?

Latour claims Temple-cleansing for Type B iconoclasm—a type of Wittgensteinian iconoclasm—because he has serious misgivings about Baconian forms of iconoclasm. To probe Latour's concerns with such iconoclasms, I want to draw Marion into the conversation as a counterpoint. Marion and Latour are both richly resonant and dissonant in how their thought helps to figure Wittgensteinian and Baconian iconoclasm. Their anxieties certainly harmonize with one another's. Marion does not talk about freeze-framing, though he does worry about the "tyranny of the image," in which the image substitutes itself for reality, the visible obscuring the invisible. These tyrannical images divorce the visible from the invisible, "walling up our eyes" and acting very *un*like an icon, which opens endlessly up.[40] And iconoclasm, we remember, cannot be a solution to this problem for Marion, for it simply reverses the situation. Maintaining the divorce between the visible and the invisible, iconoclasm simply flips the terms, privileging the invisible at the expense of the visible. Marion figures iconoclasm as aspiring to an invisibility, an impossible aniconism it will never ultimately achieve. It will never achieve it because iconoclasm simply displaces x with y; the iconoclasm that Marion worries about as the inverse of image tyranny is Baconian iconoclasm.

Marion worries about the way both image tyranny and (Baconian) iconoclasm entrench a divorce between the visible and the invisible. Latour is also troubled by the way opposite image behaviors reinforce a similar problem. On the one hand, he is concerned about a habitual, indifferent gaze, in which stagnant images do not move for the viewer but remain frozen. Like these images, the gaze, too, remains fixed, motionless, closed. This is the problem of a gaze that remains stuck, fixated on the visible. On the other hand, Latour worries about all forms of iconoclasm other than Type B iconoclasm. Such iconoclasm, for Latour, is the problem of the frozen gaze transposed. As Marion's inverse image behaviors both entrench the invisible-visible divide, Latour's inverses attempt to halt the flow of images. Baconian iconoclasm also seeks to arrest the circulation of images by offering the definitively real thing itself. The problem with Baconian iconoclasm, on Latour's terms, is not that it entails breaking an image. His worry about Baconian iconoclasm is not the moment of exposure as such—you thought this was x but it is not. It is that the moment of exposure comes with the temptation to enthrone y in x's place. The problem, in other words, is that the not-x-but-y structure of Baconian iconoclasm attempts to halt mediation. The danger is the coronation of y in x's place. If x had become an idol, then y simply becomes the new idol. If x had not been an idol, then its displacement with what is supposedly an unmediated truth potentially creates an idol where there previously was none. Baconian iconoclasm replicates the structure of the freeze-frame; it is oriented toward image tyranny, toward idolatry. In Baconian iconoclasm, the frozen structure remains, simply shifting its objects of adoration. Both Marion and Latour worry that when an image goes awry (Latour's freeze-frame, Marion's tyranny), to respond with Baconian iconoclasm (one of Latour's four types other than Type B iconoclasm or what Marion calls simply iconoclasm) risks repeating the problem.

With Latour and Marion, we can say that Baconian iconoclasm tends toward an iconoclasm of temptation to the extent that it figures itself as exposing the truth behind the image and so obviating the image itself. It tempts by promising to dispel visible, human artifice in order to reach an invisible, given reality, by desiring the non-literal without reference to the literal, by seizing presence without the acknowledgment of absence. It tempts by trying to save the invisible from the impurity or confusedness of the visible. For this is what distinguishes iconoclasms of temptation from iconoclasms of fidelity: iconoclasms of temptation erect new idols.

Yet we can imagine a more circumspect Baconian iconoclasm, one that works against this velocity to idolatry. If the Temple-cleansing, for example, might look to us like a moment of Baconian iconoclasm—a moment when Christ's body becomes the new, acheiropoietic Temple—perhaps we can affirm Marion and Latour's insights without wholly repudiating Baconian iconoclasm. It is important to observe what Latour sees following the Temple-cleansing: the resumption of a chain of mediations and images. Temple-cleansing iconoclasm is good, for Latour, because, while wielded against a specific image, it is purposed toward more, not fewer images in our lives. Whether Christ cleanses the Temple to make it a better Temple, or offers his body as the Temple, or both, the cleansing aims to get images of the divine flowing once again, not to promote that which ends all images. If this is a Baconian iconoclasm, it is a modest one, which has surrendered aspirations to dictate a larger iconoclastic program. This Baconian iconoclasm is a limited intervention within a broader culture of image affirmation, one purposed toward celebrating mediation and seeking the invisible in the visible. This is the sophisticated iconoclasm expressed in Neer's interpretation of Poussin, where an image exposes and sublimates idolatrous desire by offering itself as an object of a certain kind of desire. "Not x but y" avoids idolatry when the affirmation of y is not only an affirmation over and against x, but together with a, b, and c. There remains a possibility, even if infrequently seized, for a humble version of Baconian iconoclasm to escape Marion and Latour's critiques and become instead an iconoclasm of fidelity.

Of course, neither Marion nor Latour explicitly recommends a version of Baconian iconoclasm, however humbled it might be. Marion recommends bathing in the pool of Shiloh, and thereby gaining what amounts to immunity from the tyranny of the image. Whereas the tyrannical image walls up one's eyes, the pool of Shiloh heals them, so that they can open rightly for iconic vision. And Latour recommends his Type B iconoclasm, a type of Wittgensteinian iconoclasm in which image cascades after image. These therapies are different from one another. Marion's pool grants protection from the image's warped desire, while Latour's iconoclasm wants to affirm and refresh desire. One holds damaged desire at bay; the other wants to reinvigorate damaged desire to become better desire. Though contrasting, their solutions are not entirely at odds with one another. There is an interesting way in which Latour's image cascade mimics Marion's iconic vision, as if it were an externalized version of what for Marion an icon is supposed to do internal to itself. Wittgensteinian iconoclasm can be an iconoclasm of fidelity, faithful to what iconic vision is supposed to be. It is a kind of catechesis for Marion's iconic vision. This is a hopeful sign of convergence.

There is a darker side to this comparison of Latour and Marion as well. We have observed how Baconian iconoclasms can be either iconoclasms of fidelity or iconoclasms of temptation. I have argued that Baconian iconoclasm tends toward an iconoclasm of temptation, but that wielded within a context of image affirmation, it can be an iconoclasm of fidelity. And we have observed how Wittgensteinian iconoclasm can be an iconoclasm of fidelity, both affirming and mimicking iconic vision. But can Wittgensteinian iconoclasm also become an iconoclasm of temptation? If it can mimic iconic vision, can it not also mimic the tyranny of the image? Marion, in fact, worries that modernity's glut of images lends itself to just such a danger. What happens when the river of images freezes into a spectacular tableau? When it colonizes desire by substituting itself for the invisible? Might it simply arrest desire? Or break the gaze of the eyes without breaking the gaze of the heart? Might, in other words, this Wittgensteinian iconoclastic catechesis go awry, presenting its images as the norm for reality, and divorcing visible and invisible? Perhaps Wittgensteinian iconoclasm, too, can become an iconoclasm of temptation, freezing the viewer even as images flow.

When the gaze of the heart freezes rather than breaks, what can save us? If Baconian and Wittgensteinian iconoclasms can both become iconoclasms of temptation, what can we do? It is so easy to be mistaken, as Latour claims, and to begin molding the golden calf. Chastened, we sojourn to one last scene of Sinai. Here, desire will be the primary, rather than secondary, term of analysis.

Gregory of Nyssa and Divine Desire

Writing on the role of desire in Christian life, the poet Paul Claudel claims Christian morality as a celebration of the divine desire that courses through all life. It is pagan morality, Claudel insists, that suppresses such desire.[41] The claim is a near-comic inversion of Blake's and Nietzsche's views, but for Claudel, like the Sprite advertisement Mitchell quotes, thirst is everything. "Thirst" is the way Claudel figures desire, as does, on occasion, Gregory of Nyssa. Yet if Gregory might assent to the second part of Sprite's ad—thirst is everything— he could not endorse the first, that image is nothing. In fact, image and thirst are inextricably linked in our creaturely life with God, as Gregory displays in his own reading of idolatry at Mount Sinai. Adding Gregory's interpretation of Sinai alongside Mitchell's and Latour's helps to render intelligible Claudel's declaration that Christian morality celebrates desire more than any other moral tradition. It also illumines how negating desire can emplace it in an economy of divine desire that can recuperate all images as yielding and eliciting further desire for divine presence. Here we will see why, though Wittgensteinian iconoclasm can become an iconoclasm of temptation, it also gives us the form for our eschatological life with images.

Gregory's interpretive focal point on the stories of Sinai is not Poussin's. Where Poussin foregrounds the scenes of idolatry and dimly renders Sinai at the margins of the canvas, Gregory in his *Life of Moses* features the ascents and descents of Sinai, sketching the idolatry of the calf only in outline.[42] Appearing after Moses's first ascent and descent of Sinai, another image episode mirrors the golden calf: that of the serpent. These two images of calf and serpent are concrete accounts of a life with images, so even though their place in the narrative is much less weighty than that of Sinai, they offer some interpretive keys to the more mystical and abstract language Gregory of Nyssa uses of Sinai. So our three foci emerge—the calf as an idol, the serpent as an image of Christ, and Sinai as the place where we cultivate the desire we need to live well with images. First, the calf.

In Gregory's telling, the scene of the calf is a small moment of false worship, dwarfed by the two momentous ascents and descents of Sinai, that mysterious mountain of right worship. When the "idol-mad" (εἰδωλομανέω) Israelites worship the calf, their rejection of God breaks the tablets of the Law.[43] Scripture says that Moses breaks the tablets in fury at the Israelites' idolatry, but Gregory elides Moses's agency to focus on the idol-worshipers as the true breakers of the tablets. That sets up Gregory's reading of the tablets of the Law as signifying human nature itself.[44] For Gregory of Nyssa, the Israelites' worship of the golden calf breaks human nature. Idolatry is thus figured as a kind of iconoclasm, one directed against the image of God in the human person. And it is only in response to this iconoclastic nature-breaking that Moses himself becomes iconoclastic, breaking the golden calf image, pulverizing it, and mixing it with water to be swallowed by the Israelites.

At one level, Gregory's storytelling dramatizes what Marion and Latour contend: that certain iconoclasms are the inverse side of idolatry. Idol worship breaks the tablets, which are human nature. At another level, this story affirms that Baconian iconoclasm (Moses's calf-breaking) is at times an iconoclasm of fidelity, one that restores right desire. We learn later in Gregory's narration what it means to destroy the golden idol: it is to root out covetousness.[45] So it is a certain kind of desire—an avaricious one—that is broken in Moses's breaking of the image. This is not a Baconian iconoclasm that attempts to eradicate desire together with the image. Avaricious desire is not broken in the sense of being snuffed out; it is broken open to a much greater desire, a desire indispensable to Gregory's descriptions of Sinai.

THE DESIRE OF SINAI AND THE EXPANSIVE THREAT OF IDOLATRY

On Sinai, we learn what this restoration of desire looks like and how the image is involved in it. For Gregory, Sinai gives the larger context for our life with images and how that life is a part of our life with God. One of the most important descriptions of Moses's first journey up Sinai is that it is an ascent into "luminous darkness."[46] That dazzling darkness teaches Moses, according to Gregory, what the commandment against idolatry will later reiterate. Gregory expands the injunction against graven images. For him, it means that the divine must not be likened to any "comprehensible image," for that would be to turn the image into an idol (εἴδωλον) that no longer witnesses to God.[47] Words and concepts threaten idolatry just as much as statues and images.

For Gregory, even the words of Scripture can become idols. Gregory raises that possibility in his description of Moses, encountering in the darkness the tabernacle "not made with hands" (acheiropoietic)—an image, as readers of the fourth chapter will remember, of Christ. Gregory soothes potential readerly anxieties, asking them not to be disturbed that *tabernacle* is given as a name for God. As Gregory writes, "all names have equally fallen short of accurate description," even names like "physician, shepherd, protector, bread, vine, way" that express something important about divine power.[48] As Gregory lists assorted Scriptural names for Christ (door, mansion, water, rock, and the like—all are imagistic), it becomes apparent that the luminous darkness does not blank out all images; it suggests a regenerated sight, one that resists both blindness and enthrallment, aniconism and idolatry. Gregory is image-saturated and image-loving—and also wary of possibilities for idolatry. We need images, and we need to learn to live well with them.

The second ascent then elaborates what it might mean to have images without idolizing them. It is to ascend ever higher, never to stop in one's ascent. It is to desire the divine. It is thirst. Moses "still thirsts for that with which he constantly filled himself to capacity."[49] The ever-dilating desire by which sight increases, he writes, is like a thirst in which one drinks to capacity and then finds that the drinking expands one's capacity and desire to continue to drink. That which slakes one's thirst also expands one's thirst. Both idolatry and aniconism are failures of sight that are also failures of desire, for the true sight of God, as Gregory attests, is never to cease in the desire for God. True sight means that each image of God kindles desire to see more. The dynamic is a constantly expanding desire, a never-ending ascent into the Good, which issues in image after image.[50] The soul is drawn constantly from the beauty seen to the beauty unseen, from the visible to the hidden, as the image kindles the soul's desire for the beyond.[51] Desire draws one into image after image, into the luminous darkness.

Through ever-expanding desire, a person "receive[s] what is visible as an image of what he desires."[52] At the same time, he longs for the archetype of what he desires, to be filled with the stamp of that archetype. This is the dynamic of responding and desiring, drinking and thirsting. It is like the dynamic Jean-Luc Chrétien describes as call and response, in which the infinity of the call reveals itself in our response to it.[53] For Chrétien, as for Gregory, to respond to the call is to be wounded by the excess of it.[54] Chrétien is drawn to Claudel for his own figuration of infinite desire: thirsty water, from and to a source beyond us. It is water that longs for water, so that the longing and the fulfillment of the longing come together.

Images give the unseen in the seen by arousing a thirsty desire. They open up to an infinite desire that, in Chrétien's meditation on Claudel, "in every way exceeds us and blessedly tears us open."[55] Where do we see this wrenching thirst but on the cross? *Sitio*. I thirst. It is Christ's fourth word on the cross, long interpreted as speaking to an eschatological thirst for all humanity. Christ's thirst blessedly tears him open. It flows as water out of his wounded side and circulates through the world that we, too, might drink and become like this thirsty water. "It is God in me who is the desirer, it is God who is the desired, it is God who is the desire."[56] The circulation of thirst runs through the least of these—those thirsty ones whose thirst re-presents to us the thirst of Christ, such that to slake their thirst is to slake the thirst of Christ. The thirst is blessed in the Beatitudes, in those who thirst for justice. The thirst calls us to receive God. And as Gregory, Claudel, and Chrétien help us to see: we receive God in our thirst. The thirst for thirst, as Chrétien declares, is charity—consummate desire.[57]

The problem with our own desire is that it is too weak, too easily satiated, too quick to terminate. We are satisfied with golden calves. Our desires are closed—or too feebly open—to the circulation of divine desire that washes over our world. In a world where we are weak in desire, any image can become an idol. But images can also help to heal our desire, as the story of the bronze serpent highlights. Where the golden calf episode occurs between the two accounts of Sinai, the bronze serpent story occurs after both. This, too, is a story of a wayward desire restored, and it helps to gloss what we saw of the Baconian iconoclasm valorized in the golden calf story. A faithful version of Baconian iconoclasm does not aspire to aniconism, does not celebrate the truth that there is no image of truth. Instead, a Baconian iconoclasm of fidelity limits itself to lancing images irreparably damaged and damaging. For this time, the animal image is on the side of right desire.

THE DESIRE OF THE BRONZE SERPENT

In the story of the bronze serpent, the Israelites are poisoned by snakes, symbolic for Gregory of the Israelites' "unruly desires" and "slavish passions." Then the same Moses who destroyed the golden calf makes a bronze serpent, and the same people who broke their human nature with one image, find it healed by another. For, the image of the serpent renders the snakes powerless.[58] How could it be that, when rendered as an image, the serpent-desires are rendered salubrious? Why is it that imaging the serpent both drains the serpents of their power for evil and also mediates a new power for good? Gregory answers these questions by drawing on a tradition of interpreting the bronze serpent as a figure of Christ, found in John 3:14: "And just as Moses lifted up the serpent in the wilderness, so must the Son of Man be lifted up." To look upon the bronze serpent is to look upon the negation of one's unruly desires, just as to look upon Christ crucified is to look upon a negation of sin. The antidote for evil passions, Gregory explains, is to look upon the one who suffered the Passion.[59]

The bronze serpent healed the people of God of the unruliness of their desires because it imaged to the people of God their desires, gathering them into an image that disclosed the desire beyond their weak, slavish passions. When we were dying because of our evil desires, Christ came in our likeness, the likeness of sin, figured as the likeness of a serpent, and healed the desire of any who would look upon him. Christ comes immanent to these desires, riving the literal passions, breaking open the non-literal desire for the bronze serpent. Through these riven desires, Christ arrives, giving us himself. Christ the Image saves us. As Image, Christ restores our desire to what it might be, increasing it, and so moving it beyond idols. The people of God made the golden calf to worship it—to fashion divinity with their own hands; they made the bronze serpent to ask God to break into their sickness and rive their rivenness—to restore their desire for the divine.[60]

In casting the bronze serpent, Moses has taken up the serpents into what Marion might call a liturgy. A liturgy, for Marion, can "wrest [the image] from every spectacle" and restore it to its proper status.[61] The people of God look with hope upon an image of that to which they are enslaved, and so the image becomes an image of hope. Is it any wonder that the Gospel of John claims the bronze serpent as a figure of the cross? The cross, too, is an image of the sin to which we are enslaved; and in our looking upon it with hope, it, too, becomes an image of our hope. It negates our desires in order to open them up to the infinite circulation of desire, through the visible to the invisible. The bronze serpent typifies the thirst the people have not yet learned to receive, much like the luminous darkness figures the excess of light that Moses cannot receive. The bronze serpent redirects the gaze—in Latour's words, breaking the habitual gaze, so that the people of Israel can be seized by a new presence.

In the spirit of this bronze serpent, a twelfth-century bronze cross also redirects the viewer's gaze.[62] A cursory glance might determine that this cross memorializes the time in which Jesus hung dying on the cross. His head is bowed, the nails are driven through his hands, and he seems still attached to the cross. Yet a longer gaze can absorb a more complicated time frame. Behind the corpus, an outline of Jesus's body is traced along the cross, thus referencing the empty cross, after Jesus has died and his body has been deposed. Other details make the image difficult to place in either the moment of Jesus's dying or his entombment. His body is intact, even graceful. He wears, not a crown of thorns, but a kingly crown, signifying his eternal heavenly lordship. Etched on the cross above his crowned head is a rosette of victory, placing the time of the crucifix in Christ's triumph over death in the resurrection and the promised final triumph over sin and suffering. In displaying these overlapping time periods, the bronze cross negates the habitual gaze, manifesting the ways it cannot capture, cannot fully exhaust the divine that it images.[63] It negates itself, making clear its limitations as an image, in order to excite the desire for what it presents as image. It elicits and presents a desire greater than itself, and in this way, this bronze cross binds the *Sitio* of the cross with the bronze serpent of Moses.

The Everlasting Image Cascade: Wittgensteinian Iconoclasm in an Eschatological Register

The bronze serpent, like the luminous darkness, communicates Gregory's principal contention about sight: to see God is to desire God. This can be true because God is desire itself, and as Image, Christ reveals desire as the structure of the image. What I mean is that God gives Godself through Christ the Image. And as Image, Christ represents, mediates, and incites divine desire (desire of and for God) because Christ is divine desire (the Love that is God). This desire issues forth in images, as we learn to receive Christ through the capacities that receiving Christ develops in us. We receive Christ in image after image. To desire Christ is to generate this cascade of images.

Meditating on Gregory of Nyssa, among others, Russian Orthodox theologian Paul Evdokimov writes that Christian faith "stimulates creativity" in the world that also "shatters the world," making history "overflow its boundaries."[64] It provokes a fullness—an image stream—that opens up history to the eschaton, perhaps that it may flow like water from the side of Christ. Evdokimov quotes Gregory's claim that the impossible becomes the divine way as the totally other comes from the depths of the world, and "all forms of culture stretch toward the limit at the border of the ages."[65] In the creativity that multiplies images and stretches cultural forms, the Christian faith radically affirms images in a way that also entails their negation. It shatters and overflows, multiplying images in such a way as to convey the inadequacy of any single one of them. There are so many images of Christ because there is no image exhaustive of Christ.

This image of a fullness that shatters boundaries, no less than the thirsting-drinking dynamic, communicates no moment of arrival in which images are cast away. There is no attempt to move beyond imaging. Those metaphors convey, instead, Wittgensteinian iconoclasm in an eschatological register. This is a Wittgensteinian iconoclasm that does not end, for it is indexed, ultimately, to Christ, the Image that we always receive as a new image. This is why, further, Wittgensteinian iconoclasm gives the form of iconoclasms of fidelity. While Baconian iconoclasm is indexed to sin and so falls away with sin, Wittgensteinian iconoclasm extends everlastingly, by the everlasting desire that is Christ, the God who will be all in all (1 Corinthians 15:28)—a verse important for Gregory's eschatology. Baconian iconoclasm responds to an image that elicits a desire so malformed it is not clear how it can be recuperated; Wittgensteinian to the possibility for opening the image's desire out to the infinity of desire itself.

All images partake in a structure of desire. In Mitchell's words, pictures *want*. But that, as we have seen, does not mean that all desire as Christ desires. There are images with strongly expressed desires that seem utterly unlike the desire expressed by the Image that is Christ.[66] Advertising images, for example, geyser forth in a relentless torrent and express desire after desire. They even trade on a desire for transformation. Like the golden calf, though, they take our gold and leave us as we are, performing on us what might be called our anti-transformation, un-doing us into greediness and unhappiness. Ultimately, advertising images express the desires of their makers for us to consume a certain product, and the "transformation" is the purchase of the self we were convinced we did not have. They "have legs" that often take us into territories of temptation and idolatry. These image cascades are like Wittgensteinian iconoclasms that have become iconoclasms of temptation. They render images as idols. We are back to the problem of the spectacular tableau.

At the point at which an image becomes an idol, is Baconian iconoclasm our only option for avoiding bewitchment? It is certainly *an* option. Perhaps the image cascade has not internalized a strong negation, and so an external negation is needed to open up desire—or at least prevent it from closing. Perhaps we need to pulverize the golden calf to release ourselves from its thrall. The problem, then, is that we are simply vulnerable to the next golden calf, all the more so because the structure of Baconian iconoclasm tempts the idolatry of thinking one has the thing itself, the very truth. There is another way to freedom.

From Image to Image: The Faithful as Exemplary of Wittgensteinian Iconoclasm

The problem with the golden calf is not that it aroused Israel's love and adoration. The problem is that it arrested it. The problem with advertising images is not that they attract desire. The problem is that they divert it, siphoning it off from its path toward the divine. Such images promise a satiation they cannot deliver. They encourage a love that believes they are a final source of satisfaction—a deceived love that turns out to be too weak rather than too strong, paradoxically enslaving in its very weakness. Baconian iconoclasm can provide a moment of freedom from enthrallment, but after exposing such images, a person is immediately vulnerable to enslavement again. What one needs is for desire to grow so strong that golden calves cannot captivate it. As Gregory commends to his reader at the end of his readings of Moses, she needs to "carve in [her] own heart the divine oracles . . . from God" and "destroy the golden idol"—which Gregory interprets as eliminating covetousness from one's heart, thus allowing covetous desire to transform into the greater, stronger divine desire.[67] This is both how one waits for divine presence and how divine presence arrives to us.

At the base of Sinai, Israel waits for God's presence, as the church today continues to wait for God's presence. The Apostle Paul links these two times of waiting. He meditates on Moses veiling his glory that is so bright the people cannot bear it. And this meditation leads him to Christ: Christ's coming again in glory will be still brighter and more radiant than Moses's, yet no veil will shield us from the sight. "And all of us, with unveiled faces, seeing the glory of the Lord as though reflected in a mirror, are being transformed into the same image from one degree of glory to another; for this comes from the Lord, the Spirit" (2 Corinthians 3:18). This is the cardinal verse for Gregory's eschatology. Christ is the mirror reflecting the glory of the Lord—the Image of God—who transforms us beholders to be ever-more like him, an ever-more glorious, more perfect image. From glorious image to more glorious image. The divine presence comes to us who marred the image in which we were created, transforming us into an image with still greater likeness to God. This, at last, is what we wait for: To become the glorious image of the Lord by the glory of the one who is the Image of the Lord.[68]

This transformation of image to image turns on the transformation of desire. For what does it mean for someone to become the image of God? It is to long to receive what Gregory calls the "stamp of the archetype," receiving what is visible as a sign of what is invisible, as desire constantly expands to receive new images of the invisible, which then expand the desire further.[69] This is the gaze of love, the gaze of one enraptured, that contrasts with the gaze of contempt, which Latour describes as the habitual gaze. This contemptuous gaze believes that its object is fully known; it believes itself to be the master of the object. It is iconoclastic in the negative manner traced in Chapter 4 and expressed in much Baconian iconoclasm; it is a gaze ordered to power, expressed as exhaustively knowing, as unmasking. Gregory's gaze of love is iconoclastic in a different way. It delights in the one it beholds, who, as Christ, unfolds in image after image. The gaze of love knows that to see God is to follow God is to desire God.[70] To see the world in this way—as an image of God—requires resisting the will to master the world. It demands, instead, opening the self up to the transformations love can accomplish. This is a gaze of desire that exposes the gazer to the presence of the image, and it is maintained, for example, through ascents and descents in love described in the fourth chapter, which are not separate from the ascents and descents described by Gregory in his *Life of Moses*. In a way, then, the question of how the desire for the image resists idolatry is the question of how our desire matures into the love that binds us to Christ, making us like the Christ who is Love itself.

The presence that the gaze of desire exposes the gazer to is that of the arriving Christ. And all of us, as 1 Corinthians claims, with unveiled faces, seeing the glory of the Lord as though reflected in a mirror, are being transformed into the same image from one degree of glory to another; for this comes from the Lord, the Spirit. Gregory describes a love for images that takes the form of transcending each particular image, though never imaging as such, as one draws near the Image of God, by transforming into that Image. We are exposed to the presence of God, whose gaze, in something of an interpretive spiral, teaches us how to gaze rightly at images. For God looks upon us as clothed in Christ—as if we are God, inexhaustible and infinitely unfolding. God loves us as if we are Christ, and such love makes us little christs. Thirsty for us, Christ looks upon us as if we are Christ's very body, and so the Father looks upon us as if we are Christ, and desires us as if we are Christ. So looked upon and desired, we can become christs. We can learn to look at the world as image of God because God looks at us in this way—because, to return to a theme from Chapter 1, God wants to take our desire into the divine economy of God's desire for God.

What does the Image want? Christ the Image desires to make a person more like herself by making her more like Christ. Christ desires to make people little christs, little images of the invisible God, so that we, too, will desire like Christ desires. Becoming images of glory, a person images the freedom of perfect love (Christ's desire), desiring in perfect freedom the one who is desire itself. Christ is the Image who transforms a person into an image—the Image who draws us into a form of Wittgensteinian iconoclasm, in which we image the eternal God in our creaturely way, by becoming ourselves a cascade of images.

Christ's coming to us is identified with our becoming an image of Christ. Christ the Image arrives as we become an image of Christ. Our desiring Christ—the one who is thirst—transforms us from glorious image to glorious image. We drink in the stream of images that give us more thirst as we become thirsty for the divine, joining with God who will be, in another of Gregory's favorite verses, all in all.

Because they mediate a presence beyond them, all images bear traces of this God. In Chapter 1, I explored how the literal desires for sex and nourishment some images mediate can be opened to a spiritual desire. Now I am trying to argue something more universal about images. To the extent that they are images, they mediate a presence that is different from them. To want to see an image (to see it qua image rather than qua object) is to desire to encounter *this* presence, the one that a particular image mediates. And since to image is to mediate a presence that is more than its literal existence, a presence that arrives to us through the image, all images are structured by a desire that can open infinitely up to yield to us divine life.

When Wittgensteinian iconoclasm becomes an iconoclasm of temptation, the flood of malformed images—these images that act like idols, that freeze the viewer to dominate her—meet an image of Christ in the beholder who has opened up her small desires, her covetousness, to the unending desire of Christ. In the beholder image, the desires of the malformed images that tend toward fixity of domination are immersed into the ever-circulating desire of the Triune God—a cascade of Christic images. This is why Wittgensteinian iconoclasm gives the form of our eschatological life with images. Christ's coming again in glory transforms the beholder from image to image, into Christ the Image. Through the Image's arriving presence, the beholder becomes an image, a glorious image of divine desire and its circulations. God will be all in all. In that economy of desire, any image, any idol, can be redeemed. Even the golden calf.

The Redemption of the Golden Calf

And so we bring to Poussin's *Adoration of the Golden Calf* the additional dialogue partner of Gregory of Nyssa. What can Gregory help the picture recollect of its own desires? After Gregory, what can we say the *Adoration of the Golden Calf* wants?

I had my own encounter with an image of a golden calf recently. I was in a religious education classroom where I teach young children, and I had just received materials to help tell them a new story. I opened the story box and peeked inside to find a little golden calf, about the size of my hand. I do not know what Moses would think about this calf, but I am fairly certain Gregory of Nyssa would not be bothered by it. This golden calf has become a self-negating image, an image that returns the beholder to the luminous darkness of Sinai rather than offering itself as the bright and terminal object of desire. We might say that this little calf is supposed to work like an apophatic image of God, proclaiming for children the kind of image that God is not, and stimulating their desire for the God who lies beyond it. Of the two animal images in Exodus, this children's calf images more like the bronze serpent than the golden calf.

Perhaps Poussin's dancers, too, are children, the children of God, energized by desire for God and celebrating that theirs is a God beyond any image but who nevertheless makes Godself known through images. They dance to prepare themselves to be gripped by divine presence. Perhaps they celebrate that their golden calf has become a self-negating image that points to other images by depicting what God is not, thus inviting a cascade of images that draws them deeper into the divine life. Perhaps what the Moses figure raises are words on stone that are in danger of losing their relationship to the darkness that offers and envelops them. The Moses figure restores these stone words to the darkness so that they cannot become idols that enthrall the children and block their everlasting pursuit of God. Returning the tablets to the dark, he breaks not the tablets but the children's gaze, and in breaking the gaze he also breaks open the stone words to the reality of Christ, the Image who desires to return all images to himself, the Image whose desire will fund the children's ascent up Sinai, into its darkness and its luminosity.

CONCLUSION
The Image of the Invisible God

CATHOLICS = PRESENCE; PROTESTANTS = ABSENCE. These paired equations run like a refrain through the first chapter of Robert Orsi's beautiful book *History and Presence*. Orsi does not endorse the equations, which he calls "a caricature and polemical overstatement already in early modernity, and it remains so in the twenty-first century."[1] Instead, he traces the work they do in figuring modern imaginations about Catholicism and Protestantism. In Orsi's telling, presence is tied primarily to Eucharistic presence, though it could also speak to our life with images. Catholics (and Orthodox) are iconophiles because they endorse the presence of the divine to the image, while Protestants are iconoclasts because they do not. As with Eucharist, so also with images: Catholics = presence; Protestants = absence.

Orsi persuasively describes how this dichotomy has characterized the politics of modern Catholic and Protestant identity, but theologically, matters are more complex. Presence and absence exist in a reciprocal relationship with one another. The Protestant does not smash the image (just) to proclaim God's absence. He does so (also) to proclaim God's universal presence. He breaks to say, God does not need an image to be present to the world. Or, this image cannot contain the living God. We can hear, in these iconoclastic declarations, an affirmation of what the church celebrates on Good Friday, when it mourns the absence of Christ as a way of proclaiming the universality of Christ's presence, even unto death. Or we might also hear in such iconoclastic avowals an echo of the angel's proclamation of presence at the grave that first Easter: He is not here!

The cross, the empty tomb—these are absences that proclaim presences. The Protestant impulse to iconoclasm insists on a God who is beyond any representation, who cannot be limited by the world. But this impulse can wither into an endorsement of a more anemic absence. It may go from asserting that this image, place, or object cannot circumscribe the God who is everywhere, to suggesting that because God is everywhere, therefore God is nowhere in particular, and finally to implying that God is nowhere. Untethered from iconophilia's affirmation of presence, iconoclasm's insistence that God is not here in *that* way fades into a report that God is not here.

Iconoclasm needs iconophilia. And iconophilia, too, needs iconoclasm, as images need negation. Presbyter Martinus's medieval statue of Mary, *Madonna of the Seated Wisdom*, dramatizes this need.[2] It is meant to be hung on the wall so that Mary sits in her chair above the viewer's head. She holds on her lap the Christ-babe, who extends his arm in blessing toward the viewer, as the Madonna's fierce, open-eyed stare forbids the viewer to let her gaze linger more than a moment. The longer the viewer stares at the Madonna, the more the downward lines of Mary's lips come into focus as an expression of admonition, and the redness of her cheeks grows more striking, as if her color rises in reproach. The viewer who attempts to look at the Christ-babe dispensing blessing finds that as her gaze drifts even slightly upward, she confronts the alert, lidless eyes of the Madonna, fixing a stare on the viewer she will not break, as if reminding the viewer to look elsewhere for the divine. Circulating between these two gazes—the gaze that blesses and the gaze that deflects—the viewer receives a divine blessing from a statue that reminds the viewer that *it* is not the source of blessing. To behold it is not to behold the divine. Thus the statue both commands the viewer's veneration and deflects idolatry. *Madonna of the Seated Wisdom* reminds the viewer that images mediate a presence that is not identical with what they themselves are.

Images and iconophilia, shorn of negations and faithful iconoclasms, calcify into idolatry. Iconoclasms of fidelity, divorced from affirmations of images, dissipate into iconoclasms of temptation. This is as true of the era before Christ as after. The Old Testament is usually read as primarily iconoclastic, and yet that iconoclasm, too, takes place in the context of making, affirming, and worshiping with images. In Israel's life with God, no less than the church's, images are made and destroyed, worried about and celebrated. The golden calf is destroyed in violence; the bronze serpent brings healing and foreshadows Christ. The people of God tear down high places of worship and create an image-rich tabernacle. They design a throne for God while leaving it empty. They follow carefully scripted rituals of worship and affirm that God desires mercy, not sacrifice. Throughout the Old Testament, the people of God faithfully make and break, love and fear images. (They do all of this unfaithfully as well.) And Christ fulfills this dynamic of making and breaking. Christ is the Image of God, broken for the people of God, who reveals God in his very brokenness. Both breaking and making images are persistent features of God's life with the people of God. Together these actions say, God is here, but that does not mean God is not elsewhere. Both are needed. Without iconoclasm, iconophilia risks idolatry. Without iconophilia, iconoclasm turns to despair. The angel's proclamation that Christ is not here can only be hopeful together with an affirmation of Christ's presence in another place or in a new way.

The paradoxical togetherness of presence and absence is the paradox of the incarnation writ large. In Christ, God is uniquely present, yet God does not cease to be everywhere, to be invisible, to be uncircumscribable. The affirmation that God becomes a particular human in Christ does not vitiate God's presence to all the world as Creator. Even while God in Jesus is present as *this* human in *this* place during *this* time—say, this baby in this manger during this reign of Caesar Augustus—God remains everywhere, unbounded by space and time. Jesus is the unique bearer of divine presence who points to the invisible God; he is the Son who reveals his Father.

This dialectic of presence and absence does not end in contradiction, nor does it elevate images to the status of mini-incarnations. It generates variegated descriptions of how God is present in the world. The abiding presence of the resurrected Christ, for example, is not the same as the abiding presence of Christ prior to the resurrection. The presence of Christ to an icon is not the same as the presence of Christ to an image in Western art, nor to the presence of Christ in the Eucharist. These are all different presences generated by variations on the negation and revelation structure of Christ.

I have traced in the preceding chapters the way Christ enters, works within, and saves the world by movements of negation and revelation. Christ, I have claimed, is the Image who breaks open literal desire to non-literal desire, and non-literal desire to divine desire; who breaks open the visible image to the invisible prototype and discloses all the world as a visible image of the invisible. Christ is the Image who breaks open brokenness itself, revealing what seems to be the absence of God to mark God's unbroken presence. This paradigmatic Image discloses the iconoclastic structure of imaging. From negation, presence.

And through this Image, we become little images, transforming to be evermore like Christ, from glorious image to glorious image.

While images have their own distinct features and stories, their structure of negation and revelation is not anomalous within Christianity. Following from Christ, the logic of negation and revelation pervades the life of the church. It is the logic by which the bread becomes more than bread, as the bread is broken open to become the body and blood of Christ. It is the logic by which a saint becomes more than herself in the denial of self, thereby mediating the presence of Christ. It is the logic by which Scripture's meanings are more than literal, breaking open to include the spiritual senses. All of these are cases of the literal opening to the more-than-literal. The literal is negated to reveal the more-than-literal—and in the revelation of the more-than-literal, the literal is also revealed. The Eucharist reveals to us what our bread and wine, our fruit of the land and work of human hands, truly are and are for. The revelation of Christ in the saint reveals the lineaments of that saint's personality all the more distinctively. The spiritual senses of Scripture do not erase but consummate the literal. All of these both are and are not Christ; they speak to a complex topography of divine presence in the world.

Rather than theological monoliths, presence and absence exist in a generative relation to one another, spinning off new ways of distinguishing and responding to the divine in the world. Iconoclasm can be a way of naming an absence that testifies to a new kind of presence. Iconophilia can be a way of claiming that presence. It took the church over three hundred years to name the kind of presence God has in Christ as a consubstantial presence. Since then, Christians have found ways of naming a world replete with various divine presences.

Once we are able to move beyond identifying churches and peoples with presence or absence, iconoclasm or iconophilia, a more interesting way of describing the world is possible—a world where images mediate multiple forms of presence to us, and in which we, all of us, are both iconoclastic and iconophilic in different ways. What does this mean for our lives together in the world? To describe the world with these dialectics of presence and absence, iconoclasm and iconophilia, prepares us to draw near iconoclasms of temptation by reclaiming them as potential sites of fidelity. When *Jyllands-Posten* published iconoclastic images of Muhammed, when some Islamists iconoclastically attacked those image-makers, many Muslims fasted and prayed—a response that acknowledges injury while insisting that divine presence survives that in-

CONCLUSION 185

jury. Similarly, those Buddhists who mourned the Taliban's 2001 destruction of the Bamiyan Buddhas proclaim a presence that withstands even dynamite. These actions of the faithful Buddhists and Muslims resonate with the Christian cross's proclamation of presence in the midst of absence, love and fidelity in the midst of horror. They express faithfulness that survives violence.

Such expressions of faithfulness declare that iconoclasms of temptation can never have the final word, can never declare an absence that is ultimate, for these iconoclasms and absences are parasitic on a presence that precedes them. Performances of that ongoing presence—through prayer, fasting, worship, and love—can incorporate declarations of absence into signs of presence. They can recast iconoclasms of temptation as negations internal to images. In the Genesis story, Joseph tells his brothers that what they intended for evil, God intended for good. In the case of images, we might say, what some intended as an iconoclasm of temptation becomes by the actions of others a sign of fidelity. If the most horrific act of iconoclasm Christians know how to name—the crucifixion of the Image—can be reclaimed as the most revelatory image of divine love, then no iconoclasm of temptation is beyond redemption. Any act of violence against the image can potentially be redeemed as a negation that magnifies rather than diminishes revelation. This is the small step toward peace that grasping the iconoclastic structure of imaging can help us take. This is the first of the two hopes expressed in the introduction.

What of the second hope, the one for ecclesial unity? What could it mean for our churches, if we could recognize impulses of both iconoclasm and iconophilia as consonant with who Christ is as the Image of the invisible God? If we appreciated that many iconoclastic impulses try to affirm, however distortedly, a catholicity of presence? And that iconophilic impulses, from another angle, often attempt the same? Perhaps it would make life more complex, more entangled, and make the lines between us and them harder to draw. What might that look like?

One afternoon, following an event on images and ecumenism, I drove iconographer Dmitri Andreyev back to his hotel. He had delivered a moving tribute to the singular importance of icons within the Christian tradition. I knew that, as a teacher, he is exacting about how icons are made, what materials are used, and which patterns are appropriate. To write an icon, for Andreyev, as for many iconographers, is to join in a certain tradition with a certain history that requires certain ways of making. He takes icon-writing seriously because by icons, Christ is present to the faithful. So I wanted to know: What did he make of sacred art that is not icons? What did he think of Western art that is used in worship life? Andreyev nodded, "Yes, that happens in Orthodox churches all over, especially in Russia, where Western art is mixed in with icons." I paused and waited for a reflection that did not come. Believing he had not understood that I wanted him to assess, not just describe, the situation, I repeated my question. But what did he *think* of it? He looked at me surprised. "It happens. I'm telling you, people *do* worship with Western art."

I've thought about that exchange many times in the months since—what kind of evaluation I was seeking from him and what he, in his kind and polite way, refused to give me. I have mulled over what seems a striking contrast, Andreyev's careful attention to and love for the icon, on the one hand, and his deflection of my question about non-iconic images, on the other. The contrast suggests, it seems to me, a vibrant iconophilia, made possible by also respecting an iconoclastic impulse. It is an iconophilia that loves the special significance of icons in a way that makes possible the love of images that are not icons. It is iconoclastic in its movement toward universality, in its refusal to limit God's presence to a single class of images. It is iconoclastic in the way it affirms a negation internal to images: icons do not circumscribe Christ, nor do they form the limits of Christ's presence to images. And this iconoclastic impulse to un-limit the divine sustains a much wider iconophilia, one that also proclaims the ubiquity of divine presence.

That God is present to icons does not preclude God's presence elsewhere. Neither does God's presence in Christ. The conflict I thought I saw between Andreyev's fastidiousness about icons and the breadth of image practices is, for him, a false one. It reminded me of another seeming conflict I observed as a graduate student visiting St. Anthony's, the 1,700-year-old Coptic monastery on the Red Sea. There I observed some of the oldest sacred art in the world—and bought from the monks two-dollar fake icons, which amounted to prints shellacked onto wood bases. As I understood them, these cheap icon copies were sold by the monks at St. Anthony's as part of their ministry of hospitality, so that everyone who desires to pray with an icon can afford to, even if that icon is just a copy. While there, I watched a monk give an icon copy to a young boy, perhaps three or four years old, teaching him to kiss it and hold it with reverence, similar to the way he might treat an authentic, hand-written icon. The small icon copy almost disappeared into the monk's beard as he brought it carefully to his lips. He opened his eyes and took the boy's hands, helping him imitate his gesture. The hope expressed by both the actions of these monks and the words of

Andreyev is that God might in mercy be present even in non-canonical image forms. After all, God's presence is always a gift of mercy. And if God can do something so unexpectedly merciful as to come to us as a visible Image without ceasing to be the invisible God, and then to be present to icons without ceasing to be uniquely present in Christ the Image—who is to say where and in what way and by which images God might once again come to us, bearing unanticipated forms of divine presence?

NOTES

PREFACE

1. Marco Anelli's photographs are collected in his book *Portraits in the Presence of Marina Abramović* and also online on his website, http://www.marcoanelli.com/portraits-in-the-presence-of-marina-abramovic/. Marina sat from March 14 to May 31 during the hours MoMA was open, a total of about 730 hours. The exhibition attracted a celebrity list that included Sharon Stone, Isabella Rossellini, James Franco, Björk, Rufus Wainwright, and Lady Gaga.

2. "Marina Abramović made me cry"; O'Hagan, "Interview: Marina Abramović." Her circles of influence grew so large that Sarah Lyall, writing in the *New York Times*, saw the 2010 exhibition as bisecting Abramović's career into two stages: first, avant-garde experimentalist and, second, "celebrity darling," in which Abramović entered the cultural mainstream ("For Her Next Piece").

3. Danto, "Danger and Disturbation," 29–30.
4. Danto, "Sitting with Marina."
5. Danto, "Art, Action, and Meaning."
6. O'Hagan, "Interview: Marina Abramović."
7. Mogutin, "Legend of Marina Abramović."
8. The full epigraph reads, "Edwards's journal frequently explored and tested a meditation he seldom allowed to reach print; if all the world were annihilated, he wrote . . . and a new world were freshly created, though it were to exist in every particular in the same manner as this world, it would not be same. Therefore, because there is continuity, which is time, 'it is certain with me that the world exists anew every moment; that the existence of things every moment ceases and is every moment renewed.' The abiding assurance is that 'we every moment see the same proof of a God as we should have seen if we had seen Him create the world at first'" (Miller, *Jonathan Edwards*, 329–30, quoted in Fried, "Art and Objecthood," 148).
9. Fried, "Art and Objecthood," 168.
10. Bredekamp's attempt to trace the agency of images animates his book *Theorie des Bildakts*.
11. Contemporary picture theorists recovering the importance of the presence of the image include Gottfried Boehm, W.J.T. Mitchell, and Hans Belting. Keith Moxey traces the recent paradigm shifts in visual studies in his article, "Visual Studies and the

Iconic Turn." A German volume of essays edited by Lambert Wiesing and translated into English as *Artificial Presence: Philosophical Studies in Image Theory*, goes one step forward in an attempt to identify images as bearing a unique form of presence, which Wiesing and other contributors term *artificial presence*. From another approach, Douglas Hedley has recently attempted to recover a Platonic approach to the image over and against the critiques brought by these picture theorists. Acknowledging the problems with what he calls "'Freshman' Platonism," Hedley wants to argue that Plato's insistence that the image signifies transcendence need not denigrate the image, and in fact, "the rejection of transcendence will eviscerate rather than restore the image" (*Iconic Imagination*, 1).

12. Wood, "Iconoclasts and Iconophiles." The catalogue to an exhibit in the Menil Collection similarly uses "animism" as a category to flatten disparate attempts to locate presence and agency in the world, to the point of eliding Byzantine images with animism (Peers, *Byzantine Things in the World*).

13. In fact, theologians have long used "presence" as a central category when discussing icons. In one recent iteration of this tradition, Andreas Andreopoulos writes, "The icon takes its existence from the realized eschatology of the liturgical presence of Christ, and it tries to represent the way of seeing as it is in the Kingdom of God" (*Gazing on God*, 61). In what follows, I hope to extend such projects by arguing that presence is similarly (though not identically) central to non-iconic imaging traditions.

14. Belting, *Likeness and Presence*, 1. It is not just theologians who are subject to this temptation, of course. George Steiner voices a resonant concern about literary critics, mostly deconstructionists, when he decries the way they reduce an artwork to endless linguistic play. Such parasitic interpretation betrays its very nature as discourse. By contrast, in his essay *Real Presences*, Steiner "proposes that any coherent understanding of what language is and how language performs . . . is, in the final analysis, underwritten by the assumption of God's presence." He continues, "I will put forward the argument that the experience of aesthetic meaning in particular, that of literature, of the arts, of musical form, infers the necessary possibility of this 'real presence'" (3). My similarities with and differences from Steiner will, I hope, become clearer in the Introduction. Steiner's claim that "the wager on the meaning of meaning" is "a wager on transcendence" may prove less compelling in today's literary climate, which is dominated not by deconstruction but by the new materialism and object-oriented ontology. I do not want to claim that we need God to secure either our language or our images, as if they are meaningless absent a divine referent. Yet I am sympathetic to the idea that there is an excessiveness to images analogous to and suggestive of the divine—an argument very similar to what Rowan Williams claims about language in *The Edge of Words: God and the Habits of Language*.

INTRODUCTION

1. An overview of the events surrounding the *Charlie Hebdo* attacks can be found on the BBC website ("Charlie Hebdo Attack").
2. Anderson, "Cartoons of Prophet Met with Outrage."
3. Ghorashi, "A Look at the Full Scope of ISIS's Destruction."
4. *Modern West* is a problematic and not entirely accurate term. To the extent it is

located geographically, it denotes not "the West" but the North Atlantic region—Europe, the United States, and Canada, really. While it might suggest that the rest of the world is less "modern," I mean only to name that many of the modernities prevalent in this region are not identical to the modernities prevalent in other regions. The phrase also obscures some of the modernities present in the North Atlantic region. Still, the term Modern West is important because it has formed cultural imaginations and because it has a literary history that has helped to create a certain people's understanding. I mean Modern West to name a self-understanding registered in the literature and institutions of a people that have often claimed that term. Even as I use the term, I hope to indicate the complications and multitudes that the category masks.

5. Saba Mahmood ("Religious Reason and Secular Affect") has written insightfully about these polarities of the free-speaking Modern West and the blasphemous others, with respect to the Danish cartoon controversy especially. Mahmood's article is engaged at some length in Chapter 1.

6. Chrisafis, "Attack on 'Blasphemous' Art." I return to this image and attacks on it in Chapter 3.

7. "The Islamic Veil Across Europe" outlines the state of the veil across Europe. This 2014 article does not have the latest laws and challenges—for example, the 2015 law in France—but it does give some sense of how France compares with other countries in Europe.

8. I explore the role of the museum further in Chapter 1 of my book *Beauty: A Theological Engagement with Gregory of Nyssa*. I further probe the iconoclasms rife in the Modern West in "Making, Breaking, Loving, and Hating Images."

9. I speak here in generalities. There are also many movements within museums that try to respect the religious and political claims of the objects they protect. Children's museums often lead the charge in this area. For example, the Children's Museum of Indianapolis created "Sacred Journeys," an exhibit in which religious objects are introduced by characters who represent the faithful in the same tradition as each object. They introduce children to the objects through narratives of their own religious life with each object. This exhibit aims explicitly at the transformation of the audience members, to make them more understanding, peaceful, and tolerant.

10. Wood, "Iconoclasts and Iconophiles." In his recent book *The Iconic Imagination*, Douglas Hedley makes a similar point, quoting as an epigraph to his sixth chapter the renowned scholar of Neoplatonism A. H. Armstrong: "The true Neoplatonist is at once an idoloclast and an iconodule" (149). Hedley elaborates his point with the philosophy of Jean-Luc Marion, contrasting idols that "domesticate" God with icons that admit of the transcendent invisible; recognizing the latter requires recognizing the former. Hedley goes on to critique the strong opposition between the two, pointing to the transformation and incorporation of pagan idols into Christian worship, as well as the antecedents for the iconic tradition in Israel.

11. Here is a sampling of the works in which one finds such arguments about images: von Balthasar, *You Have Words of Eternal Life*; Ratzinger, *Spirit of the Liturgy*; Jenson, "Christ-Dogma and Christ-Image"; and Yoder, "Politics: Liberating Images of Christ."

12. See, for example, Ouspensky, *Theology of the Icon*; and Evdokimov, *Art of the Icon*.

13. The distinction I draw between picture and image is purely stipulative. I use it to underscore that by *image*, I mean a type of sign. One might have good reason to use the words differently, interchangeably, even. Hans Belting, in "Iconic Presence," an essay that previews a planned book of the same title, uses *picture* and *image* as synonyms, which certainly makes sense for one whose native language has one word (*Bild*) for both.

14. Though images can be auditory, it may be the case that images are more often visual than related to any other sense. I will most often use visual-metaphorical language to discuss them—*beholders*, for example—as many do, because the terminology we favor seems to register our greater familiarity with visual images.

15. Likeness is especially important in distinguishing images from symbols. The two can be confused because both are often visual, but symbols do not bear likeness qua their status as symbols. A red octagon symbolizes stopping and smoke axiomatically signifies fire, even though there is no likeness between these symbols and what they symbolize. To the extent that a symbol does bear some resemblance to what it signifies—as, for example, the woman on the door of a women-only restroom—it is also an image.

16. Theodore the Studite was the first to make this argument. It will be further explicated in Chapter 4.

17. This is why I will diverge in my account of images from Nicholas Wolterstorff's approach in his intelligent article "Would You Stomp on a Picture of Your Mother? Would you Kiss an Icon?" Wolterstorff seeks an account of all images that will explain how we relate to them, and so he finds the Byzantine account wanting. But the Byzantine account, as expressed, for example, by Theodore the Studite, does not mean to be a one-size-fits-all account of images, precisely because internal to the account is a way of describing the *different* presences and likenesses found, for example, in photos of one's mother and icons of Christ (or closer to Theodore, images of the emperor and icons of Christ).

18. John of Damascus, *Three Treatises on Divine Images*, 95.

19. Drawing on this same point by John of Damascus about likeness and unlikeness, Father Maximos Constas makes a similar point about the image, one that gives rise to the subtitle of his recent book *The Art of Seeing: Paradox and Perception in Orthodox Iconography*: "This is the great paradox of the icon, at once its weakness and its strength. As the 'likeness' of something else, icons bear certain formal points of resemblance to that which they portray. Yet the very word 'likeness' implies that their resemblance is not absolute, and so the Damascene says that they are also '*unlike* their prototypes.' By definition then, every icon is both continuous and discontinuous with its source; both similar and dissimilar to that which it reflects" (25).

20. Hans Belting, in *An Anthropology of Images*, argues, in fact, that images are born in the ultimate absence of the loved one: death.

21. Also influenced by Michael Fried, Carolyn Walker Bynum finds a similar dynamic of negation in both the medieval art she studies and modern art: "Paint, wood, steel, and so forth present to us as if they were, for example, apples or the color red, but they are not, and thus they call attention to the 'not-ness.'" (Bynum, *Christian Materiality*, n7).

22. Horst Bredekamp discussed the Dangolsheim Madonna from Strasbourg (1460/65) in a talk he gave to a SIAS workshop hosted by Wissenschaftskolleg on July 18, 2014. I anticipate the larger claims about images, art, and religion will be further substantiated in his forthcoming book that treats an eleventh-century Spanish church building.

23. Bynum, *Christian Materiality*, 62.

24. Bynum, *Christian Materiality*, 62.

25. See, for example, Marion, *Crossing of the Visible*, 58–9.

26. Brubaker, *Inventing Byzantine Iconoclasm*, 3–4, 120.

27. Bremmer, "Iconoclast, Iconoclastic, and Iconoclasm."

28. Simpson, *Under the Hammer*.

29. I pointed out earlier such modern forms of iconoclasm as the museum, which make identifying contemporary iconoclasts a difficult and freighted task. Some acts of iconoclasm are also attempts to protect the image; others both destroy the image and respect its capacity to make claims. That is one argument for distinguishing forms of iconoclasm. There are others, just as there are additional complexities with the term *iconoclasm* in our modern world.

30. People both lauded and denounced Pope Francis as an iconoclast for his iconoclastic foot washing. For a more laudatory account, see Powell, "Pope Francis and the Beautiful Iconoclasm."

31. All quotations from the Bible are from the New Revised Standard Version (NRSV), unless otherwise indicated.

32. Links to the four articles comprising this conversation can be found on the University of Chicago's Martin Marty Center website, https://divinity.uchicago.edu/tags/charlie-hebdo.

33. Marion, "After the 'Charlie Hebdo' Massacre."

34. Marion, "After the 'Charlie Hebdo' Massacre."

35. Lincoln and Yu, "Reply to Jean-Luc Marion."

36. Lincoln and Yu ("Reply to Jean-Luc Marion") write: "It is one thing for *Charlie Hebdo* to mock the Pope, and quite another to mock Muhammad. To poke fun at the icons revered by the powerful is a courageous act of iconoclasm; to ridicule those of the weak is cheap bullying, as it subjects people who already suffer abuse of multiple sorts to public humiliation, making sport of their (perceived) inability to defend the things they hold sacred." This might sound as though they are contrasting the *Charlie Hebdo* cartoons with iconoclasm, but they go on to write, "We understand the need to rally in defense of *liberté* and we also understand that free speech includes forms of critical speech that may be cruel and offensive, such as iconoclasm, blasphemy, ridicule and derision. But one also has to realize that when those who enjoy the full benefits of citizenship use their *liberté* to mock others to whom basic rights are abridged or denied, something has gone badly amiss."

37. The question of Islam's relation to critique comes to the fore in Asad et al., *Is Critique Secular?*

38. It is worth noting that in some of Marion's most virulent critiques, the French word he uses is *iconomaque* (see the chapter "Prototype and the Image" in *Crossing of*

the Visible, 66–87). At other points, though, Marion criticizes iconoclasm (*iconoclasme*), especially in the chapter "Blind at Shiloh" in *Crossing of the Visible*, 46–65.

39. Marion, *Crossing of the Visible*, 58. Ironically, some have accused Marion himself of being an iconoclast (see, for example, Benson, *Graven Ideologies*, 222).

40. Marion, *Crossing of the Visible*, 58.

41. Marion, *Crossing of the Visible*, 59.

42. Janet Martin Soskice (*Kindness of God*) makes a point importantly complementary to this one about how the Son images the Father by negation, when she claims that any attempt to lay claim to the Father without the Son renders the Father an idol. She writes: "In Christian teaching it is because Jesus is 'Son' that God is 'Father.' Already in the New Testament the hierarchical understanding of Father and Son is rendered unstable by Jesus who says, 'I and the Father are one.' The force of this subversion will only be felt, in due course, in the out-workings of the doctrine of the Trinity, but in the meantime, suffice it to say that, within the religious dynamics of Christianity, only the Son can show us the Father. Without the Son 'the Father' is not God, but an idol" (83).

43. Sheryl Overmyer ("Three More Jigs in the Puzzle") has a rich discussion of how image functions analogously in Thomas Aquinas's work, with Image properly speaking of Christ and derivatively speaking of humanity. It is just such an analogical understanding of image that I hope to retrieve.

44. All of the creedal claims that follow are, in some form, in the Nicene or the Apostle's Creed. Though they follow the former closely, I have taken minor liberties in arranging them. The recently official Catholic version (the English translation implemented in Advent 2011), for example, declares Christ was "Incarnate" of the Virgin Mary, but I have kept "born" as in the pre-2011 Nicene Creed (and in the Apostle's Creed) so as not to confuse the interpretive foci of Chapters 1 and 2. The first centers on Christ coming to and from Mary, while the second treats the incarnation more broadly.

CHAPTER 1: *BORN OF THE VIRGIN MARY*

1. Leo Steinberg's important book *The Sexuality of Christ* extensively treats images of the phallic infant and adult Christ. At one point, he names three theological reasons for the *ostentatio genitalium* of both the infant and adult Christ: that it emphasizes the humanity of Christ, that it exemplifies Christ's consecration of chastity and defeat of concupiscence, and that it calls to mind Adam's lost innocence. It is especially the first that he identifies with images of the infant Christ (24).

2. The scenes in which Correggio depicts the naked breasts of Mary, Mother of Christ and Mary Magdalene are ones of nourishing an infant and penitence, respectively, while scenes depicting the nakedness of mythological figures are often ones of sexual delight or conquest. The naked breast, in these latter depictions, is often not the only naked part of the woman's body.

3. Margaret Miles claims, "I have not been able to find a single religious image of the breast painted after 1750" ("God's Love, Mother's Milk," 23).

4. Council of Trent, "Invocation, Veneration, and Relics of Saints," 236.

5. Scaraffia, "Quelle Marie troppo umane censurate dall'età moderna," 4; Covolo, "I paradossi iconografici della *Madonna guerriera* e della *Vergine che allatta*," 4.

6. Alex Dobuzinskis ("Nude Virgin Mary Cover") reported that "in a statement, Chicago-based Playboy Enterprises Inc. said the Mexican edition of the magazine is published by a licensee, and the company did not approve or endorse the cover. 'While Playboy Mexico never meant for the cover or images to offend anyone, we recognize that it has created offense, and we as well as Playboy Mexico offer our sincerest apologies,' the statement said. Raul Sayrols, publisher of Playboy Mexico, said in a further statement, 'The image is not and never was intended to portray the Virgin of Guadalupe or any other religious figure. The intent was to reflect a Renaissance-like mood on the cover.'"

7. Coetzee, "Lesson 5: The Humanities in Africa."

8. What does Elizabeth Costello miss, in ignoring Sister Bridget's chosen name? Saint Bridget of Ireland (Bridget of Kildare), according to an old saint's tale, was known for her love of the poor, her love of God, and her great beauty. As she grew up, she longed to live a consecrated life of holy virginity in which she could be devoted to both the poor and the Lord. However, her father, eager to reap the rewards of her beauty, schemed to marry her off. Bridget prayed to God and her prayers were answered when she lost her beauty and became, if not ugly, then at least safely plain. Seeing she had lost her beauty, her father relinquished his scheme to have her married and allowed her to pursue holy virginity. Bridget was consecrated to her life of celibacy, and then her beauty miraculously returned. The story goes that this patron saint of Ireland was also the island's first religious woman. In early documents she is known as Mary of the Gael—another Mary for this story—who founded a convent for young girls who wanted to become nuns.

9. Coetzee, "Humanities in Africa," 144.
10. Coetzee, "Humanities in Africa," 145.
11. Coetzee, "Humanities in Africa," 148.
12. Coetzee, "Humanities in Africa," 149.
13. Coetzee, "Humanities in Africa," 154.
14. Coetzee, "Humanities in Africa," 155.
15. Coetzee, "Humanities in Africa," 155.

16. I press the point of what presences the images in "The Humanities in Africa" do loose in the narrative in "Embracing Beauty in a World of Affliction."

17. Gregory of Nyssa, *Life of Saint Macrina*. A critical edition of this work is also available: Maraval, *Grégoire de Nysse: Vie de sainte Macrine*.

18. Gregory of Nyssa (*Life of Saint Macrina*) notes Macrina's especially close relationship to her mother in his *vita*, as he records Emmelia's joke that she bore all her other children in her womb for the usual nine months, but Macrina "she bore her always and everywhere, embracing her, as it were, in her womb" (25).

19. The literal meaning of the name El Shaddai has been debated by scholars, but David Biale makes a convincing case for "God with Breasts," based on that meaning's association with fertility blessings and a key passage in Genesis 49:25, which makes a wordplay with Shaddai and breasts (*shadayim*). Biale translates this passage: "[A]nd El

Shaddai will bless you with the blessings of the heavens above, blessings of the deep lying below, blessings of breasts [*shadayim*] and womb [*rahem*]" ("God with Breasts," 248).

20. Scholars believe the fertility goddess statue Artemis (Diana) of Ephesus predates classical Greek culture.

21. This discussion is especially indebted to the work of Marilyn Yalom in her *History of the Breast* and of Margaret Miles in *A Complex Delight*.

22. James Bruce Ross has done important work on *balía* and their influence on childhood in Italy in "The Middle-Class Child in Urban Italy."

23. Yalom, *History of the Breast*, 42–3.

24. Miles's *A Complex Delight* traces primarily the shift from the "religious" to the "secular" breast (24).

25. Yalom traces a series of shifts in her *History of the Breast*, from the erotic bosom of the sixteenth century through the political breasts of the eighteenth century to the myriad, though primarily sexual, meanings of the twentieth century.

26. *Time*, front cover.

27. It is interesting to contrast this pose with the more familiar maternal pose of a seated mother cradling her nursing child, a pose featured both in the photographs *Time* chose not to use for its cover and in the "visual references" (paintings of nursing mothers and infants) that guided its photographic choices. Appearing on NBC's *Today Show* to discuss the cover, the model, Jamie Lynn Grumet, said: "I understand [why] some of the breastfeeding advocates are actually upset about this, because I feel like [the pictures] don't show the nurturing side to attachment parenting. This isn't how we breastfeed at home. It's more of a cradling, nurturing situation. And I understand what they're saying, but I do understand why *Time* chose this picture." *Time* managing editor Rick Stengel clarified that point for those who were not as understanding. On MSNBC's *Morning Joe*, he said, "The point of a cover is to get your attention," adding, "and this gets your attention" (Manker, "*Time* Magazine Cover"). For the photographs *Time* considered in choosing the cover, see Sun, "Behind the Cover."

28. For Freud's work along these lines, see his *Outline of Psychoanalysis*, which describes the breast's significance as the infant's first sexual object.

29. Sarah Coakley's work ("Batter my heart" and "Living into the Mystery of the Holy Trinity") taught me to see Freudianism's nearness to and distance from patristic configurations of desire. Also see note 77 for this chapter, below.

30. Sarah Jane Boss tells a similar story of the decline of *Maria lactans*, and though we are largely in agreement, her conclusion is more definitive. She offers little hope of rehabilitating the bare-breasted Mary, nor does she find the traces of other meanings for breasts still present today. She writes, "I suggest that it is precisely in consequence of the breast's association with the narrowly sexual and the medical that it is no longer possible for it to feature in Christian art; for Christianity has always excluded from the realm of the sacred that which is understood to be predominantly sexual, while scientific medicine is a practice which is not itself sacred, and its imagery would have no meaning in works of a devotional or theological nature" (*Empress and Handmaid*, 38).

31. Irenaeus, *Against Heresies*, I.7.2.

32. Much of what follows about Nestorius retraces ground I covered in "Reconsideration of Religious Authority."
33. McGuckin, *Saint Cyril of Alexandria*, 24.
34. McGuckin, *Saint Cyril*, 28.
35. McGuckin, *Saint Cyril*, 24–38.
36. Cyril quotes this phrase of Nestorius's throughout his writings "Against Nestorius," sometimes using the exact phrase Nestorius used (*parelthen*), sometimes blurring it into the term associated with the Gnostics (*dielthen*) (Russell, *Cyril of Alexandria*, 233, n25).
37. See, for example, Cyril of Alexandria, "Dispensation of the Incarnation."
38. The death God can die in Christ is, of course, a human, not a divine death. For more on impassibility in Cyril's theology, see Smith, "Suffering Impassibly." For more on impassibility's connection to love, see Hart, "No Shadow of Turning." Impassibility will be a motif in Chapter 3 as well.
39. Not all churches submitted to the authority of these councils. Some left communion with Constantinople, and to this day, Nestorian Christianity survives in the Assyrian Church of the East, which is found in countries throughout Asia as well as diaspora communities around the world.
40. Skalova, "Icon of the Virgin Galaktotrophousa."
41. Jean-Luc Chrétien points to the way seventeenth-century theologians Cardinal de Bérulle and François Bourgoing drew this connection by contemplating the silence of the *Verbum infans* who could not speak, the Speech deprived of speech, and claiming it is just as humiliating as the cross (Chrétien, *Hand to Hand*, 44).
42. Cavell, *Disowning Knowledge*, 13.
43. Cavell, *Disowning Knowledge*, 188–9.
44. Cavell, *Disowning Knowledge*, 189.
45. Paola Marrati draws out this theme in Cavell's work, particularly his memoir *Little Did I Know*, in her article "Childhood and Philosophy."
46. Asad et al., *Is Critique Secular?*
47. Mahmood, "Religious Reason and Secular Affect," 78.
48. Mahmood, "Religious Reason," 71.
49. Mahmood, "Religious Reason," 90.
50. Mahmood makes this connection herself, in her discussion of Protestant missionaries and their encounter with the animism of the people they proselytize ("Religious Reason," 66–7).
51. Brown, "Introduction," 16.
52. Asad, "Free Speech, Blasphemy, and Secular Criticism," 33.
53. Asad ("Free Speech," 33) is quoting French historian Alain Cabantous, *Blasphemy*, 5.
54. The case in which seduction *is* a cause for concern in the contemporary United States is that of children, whom U.S. law deems worthy of special protection, perhaps because their capacity for reason is not considered fully formed and therefore they, like the inebriated, cannot legally give consent to sex.

55. Asad, "Free Speech," 31.

56. Asad, "Free Speech," 32.

57. For an example of how artworks elicit or defer desire, see the complicated analysis of desire and art in James Elkins's *The Object Stares Back*, especially his first two chapters. For an example of how advertising images provoke philosophy, see W.J.T. Mitchell's sophisticated engagement with the marketing campaigns of Canon camera and Sprite in *What Do Pictures Want?*, especially his Introduction and Chapter 4. Mitchell's analysis of these advertising images is also important to Chapter 5 in this book.

58. As David Freedberg pointed out in 1989:

> Notions of canonicity, now, seem to expand; but however much we (as sophisticated critics and consumers of art) may be pleased with the processes of liberalization and liberation, it is clear that the dismissal of artists who represent subjects commonly subsumed under the category of pornography is predicated on just the position that the images are not art but pornography. On the other hand, we sophisticated deal with our greater or lesser discomfort in perceiving the images as straightforwardly erotic by putting them into a loftier category, by granting them the higher status of art. Hang them in galleries and exhibit them in the art museum. (*Power of Images*, 349–50)

59. This history is traced more fully in Carnes, *Beauty*, ch. 1.

60. For more on this history, see Guyer, "History of Modern Aesthetics" and "Origins of Modern Aesthetics."

61. In his book *The Invisible Dragon*, Dave Hickey explores the separation of art from pleasure, beauty, and desire, describing it as an elitist and anti-democratic move on the part of the artworld that is motivated by an anxiety about being associated with the marketplace. In his book *The Secret Museum*, Walter Kendrick offers some support for this observation. He argues that the secret museum, like the category of pornography more broadly, was developed in modernity in response to anxieties about democratization.

62. For more on the development and consolidation of the category of art, see Shiner, *Invention of Art*.

63. For more on the development of the secret museum, see Kendrick, *Secret Museum*.

64. There is an interesting parallel between, on the one hand, desire's absence in the museum and return through the secret museum of yore, and on the other hand, its absence in the museum and return through the museum gift shop today.

65. Miles, *Complex Delight*, 122.

66. Miles, *Complex Delight*, 122. According to Miles, Jacob Burckhardt called Aretino the "father of journalism" because he deployed print technology to reach a popular audience.

67. Miles, *Complex Delight*, 123.

68. Miles, *Complex Delight*, 124–6.

69. Miles (*Complex Delight*, 126) gives as one prominent example *Thérèse philosophe* (1748), a popular book that references the Enlightenment work *Le philosophe* (1743), a book that described the ideal freethinker type. In *The Forbidden Best-Sellers of Pre-*

Revolutionary France, Robert Darnton discusses books like *Thérèse philosophe*, making some of these connections between pornography and philosophy.

70. In *Putting Liberalism in Its Place*, Paul Kahn claims that pornography presents the body "detached from family, state, and market. If we ask, who owns the pornographic body? the answer is, the individual." This claim is made, according to Kahn, "against the claims of the ordinary institutions of institutionalized power: family, government, and markets." Further, Kahn claims that in dramatizing the individual taking possession of her body, pornography also presents this act of possession as an act of self-discovery, such that the individual's bodily experience reveals her subjecthood (203–04).

71. Hunt, "Introduction," 13. Hunt writes, "[I]f we take pornography to be the explicit depiction of sexual organs and sexual practices with the aim of arousing sexual feelings, then pornography was almost always an adjunct to something else until the middle or end of the eighteenth century" (10).

72. Hunt, "Introduction," 14–6.

73. Hunt, "Introduction," 13.

74. Miles, *Complex Delight*, 122.

75. See, for example, philosopher Arthur Danto's famous piece "The Artworld," in which he argues that Warhol's *Brillo Boxes* presents the question toward which all Western art and philosophy had been tending: what makes the difference between X (art) and not-X (not-art) when there is no interesting perceptual difference between them? It is a question he likens to Descartes's contemplations on what distinguishes reality from dreams (581).

76. The differences between pornographic and advertising images are interesting in part because advertising images have a range of ways in which they can work on desire. For example, rather than literalizing desire, they might figure a non-literal desire (for familial intimacy) as if it were a literal one (the consumption of a particular brand of gravy). I treat different perversities of desire aroused by advertising images in Chapter 5.

77. I have learned much from Sarah Coakley, whose work on desire both diagnoses and offers therapy for the disjunction of sexual and divine desire. Drawing on Gregory of Nyssa, she proposes a kind of inverse Freudianism, not unlike what I see in *Maria lactans*. And she does so using the language of "disjunction." She refers, for example to the "tortured disjunction between human sexual love and the love for God" in an essay on the Trinity and sexual desire ("Batter my heart," 74). She treats this theme again in an essay in which she seeks to see sexual desire and desire for God "no longer seen as disjunctive alternatives" but as part of "a renewed vision of divine desire . . . rooted in, and analogously related to, Trinitarian divine relations" ("Living into the Mystery of the Holy Trinity," 224.) The theme is traced in several other articles as well and then treated at much greater length in her book *God, Sexuality, and the Self*.

78. While I use *eros* broadly to name all desire, Elizabeth Costello distinguishes *eros* from *caritas* and *agape*, which indicates she intends it in a sexual key.

79. Something like this is behind the statement often attributed to Pope John Paul II and recently endorsed by secular comedian Russell Brand: "The problem with pornography is not that it reveals too much of a person, but that it reveals far too little"

(West, *Theology of the Body Explained*, 235). This statement is West's gloss on Pope John Paul II's actual comments about pornography in a 1981 address to a general audience, "Art Must Not Violate the Right to Privacy."

80. Michael Fried, "Art and Objecthood, 168."

81. For more on sacrifice and on God entering the economy of desire and need in the Old Testament, see Anderson, "Redeem Your Sins by the Giving of Alms."

82. Ephrem the Syrian, *Hymns on the Nativity* 4:203–5, 103; quoted in Anderson, "Redeem Your Sins," 59.

83. As it appears in Italian on the painting: DOLCIXIMO FIGLIUOLO PELLAC: / TE CHIO TIDIE ABBI MIA DI CHOSTORO.

84. As it appears in Italian on the painting: PADRE MIO SIENO SALVI CHOSTORO PEQUALI TU / VOLESTI CHIO PATISSI PASSIONE.

CHAPTER 2: *CAME DOWN FROM HEAVEN AND WAS MADE HUMAN*

1. I use the term *iconomach* to refer specifically to the Byzantine image fighters and *iconodule* to refer to the image defenders, while *iconoclast* and *iconophile* refer to image resisters and image lovers across times, places, and images. As described in the Introduction, *iconoclasm* as a word postdates the Byzantine image controversy, which contemporaries referred to as an *iconomachy*, a struggle over images.

2. I use *icon* specifically to denote a material image of Christ—one that is kin to the painted wood images that the iconomachy addressed, whereas *image* refers broadly to all images of Christ, material or immaterial and including, for the iconomachs, the Eucharist.

3. The Seventh Ecumenical Council did not settle the issue of the image, even for the East. Not only did the struggle over the image continue during the decades immediately following that council, reaching some settlement in the Triumph of Orthodoxy (in 843), but iconoclastic energies returned with new force in the eleventh century. Charles Barber traces this history in his book *Contesting the Logic of Painting*.

4. The writings and transcripts of those deemed heretics by the church have been destroyed, so we have access to the iconomachs' positions largely through the iconodules' quotations from these materials.

5. Sahas, *Icon and Logos* ("Introduction," 30).

6. Sahas, *Icon and Logos*, 244D. While both translate as "one nature," *Monophysitism* and *Miaphysitism* resonate differently in theological conversation. The term Monophysite denotes the heretical position taken by Eutyches and his heirs, while the Miaphysite position is associated less with Eutyches and regarded more as a gloss on Cyril's position as he defended the church from Nestorianism. Professed by oriental Orthodox churches today, Miaphysitism is considered in principle reconcilable with the two natures position of the Council of Chalcedon.

7. Sahas, *Icon and Logos*, 30.

8. Sahas, *Icon and Logos*, 260A/B, 341E. Just as *circumscribe* and *scribe* share the Latin root word *scribere*, in ancient Greek, *perigraphein* (to circumscribe) uses the same root as the term meaning "to write" (*graphein*) something, such as an icon.

9. Hedley, *Iconic Imagination*, 1–11.
10. Sahas, *Icon and Logos*, 264C. Jaroslav Pelikan narrates it this way:
But Constantine V developed this definition further by asserting that a genuine image was 'identical in essence with that which it portrays.' The term used here, 'identical in essence' [*homoousios*], came from the Trinitarian language of orthodox dogma, where it had been used to define the deity of the Son in relation to the Father; it was in this sense that the Son was 'the image of the Father.' . . . The very definition of a true image necessarily implied for the iconoclasts that no painting or statue could ever be an image of Christ. But the Eucharist could be, and in fact was, a true image, for only it was identical in essence with Christ. . . . At their [iconoclastic] council in 754, he and his fellow believers declared that apart from the Eucharist there was 'not any other form or type capable of representing his incarnation of an image. (*The Spirit of Eastern Christendom*, 109–10)
Stephen Gerö claims that more attention should be paid to the role of the Eucharist in the iconomachy: "Less attention than it deserves has been paid by modern scholarship to the fact that this second phase of iconoclasm is also characterized by the emergence of a eucharistic argument: the bread and wine of the eucharist are the only true images of Christ" ("Eucharistic Doctrine of the Byzantine Iconoclasts," 4).
11. Charles Barber describes the force of the iconoclasts' argument as an issue of "truth in painting," and he traces that idea in *Figure and Likeness*, ch. 3.
12. Sahas, *Icon and Logos*, 253E.
13. Constas, *Art of Seeing*, 106.
14. In the Introduction, I distinguished pictures from images by claiming that the latter are always signs, which point to a signified. The movies are commonly called moving pictures, but Binx is particularly interested in the way they are images—and the way they might be images of the excess of vitality in the world.
15. Walker Percy, *Moviegoer*, 69, 82.
16. Percy, *Moviegoer*, 70. Ralph Wood (*Comedy of Redemption*) notices the echo here of Kierkegaard's criticism of Hegel. He writes: "Percy discovered that Kierkegaard's critique of Hegel helped clarify his own misgivings about secularist science. 'The same thing he said about the Hegelian system,' Percy notes, 'might be said about a purely scientific view of the world that leaves out the individual.' Percy takes delight in Kierkegaard's description of Hegel as the philosopher who, upon completing the magnificent crystal palace of his philosophical system, had to build a shanty wherein he could actually live" (146). Wood quotes Walker's remarks from Dewey, "Walker Percy Talks About Kierkegaard," 288.
17. Percy, *Moviegoer*, 70, 135.
18. Percy, *Moviegoer*, 135.
19. O'Connor, "Parker's Back," 657.
20. O'Connor, "Parker's Back," 659.
21. O'Connor, "Parker's Back," 666–7.
22. O'Connor, "Parker's Back," 670.
23. O'Connor, "Parker's Back," 673.

24. O'Connor, "Parker's Back," 674–5.
25. Percy, *Moviegoer*, 10–11.
26. Percy, *Moviegoer*, 13.
27. Percy, *Moviegoer*, 63.
28. Percy, *Moviegoer*, 15–18.
29. Percy, *Moviegoer*, 216.
30. Percy, *Moviegoer*, 75.
31. For example, Percy, *Moviegoer*, 70, 126.
32. Marion, *Crossing of the Visible*, 46.
33. Marion, *Crossing of the Visible*, 53.
34. Marion claims to be less worried about film than television, offering the unconvincing reason that one could find the actors at a film festival or film shoot, or learn who those actors were, thus maintaining a relationship between image and original. It is not entirely clear why this would be less true of television. It seems when he first wrote those remarks in 1996 (the date of the original French edition), he understood television actors to be more anonymous and less publicly accessible. More fundamentally, though, it seems strange to understand the actors as the original or prototype, rather than the medium. The classical understanding of drama, as in Aristotle's discussion of tragedy, for example, is that it is a *mimesis* (imitation or representation) of an action, and that seems a more illuminating and intuitive way to go. Audrey Hepburn is not the prototype for the scenes in *Breakfast at Tiffany's*; she is more like the medium for creating the character Holly Golightly, much as oil paints are the medium for the *Mona Lisa*. What *Breakfast at Tiffany's* images is, rather, something more complex, which we might describe as the competing and interweaving desires for love and social status in mid-twentieth-century New York City.
35. Percy, *Moviegoer*, 74.
36. Percy, *Moviegoer*, 63, 75.
37. Marion, *Crossing of the Visible*, 53.
38. Percy, *Moviegoer*, 13.
39. Percy, *Moviegoer*, 70.
40. Percy, *Moviegoer*, 23.
41. Percy, *Moviegoer*, 54, 224.
42. Percy, *Moviegoer*, 58.
43. Percy, *Moviegoer*, 201.
44. Percy, *Moviegoer*, 26–7.
45. Percy, *Love in the Ruins*.
46. Cavell, *Pursuits of Happiness*, 80–3.
47. Cavell, *Pursuits of Happiness*, 100.
48. Cavell, *Pursuits of Happiness*, 109.
49. Percy, *Moviegoer*, 228.
50. Percy, "Holiness of the Ordinary." The idea of the human as a "pilgrim" is so central to Percy's way of thinking that a famous biography of him, by Jay Tolson, is titled *Pilgrim in the Ruins*. Robert Coles wrote an article on Percy for the *New York Times* and called it "The Doubtful Pilgrim."

51. Percy, "Holiness of the Ordinary," 369.
52. Percy, *Moviegoer*, 228.
53. Percy, *Moviegoer*, 235.
54. Percy, *Moviegoer*, 228.
55. Percy, *Moviegoer*, 234–5.
56. John of Damascus, *Three Treatises on the Divine Images*, 26; emphasis added.
57. Schaff, *St. Augustine*, Tractate 75.2.
58. Pseudo-Dionysius, "Letter Three: To the same Gaius," in *Pseudo-Dionysius: The Collected Works*, 264.
59. Lossky, *Image and Likeness of God*, 14–5.
60. Lossky, *Image and Likeness of God*, 13.
61. There is an interesting convergence of readers insistently reading Kate as the disaster whom Binx saves and so saves himself—a reading I find mystifying given Kate's earlier observation that Binx is "nuttier than she" and given the way she saves him in her arrival. Why is it that readers of *The Moviegoer*—insightful, sensitive readers—insist on reducing Kate to the role of damsel in distress, when she arrives on her bright and shining Plymouth to save Jack from the howling despair of desire?
62. Percy, *Moviegoer*, 237.
63. Percy, *Moviegoer*, 224.
64. Percy, *Moviegoer*, 233.
65. Percy, *Moviegoer*, 234.
66. Percy, *Moviegoer*, 235.
67. O'Connor, "Parker's Back," 672.
68. This theme emerges in Gregory of Nyssa's *Homilies on the Song of Songs*, especially his fourth homily, which I treat in *Beauty*, ch. 4.
69. Percy, "Holiness of the Ordinary," 369.
70. Thomas Aquinas treats the issues of change and annihilation in the second and third articles of Question 75 in the Third Part of his *Summa Theologica*. Mark Jordan has stressed to me the importance of understanding this change as occurring for Thomas at the level of substance—as *conversio* rather than *mutatio* (simple alteration) or *motus* (movement). My thanks to him and Matthew Whelan for helping to clarify Thomas's view for me.
71. Evdokimov, *Art of the Icon*, 204.
72. Williams, *Ponder These Things*, 45.
73. Williams, *Ponder These Things*, 49.
74. Williams, *Ponder These Things*, 54, 55.

CHAPTER 3: CRUCIFIED, DIED, AND WAS BURIED

Portions of this chapter are adapted from Natalie Carnes, "'Our Cross's Children Which Our Crosses Are': *Imitatio Christi, Imitatio Crucis*," © 2016 Cambridge University Press. Originally published in the *Scottish Journal of Theology* 69:1 (2016): 63–80. Reprinted with permission.

1. Koerner, *Reformation of the Image*, 83.

2. Koerner, *Reformation of the Image*, 124.

3. Marion, *Crossing of the Visible*, 75. The discussion that follows in this paragraph draws on pp. 68–75 of Marion's work.

4. Koerner, *Reformation of the Image*, 132; here Koerner draws upon the *Basler Chroniken*, I (1874), 447.

5. The taunt alludes to Matthew 27:40, Luke 23:37, and Mark 15:29.

6. Koerner, *Reformation of the Image*, 132.

7. Koerner, *Reformation of the Image*, 132.

8. Gutiérrez, *Las Casas*, 62.

9. Chrisafis, "Attack on 'Blasphemous' Art Work."

10. Chrisafis, "Attack on 'Blasphemous' Art Work." In the wake of the *Charlie Hebdo* attacks, Serrano wrote an editorial in which he said:

> For me, *Piss Christ* was always a work of art and an act of devotion. I was born and raised a Catholic and have been a Christian all my life. As a child and especially as I was preparing for my Holy Communion and confirmation, I often heard the nuns speak reverentially of the "body and blood of Christ." They also said that it was wrong to idolize representations of Christ since these were only representations and not holy objects themselves. My work was, in part, a comment on that paradox. I am neither a blasphemer nor "anti-Christian," as some have called me, and I stand by my work as an artist and as a Christian. Where the photograph has ignited spirited debate, that has been a good thing. Perhaps it reminds some people to question what we unthinkingly fetishize (and thereby often minimize) in lieu of pondering seriously what the crucifix actually symbolizes: the unimaginably torturous death of Christ, the Son of God. (Serrano, "Protecting Freedom of Expression")

11. This image from the Khludov Psalter is reproduced in multiple places, including Karlin-Hayter, "Iconoclasm," 156.

12. Mochizuki, *Netherlandish Image After Iconoclasm*.

13. Koerner, *Reformation of the Image*, 111.

14. Latour, *Modern Cult of the Factish Gods*, 83.

15. In this way, it repeats what Koerner ("Icon as Iconoclash") calls "the antagonism between appearance and truth" (196).

16. In her book on the history and historiography of Byzantine iconoclasm, *Inventing Byzantine Iconoclasm*, Leslie Brubaker points out that the three written testimonies of this account are all fictionalized and problematic in many ways—specifically in their ability to corroborate whether Leo III took sides in the icon struggle. Although we do not know exactly who the actors were at Chalke Gate, we do know that it was the site of an iconoclastic skirmish, and we have the five poems that were placed there by an iconoclastic faction (26–28). A detailed discussion of the historicity of the event can be found in Brubaker and Haldon, *Byzantium in the Iconoclast Era*, 128–135.

17. Translated by Barber, *Figure and Likeness*, 94–5. The poem was written by Sergios, and the acrostic reads, "The Cross raised Sergios as it has already saved [him]" (Pentcheva, *Sensual Icon*, 81).

18. Marion, *Crossing of the Visible*, 78–9.

19. Aston, "Cross and Crucifix," 269.
20. Aston, "Cross and Crucifix," 272.
21. Quoted in Aston, *England's Iconoclasts*, 314, from Peel, *The Seconde Parte of a Register*, ii.53. I have modernized the spelling in quotations from English works of this period.
22. Zwingli, *Huldreich Zwinglis Sämtliche Werke*, 258.
23. Mure, "True Crucifix for True Catholics," lines 42, 43–4, in *The Works of Sir William Mure of Rowallan*, 197–300.
24. Mure, "True Crucifix," line 55.
25. Mure, "True Crucifix," lines 279, 284.
26. Mure, "True Crucifix," lines 683–7. An *oblishment* is "a legally binding or contractual promise or undertaking" (*A Dictionary of the Older Scottish Tongue*).
27. Mure, "True Crucifix," line 33.
28. Mure, "True Crucifix," line 68.
29. Mure, "True Crucifix," line 22.
30. Mure, "True Crucifix," line 9.
31. Mure, "True Crucifix," side note, 198.
32. Simpson, *Under the Hammer*.
33. Pentcheva, *Sensual Icon*, 77.
34. Yoder, "Politics."
35. Yoder, *Politics of Jesus*, 95, 131.
36. Yoder, *Revolutionary Christianity*, 42.
37. Kempe, *Book of Margery Kempe*, 72.
38. Margery responds not just to the suffering of Christ but also to Christ's humanity, Mary's pity, and Mary's love for Christ. She seems, however, especially focused on Christ's suffering.
39. During Kempe's lifetime, the Wycliffites and the Lollards had their own iconoclasms that sometimes led them to attack crosses, but such cross iconoclasm was not widespread nor the cross so politicized as it would later become (Aston, "Cross and Crucifix," 253).
40. Kempe, *Book*, 103.
41. Bernard McGinn explores the extent and nature of the union of outer and inner sensation in five medieval mystics in "Late Medieval Mystics." Noting their internal differences, he claims that "there was an impetus during these times towards presenting an integrated notion of the mystical self that saw outer and inner aspects of sensation—feeling, desiring, perceiving, and knowing—as part of a continuum of conscious and progressive reception of divine gifts" (209).
42. Kempe, *Book*, 50.
43. Kempe, *Book*, 50.
44. Within the next couple of pages, Kempe describes this event graphically, declaring of herself:
    She had such very contemplation in the sight of her soul, as if Christ had hung before her bodily eye in his manhood. And, when through dispensation of the high mercy of

our sovereign savior Christ Jesus, it was granted this creature to behold so verily his precious tender body, completely rent and torn with scourges, more full of wounds than ever was a dove house of holes, hanging upon the cross with the crown of thorns upon his head, his blissful hands, his tender feet nailed to the hard tree, the rivers of blood flowing out plenteously from every member, the grisly and grievous wound in his precious side shedding out blood and water for her love and her salvation, then she fell down and cried with loud voice, wonderfully turning and twisting her body on every side, spreading her arms abroad, as if she should have died, and could not keep herself from crying out from these bodily movings, for the fire of love that burns so fervently in her soul with pure pity and compassion. (Kempe, *Book*, 51–2)

45. Kempe, *Book*, 50.
46. Kempe, *Book*, 52.
47. Kempe, *Book*, 129.
48. Ebner, *Revelations*, 85.
49. Ebner, *Revelations*, 96.
50. Ebner, *Revelations*, 96.
51. Ebner, in fact, also describes perceiving a "sweetness" in drinking from the chalice (*Revelations*, 91).
52. Ebner, *Revelations*, 96.
53. Ebner, *Revelations*, 95.
54. As Amy Hollywood writes, in "Practice, Belief, and Feminist Philosophy of Religion": "Ebner explicitly articulates the way in which her intense meditation on Christ's Passion leads to her inability not to see, hear, and feel Christ's Passion and ultimately to experience it in and on her own body. The process begins with a conscious concentration of Ebner's energies on visual representations of Christ's suffering" (62).
55. Ebner, *Revelations*, 116.
56. Ebner, *Revelations*, 90.
57. Amy Hollywood describes the transformation as being from "a lone, ill woman mourning the loss of her fellow sister and caretaker" to "a woman thoroughly identified with Christ's salvific suffering" ("Acute Melancholia," 400).
58. Kempe, *Book*, 18.
59. Ebner, *Revelations*, 148–9.
60. Ebner, *Revelations*, 149.
61. Rowan Williams uses this phrase as he explores the world as cross-saturated, as *signa* of the *res* of God, in "Language, Reality, and Desire," a classic and brilliant reading of Augustine's *De Doctrina Christiana*.
62. Stories that turn on the violent restoration of order are unfortunately common in the corpus of hagiographies about female saints. These stories often tell of a vulnerable, beautiful, and frequently intelligent or gifted woman (who is usually also socially privileged) who desires to commit to a life of holy virginity. A lascivious man attempts to wrest her from that vocation, is thwarted, kills her, and meets a violent fate himself in the killing. See, for example, the story of St. Katherine and her wheel, intended to torture her, but by divine hand exploding to kill a thousand heathen. There is also the story

of St. Agnes, in which men who tried to touch her were blinded or killed. These and other stories are featured in Osbern Bokenham's fifteenth-century *Legendys of Hooly Wummen* and Jacobus Voragine's thirteenth-century *Legenda Aurea*.

63. One of the places the phrase "with the grain of the universe" shows up in Yoder's corpus is, ironically, just before his call to renew Mosaic iconoclasm (Yoder, "Politics," 179).

64. Yoder, *Christian Attitudes to War*, 134.

65. Ratzinger, *Spirit of the Liturgy*. Ratzinger's writings on the sign are an important source for this paragraph and the following one.

66. Quoted in Ratzinger, *Spirit of the Liturgy*, 182.

67. Augustine makes this point in many places; see, for example, Schaff, *St. Augustine*, Tractate 118.5.

68. Donne, "The Cross," lines 1–2.

69. Donne, "The Cross," lines 11–2.

70. Donne, "The Cross," line 14.

71. Donne, "The Cross," lines 60–4.

72. Wiman, "Every Riven Thing"; see lines 1, 6, 11, 16, and 21.

73. Wiman, "Every Riven Thing," lines 1–3.

74. Wiman, "Every Riven Thing," lines 16–8.

75. Lydon, "Whose Words These Are."

76. Gregory of Nyssa, "An Address on Religious Instruction."

77. Father Maximos Constas (*The Art of Seeing*) makes a similar point as he reflects on the iconographic tradition and the way all the scenes in the life of Christ speak to the crucifixion: "Seen from this point of view, the Crucifixion is not simply another icon within a series of icons, but rather the matrix from which all icons emerge, the focal point on which their divergent forms converge" (105).

78. Quoted in Gutiérrez, *Las Casas*, 63.

79. Koerner, *Reformation of the Image*, 127.

80. Wiman, "Every Riven Thing," lines 11–6.

81. The first Cristo Negro dates back to 1595. Other early Cristo Negro images date back to the early seventeenth and eighteenth centuries.

82. I draw here on Sullivan-González, *The Black Christ of Esquipulas*, 7–11, 155–8. Sullivan-González quotes the official report: González de Flores and Carías Ortega, *Restauración en Esquipulas*.

83. Gutiérrez, *On Job*, xvi.

CHAPTER 4: ROSE AGAIN ON THE THIRD DAY

1. This point has been recently made by Rowan Williams (*Dwelling of the Light*, 23–4) and Paul Evdokimov (*Art of the Icon*, 325). There are exceptions. For example, the nineteenth-century Russian Menaion icon for the month of March depicts the resurrection as one of its many scenes. Some other multi-scene Russian icons feature the risen Christ holding a banner (a scene more familiar to Westerners). These, too, are post-medieval. Though some Byzantine icons attempted to show the resurrection through a

tomb exploding with light, these did not find a prominent place in the church and have largely fallen out of the tradition (Karstonis, *Anastasis*, 19–39).

2. Evdokimov translates this quotation from Epiphanius's homily on Holy Saturday in *The Art of the Icon*, 322.

3. Evdokimov, *Art of the Icon*, 190; Ratzinger, *Spirit of the Liturgy*, 116.

4. "[T]he same quality of Presence is inherent in every icon: Yahweh appears on the throne of mercy and speaks from it" (Evdokimov, *Art of the Icon*, 190).

5. I refer to him as Joseph Ratzinger in relation to his writings before he assumed the papacy, and as Pope Benedict XVI in relation to his acts and writings issued after that.

6. Ratzinger, *Spirit of the Liturgy*, 117.

7. Von Balthasar, *Mysterium Paschale*, 200.

8. Basil began using the word *prosopon* for the Trinity, qualifying it with *teleios*, "perfect" or "complete" (Turcescu, "'Person' Versus 'Individual'").

9. Turcescu, "*Prosōpon* and *Hypostasis* in Basil." For *prosopon* and *hypostasis* in Gregory of Nyssa, see Turcescu, "'Person' Versus 'Individual.'" The Metropolitan of Nafpaktos Hierotheos has a nice overview of the use of *hypostasis* and *prosopon* in *The Person in the Orthodox Tradition*, as does Gerald O'Collins in *The Tri-Personal God*. See also "Prosopon" in Astley, Brown, and Loades, *Christology: Key Readings*.

10. Lucian Turcescu dates Basil's shift in terminology to around the same time as the famine sermons (the shift occurred between 364 and 376; the famine sermons were delivered in 368–9). See Turcescu, "'Person' Versus 'Individual'" and "*Prosōpon* and *Hypostasis* in Basil."

11. In his "79th Homily on the Gospel of Matthew," St. John Chrysostom justifies the logic of Matthew 25:31–41 by explaining that baptism makes a person a brother (456). In his book *The Least of My Brothers*, tracing the history of the reception of the verse, Sherman Gray devotes most of his analysis of the patristic era's invocation of these verses to cataloguing when the passage is interpreted to refer universally to all poor and when specifically to the Christian poor.

12. Basil of Caesarea, "In Time of Famine and Drought," 190.

13. Gregory of Nyssa, "Love of the Poor, 1," 195.

14. Grillmeier, *Christ in Christian Tradition*, 126.

15. Like Theodore, John of Damascus emphasized the unity of image and prototype, but Theodore, unlike the Damascene, also underlined their difference, by distinguishing kinds of veneration—one for Christ himself and one for images of Christ. This second line of argument strains against the first and, ultimately, did not find its way into the thought of later Byzantine iconodules. For more on these arguments and their transformations, see Carnes, "How Love for the Image Cast Out Fear of It."

16. Evdokimov (*Art of the Icon*) makes this point: " to worship an icon, to adore it as though it were of the same nature as the person it represents would be to destroy it, for that would be to enclose a presence in the wooden board. It would be to make an idol and make the person represented absent" (200–1).

17. Jasper, *Sacred Body*, 22.

18. Jasper, *Sacred Body*, 30. Jasper is here drawing on the language of both Nikephoros and Jean-Luc Marion.
19. Evdokimov, *Art of the Icon*, 195.
20. Evdokimov, *Art of the Icon*, 87.
21. Lossky, *Image and Likeness of God*, 66. Leonid Ouspensky writes of the connection between iconography and the transfiguration:

> The light of the transfiguration on Mount Tabor is already the glory of the world to come. For the power which resurrects the saints after their death is the Holy Spirit. It is the Holy Spirit who, during the terrestrial life of the saints, vivifies not only their souls but also their bodies. This is why we say that the icon transmits not the everyday, banal face of man, but his glorious and eternal face. For the very meaning of the icon is precisely to depict the heirs of incorruptibility, the heirs of the Kingdom of God, of which they are the first-fruits from the time of their life here on earth. (*Theology of the Icon*, 166)

22. Florensky, *Iconostasis*, 64.
23. It is certainly true that the icon has no reality of its own. In itself, it is only a wooden board. The icon gets all its theophanic value from its participation in the Wholly Other; the icon is a mirror of the Wholly Other. It can therefore contain nothing in itself but becomes rather a grid, a structure through which the Other shines forth. The absence of three-dimensional volume in two-dimensional icons excludes all materialization. The icon thus expresses an energetic presence which is not localized nor enclosed but which shines out from a point of condensation. (Evdokimov, *Art of the Icon*, 179)
24. Theodore the Studite, *Holy Icons*, 33.
25. Florensky, *Iconostasis*, 61.
26. Florensky, *Iconostasis*, 60.
27. Ouspensky, *Theology of the Icon*, 162.
28. Florensky, *Iconostasis*, 65.
29. Drawing on the thought of Gregory Palamas, Father Maximos Constas expresses the way icons inhabit the visible and invisible realms: "These two worlds, the immanent and the transcendent, the visible and the invisible, are connected by a boundary that simultaneously separates and unites them. This boundary is symbolized architecturally by the icon screen, 'which manifests the distinction between the sensible and the intelligible, and is thus like a 'firmament' (Gen 1:6) marking the frontier between the intelligible reality and material phenomenon'" (*Art of Seeing*, 235).
30. Evdokimov, *Art of the Icon*, 179.
31. Evdokimov, *Art of the Icon*, 200–1.
32. In *Icons in Time, Persons in Eternity*, Cornelia Tsakiridou analyzes the aesthetics of specific icons, arguing for the importance of what she calls their *enargeia* (liveliness, vivacity) in a way that connects them to important streams in Zen art and Russian modernism. Distinct from *energeia*, which names God's activity and became an important concept in late ancient debates about Christ, *enargeia* speaks to the way some images "behave as facts or realities . . . rather than mental objects" (50). "Enargeia,"

Tsakiridou writes, "bring to an art object the dynamism implicit in hypostasis. . . . It 'asks' to be treated as a part of life rather than its detached copy" (7). Her impressive work is in many ways a corrective to twentieth-century theological approaches like that of Sergei Bulgakov—and many of the Russian theologians I engage in Chapter 4. Where they argue for the distinctiveness of icons, she argues for both distinctiveness and continuity.

33. Evdokimov, *Art of the Icon*, 199.

34. Those attentive to race and its dynamics will be familiar with this point, which is eloquently made in Ralph Ellison's 1952 novel *Invisible Man*.

35. These descriptions all come from Gregory of Nyssa, "Love of the Poor, 1," 195.

36. Gregory of Nyssa, "Love of the Poor, 2."

37. Gregory of Nyssa, "Love of the Poor, 2."

38. Gregory of Nazianzus, Oration 14.40, 97.

39. Coakley, "Identity of the Risen Jesus," 318.

40. Coakley, "Identity of the Risen Jesus," 307, 313, 319.

41. Gregory of Nyssa, "Love of the Poor, 1," 195.

42. Williams, *Resurrection*, 74.

43. Williams, *Resurrection*, 85.

44. Evdokimov, *Art of the Icon*, 211.

45. As Ouspensky writes, "Like the deification which it conveys, the icon suppresses nothing that is human: neither the psychological element, nor a person's various characteristics in the world. Thus the icon of a saint does not fail to indicate his occupation in the world" (*Theology of the Icon*, 181, 183–4).

46. Evdokimov, *Art of the Icon*, 87.

47. I am grateful to the monks at Holy Cross Monastery—Father Maximos, Father Silouan, and Father Parthenios—for pluralizing my understanding of these traditions.

48. Evdokimov, *Art of the Icon*, 206.

49. Lossky, "Saviour Acheiropoietos," 72.

50. Evdokimov, *Art of the Icon*, 199. Note that the word *man* is often used to mean *humanity*. I won't note all the instances, but I hope the reader will understand that these modern writers mean *humanity* when they use *man*.

51. Christ's resurrected body is described so in Mark 14:58, John 2:21, and 2 Corinthians 5:1. Thomas de Wesselow argues, in *The Sign*, that the resurrection appearances of Christ were actually appearances of the Shroud.

52. John Paul II, Address, Pastoral Visit.

53. Benedict XVI, "Veneration of the Holy Shroud."

54. Benedict XVI, "Veneration of the Holy Shroud."

55. Francis, "Exposition of the Holy Shroud."

56. The other thread of this story involves a prior sign for Juan Diego: the sickness and miraculous healing of his uncle, Juan Bernadino. This story was first published by Miguel Sanchez in 1648 in his *Image of the Virgin Mary, Mother of Guadalupe. Miraculously Appeared in the City of Mexico. Celebrated in her History, with the prophecy of Chapter Twelve of the Apocalypse*. I follow here D. A. Brading's retelling in *Mexican Phoenix*.

57. John Paul II, translated by and quoted in Brading, *Mexican Phoenix*, 340.

58. There is another, darker layer to this story. Devotion to the Virgin of Guadalupe physically and spiritually supplants devotion to the indigenous god Tonantzin, the mother of the gods. The altar to Tonantzin is razed and devotion to the mother of gods ceases, but in the death of this piety a new piety is raised: the devotion to the Mother of God, whose chapel stands where Tonantzin's altar once stood. Nearby is a chapel that testifies to the traces of this death: the "chapel of the Indians." It recognizes the people who offered up their devotion to Tonantzin, suffered that devotion's death, and received it back as devotion to Mary, who comes as one of their own. The image thus testifies to its deep roots in the resurrection: we die like the mother of the gods to be raised like the God whose Mother witnesses to this rising. The history of the players here is complex, and I do not glorify, condone, or praise the conquistadors for destroying Tonantzin's temple, any more than I would praise those who crucified Christ. I mean instead to note the way God raises Aztec piety to new life, and the way the people received the new life of their piety in their miraculously quick conversion to the Roman Catholic Church. For their part, the Franciscans—the original custodians of the chapel to Guadalupe—vocally worried about the purity of the devotion, so their custodianship passed on to the Dominicans, who defended veneration of the Virgin of Guadalupe (Brading, *Mexican Phoenix*, 1–5).

59. Francis, "Message to the Americas."

60. The history of this mandylion of Edessa seems to intertwine at moments with the histories of both the Veil of Veronica and the Shroud of Turin, and it is thought that the stories of the Veil and of the Image of Edessa share a common source.

61. Other Scriptural references commonly given are Isaiah 52:14, Isaiah 53:2–3, Psalm 27:8–9, John 14:9, and Matthew 5:8.

62. Ratzinger, "Way of the Cross at the Colosseum."

63. Ratzinger, *Spirit of the Liturgy*, 123.

64. Ouspenksy, *Theology of the Icon*, 181.

65. Ratzinger, *Spirit of the Liturgy*, 133. Evdokimov makes a similar point: "To contemplate the icon, we must have an ascetical conditioning, the liturgical fine tuning of purified senses, and the creative elevation of the spirit" (*Art of the Icon*, 197).

66. Ratzinger, *Spirit of the Liturgy*, 133.

67. Ratzinger, *Spirit of the Liturgy*, 121–2.

68. Ratzinger, *Spirit of the Liturgy*, 123.

69. Ratzinger, *Spirit of the Liturgy*, 122.

70. Ratzinger, *Spirit of the Liturgy*, 122.

71. Evdokimov, *Art of the Icon*, 76.

72. Evdokimov, *Art of the Icon*, 77.

73. Evdokimov, *Art of the Icon*, 77.

74. Lossky, *Image and Likeness of God*, 168.

75. There are many kinds of images, just as there are many iconoclasms and negations. I understand this mapping out of the relationship of icons to other resurrection images and to images more broadly to support the argument made by many Orthodox theologians for icons as a distinct and privileged class of Christian images—even as I

moderate the stronger version of this claim that dismisses all other attempts at Christian imaging. There are both important continuities and important differences between icons and traditional Western art, not least of which is that while icons also have ways of expressing internal negation, some of these ways are unique to their iconic form. They have their own forms of negation, which hearken distinctively to the breaking of the resurrection.

CHAPTER 5: WILL COME AGAIN IN GLORY

1. Marion, *Crossing of the Visible*, 58.
2. Marion, *Crossing of the Visible*, 65.
3. Two recent books testify to and explore modern anxieties about images: Ellenbogen and Tugendhaft, *Idol Anxiety*; and Simpson, *Under the Hammer*.
4. One reason for framing this iconoclasm with Francis Bacon is that Mitchell himself claims Bacon's idols of the mind as "a foundational trope for subsequent attempts to stage criticism itself as an iconoclastic practice" (Mitchell, *What Do Pictures Want?*, 90). He then returns to Bacon as significant for iconoclasm in his essay "Idolatry: Nietzsche, Blake, Poussin."
5. In *The New Organon*, Bacon describes four types of idols of the mind: idols of the tribe (from limits of the senses), idols of the cave (from limits of an individual's experiences), idols of the marketplace (from limits of language), and idols of the theater (from human-made philosophies) (48–9).
6. Many of the iconoclasms discussed in Chapter 3 and related to the Reformation project of eradicating or unmasking superstitions are Baconian iconoclasms.
7. Wittgenstein, *Philosophical Investigations*, 98.
8. Mitchell, *Picture Theory*, 12, 49. In this text, Mitchell also describes Wittgenstein's iconophobia, turning to Charles Altieri who writes, in an October 1992 private correspondence with Mitchell, "that the 'anxiety' here lies in Wittgenstein's realization that 'analytic philosophy was itself based on a radically pictorial notion of self-evidence and representability'" (13, n2).
9. In the preface to his *Philosophical Investigations*, Wittgenstein says, "The philosophical remarks in this book are, as it were, a number of sketches of landscapes . . ." He pursues the metaphor of sketching until he writes, "So this book is really just an album" (4).
10. Wittgenstein's strategy with Augustine contrasts with his response to what he perceives Sir James George Frazer doing in *The Golden Bough*, a work that unmasks in religions a universal impulse to reckon with death. Robert Orsi's discussion of Wittgenstein's reading of *The Golden Bough* helped me to see that what Wittgenstein chafes against in Frazer is the way he strives to translate religious practices into his own idiom—to claim that x is really y: "How impossible of him to understand a different way of life from the English one of his time!" (see Orsi, *History and Presence*, 63–4; Orsi quotes Wittgenstein's remark from Wittgenstein, *Remarks on Frazer's Golden Bough*, 5e). Wittgenstein, by contrast, wants to resist unmasking the strange as the familiar. He wants to avoid, that is, a kind of Baconian iconoclasm.

11. Of course, in practice, it is difficult to distinguish responding to falsity from responding to truthfulness. Pseudo-Dionysius, for example, finds Scripture referring to God as a drunkard. This sounds straightforwardly false, but for Pseudo-Dionysius, it is true, just less true than referring to God as light and life and love. So he emplaces it in a way of properly affirming and denying aspects of God—a strategy very like Wittgensteinian iconoclasm. The claim that God is a drunkard is found in his *Divine Names*; the strategy of affirmation and negation is found in his *Mystical Theology* (see *Pseudo-Dionysius: The Complete Works*).

12. Mitchell, *What Do Pictures Want?* Mitchell does not differentiate between images and pictures, as I do in the Preface to this book. What he calls a picture is, by and large, what I would identify as being at the intersection of image and picture—a type of visual sign.

13. Mitchell, *What Do Pictures Want?*, 7.

14. Examples of the consternation at and applause for the circulations and circumscriptions of images abound: the Corcoran Gallery's cancellation of the exhibition of Robert Mapplethorpe's *X Portfolio*; France's right of image law; the Danish cartoon controversy and the debates over the *Charlie Hebdo* illustrations; the American debates over displays of the Ten Commandments near statehouses; the restrictions on *hijabs*, large crosses, and yarmulkes in public spaces in France, and so forth.

15. Mitchell develops the approach of interrogating the desire of the picture in *What Do Pictures Want?*, 10.

16. Mitchell, *What Do Pictures Want?*, 67.

17. Mitchell, "Idolatry," 67; Neer, "Poussin and the Ethics of Imitation," 317.

18. Neer, "Poussin and the Ethics of Imitation," 317.

19. Neer, "Poussin and the Ethics of Imitation," 340.

20. Mitchell, *What Do Pictures Want?*, 70.

21. Mitchell, *What Do Pictures Want?*, 67; quoting Nietzsche, *Thus Spake Zarathustra*, 317.

22. Mitchell, *What Do Pictures Want?*, 70.

23. William Blake, "To Nobodaddy," in *The Complete Poetry and Prose of William Blake*, 471.

24. William Blake, "Let the Brothels of Paris Be Opened," in *The Complete Poetry and Prose of William Blake*, 499.

25. In fact, Blake also painted his own scene of the golden calf, *Moses Indignant at the Golden Calf* (1799–1800), now on display at the Tate Gallery in London. Presenting Moses's horror at the idolatrous scene, Blake depicts the moment just after the breaking of the tablets, which lie in fragments at Moses's feet.

26. Mitchell, *What Do Pictures Want?*, 72.

27. Mitchell, "Idolatry," 72.

28. Mitchell, "Idolatry," 73.

29. Zarathustra's iconoclasm is a Baconian iconoclasm—at least early in Nietzsche's text—and it is interesting to watch Mitchell subsume such iconoclasm into Wittgensteinian iconoclasm.

30. It is interesting to consider the irony of Poussin's painting as an image about the danger of images together with the tendency of art historians to, in Richard Neer's estimation, decode Poussin in terms of literary allusions and claim him as the most literary of painters. It is as if, for Neer, Poussin is often interpreted as a painter whose images elevate words about images (Neer, "Poussin and the Ethics of Imitation," 297).

31. Mitchell, *What Do Pictures Want?*, 11.
32. Mitchell, *What Do Pictures Want?*, 87–9.
33. Latour, *Modern Cult of the Factish Gods*, 86.
34. Latour, *Modern Cult of the Factish Gods*, 84.
35. Latour, *Modern Cult of the Factish Gods*, 115.
36. Latour, *Modern Cult of the Factish Gods*, 122.
37. Latour, *Modern Cult of the Factish Gods*, 122.
38. Latour, *Modern Cult of the Factish Gods*, 85.
39. Jesus is reported to have had said something like this in three of the Gospels. Only in Mark (14:58) is the word "acheiropoietic" added and contrasted with the human-made Temple, and only in John (2:19) does Jesus say these words at the scene of the Temple cleansing.
40. Marion, *Crossing of the Visible*, 65.
41. Paul Claudel (1868–1955) was a French poet, dramatist, and diplomat whose writings influenced Hans Urs von Balthasar and Jean-Louis Chrétien, among others. He writes about water throughout his *oeuvre*. I follow Jean-Louis Chrétien's discussion of Claudel in "Like a Liquid Bond."
42. Gregory of Nyssa, *Life of Moses*, 95.
43. Gregory of Nyssa, *Life of Moses*, 107.
44. Gregory of Nyssa, *Life of Moses*, 110.
45. Gregory of Nyssa, *Life of Moses*, 136.
46. Pseudo-Dionysius famously picks up on that phrase, also translated "dazzling darkness," in his *Mystical Theology*, which then funds an important stream of Western theological thought on the unknowability of God.
47. Gregory of Nyssa, *Life of Moses*, 95–6. Literally, into a comprehensive/comprehending phantasm (περιληπτική φαντασία).
48. Gregory of Nyssa, *Life of Moses*, 99.
49. Gregory of Nyssa, *Life of Moses*, 114.
50. Gregory of Nyssa, *Life of Moses*, 115, 116.
51. Gregory of Nyssa, *Life of Moses*, 114.
52. Gregory of Nyssa, *Life of Moses*, 114.
53. Jean-Louis Chrétien explores this theme at length in *The Call and the Response*.
54. Chrétien, *Hand to Hand*, 140. I explore this theme of wounding in the anthropology of Gregory of Nyssa in *Beauty*, ch. 4.
55. Chrétien, *Hand to Hand*, 139.
56. Chrétien, *Hand to Hand*, 139.
57. Chrétien, *Hand to Hand*, 140.
58. Gregory of Nyssa, *Life of Moses*, 124.

59. Gregory of Nyssa, *Life of Moses*, 124.

60. Idols can become images—a point Douglas Hedley makes when he describes Christians as transforming pagan idols rather than obliterating them (Hedley, *Iconic Imagination*, 151).

61. Marion, *Crossing of the Visible*, 65.

62. Bredekamp discusses this image in *Theorie des Bildakts*, 73–6.

63. Caroline Walker Bynum describes a similar phenomenon in the Christ cradle that is also a cathedral, described in the Introduction. Of it she writes, "That an object can simultaneously *be* (not merely signify) two objects—both bed and church—calls attention to the simultaneity of Christ's life stages" (*Christian Materiality*, 62).

64. Evdokimov, *Art of the Icon*, 69.

65. Evdokimov, *Art of the Icon*, 69.

66. Marie-José Mondzain's work seems especially attuned to negative image flows, and not as attentive to how the proliferation of images also proliferates new sources of authority in complex relation to institutional authority (see Mondzain, *Image, Icon, Economy*).

67. Gregory of Nyssa, *Life of Moses*, 135.

68. Gregory of Nyssa, *Life of Moses*, 135, 136.

69. Gregory of Nyssa, *Life of Moses*, 114.

70. Gregory of Nyssa, *Life of Moses*, 119.

CONCLUSION

1. Orsi, *History and Presence*, 25.

2. Presbyter Martinus, *Madonna as Sedes Sapientiae* from Borgo S. Sepolcro, 1199, now in the Staatliche Museen Preussischer Kulturbesitz in Berlin. Horst Bredekamp discussed this statue (along with the Dangolsheim Madonna, as mentioned in the Introduction), in a talk he gave to a SIAS workshop hosted by Wissenschaftskolleg, on July 18, 2014. The forbidding eyes may remind the reader of those that Flannery O'Connor's character O. E. Parker sees in the Byzantine Christ, which remind Parker of the icepick eyes of his wife, Sarah Ruth, as discussed in Chapter 2.

WORKS CITED

Anderson, Gary. "Redeem Your Sins by the Giving of Alms: Sin, Debt, and the 'Treasury of Merit' in Early Jewish and Christian Tradition." *Letter & Spirit* 3 (2007): 39–69.

Anderson, John Ward. "Cartoons of Prophet Met with Outrage." *Washington Post*, January 31, 2006. Accessed March 28, 2016, http://www.washingtonpost.com/wp-dyn/content/article/2006/01/30/AR2006013001316.html.

Andreopoulos, Andreas. *Gazing on God: Trinity, Church and Salvation in Orthodox Thought and Iconography*. Cambridge: James Clarke, 2013.

Anelli, Marco. *Portraits in the Presence of Marina Abramović*. Bologna: Damiani, 2012.

Asad, Talal. "Free Speech, Blasphemy, and Secular Criticism." In *Is Critique Secular?: Blasphemy, Injury, and Free Speech*, by Talal Asad, Wendy Brown, Judith Butler, and Saba Mahmood, 20–63. Berkeley: University of California Press, 2009.

Asad, Talal, Wendy Brown, Judith Butler, and Saba Mahmood. *Is Critique Secular?: Blasphemy, Injury, and Free Speech*. Berkeley: University of California Press, 2009.

Astley, Jeff, David Brown, and Ann Loades. *Christology: Key Readings in Christian Thought*. Louisville, KY: Westminster John Knox Press, 1999.

Aston, Margaret. "Cross and Crucifix in the English Reformation." *Historische Zeitschrift* 270:2 (2000): 253–72.

———. *England's Iconoclasts*. New York: Oxford University Press, 1988.

Bacon, Francis. *The New Organon*. Edited by Fulton H. Anderson. Indianapolis, IN: Bobbs Merrill, 1960 [1620].

Barber, Charles. *Contesting the Logic of Painting: Art and Understanding in Eleventh-Century Byzantium*. Boston: Brill, 2007.

———. *Figure and Likeness: On the Limits of Representation in Byzantine Iconoclasm*. Princeton, NJ: Princeton University Press, 2002.

Basil of Caesarea. "In Time of Famine and Drought." In *The Hungry Are Dying: Beggars and Bishops in Roman Cappadocia*, by Susan R. Holman, 183–92. New York: Oxford University Press, 2001.

Belting, Hans. *An Anthropology of Images: Picture, Medium, Body*. Princeton, NJ: Princeton University Press, 2011.

———. "Iconic Presence: Images in Religious Traditions." *Material Religion: The Journal of Art, Objects, and Belief* 12:2 (2016): 235–7.

———. *Likeness and Presence: A History of the Image Before the Era of Art*. Translated by Edmund Jephcott. Chicago: University of Chicago Press, 1994.

Benedict XVI. "Veneration of the Holy Shroud." Pastoral Visit to Turin, Italy, May 2, 2010. Accessed July 11, 2016, http://www.vatican.va/holy_father/benedict_xvi/speeches/2010/may/documents/hf_ben-xvi_spe_20100502_meditazione-torino_en.html.

Benson, Bruce Ellis. *Graven Ideologies: Nietzsche, Derrida & Marion on Modern Idolatry*. Downers Grove, IL: InterVarsity Press, 2002.

Biale, David. "The God with Breasts: El Shaddai in the Bible." *History of Religions* 21:3 (1982): 240–56.

Blake, William. *The Complete Poetry and Prose of William Blake*. Edited by David V. Erdman. New York: Random House, 1988 [1965].

Boss, Sarah Jane. *Empress and Handmaid*. New York: Cassell, 2000.

Brading, D. A. *Mexican Phoenix: Our Lady of Guadalupe: Image and Tradition Across Five Centuries*. Cambridge: Cambridge University Press, 2001.

Bredekamp, Horst. *Theorie des Bildakts*. 2nd ed. Berlin: Suhrkamp, 2013.

Bremmer, Jan. "Iconoclast, Iconoclastic, and Iconoclasm: Notes Toward a Genealogy." *Church History and Religious Culture* 88 (2008): 1–17.

Brown, Wendy. "Introduction." In *Is Critique Secular?: Blasphemy, Injury, and Free Speech*, by Talal Asad, Wendy Brown, Judith Butler, and Saba Mahmood, 7–19. Berkeley: University of California Press, 2009.

Brubaker, Leslie. *Inventing Byzantine Iconoclasm*. London: Bristol Classical Press, 2012.

Brubaker, Leslie, and John Haldon. *Byzantium in the Iconoclast Era, c. 680–850: A History*. Cambridge: Cambridge University Press, 2011.

Bynum, Caroline Walker. *Christian Materiality: An Essay on Religion in Late Medieval Europe*. New York: Zone Books, 2011.

Cabantous, Alain. *Blasphemy: Impious Speech in the West from the Seventeenth to the Nineteenth Century*. Translated by Eric Rauth. New York: Columbia University Press, 2002.

Carnes, Natalie. *Beauty: A Theological Engagement with Gregory of Nyssa*. Eugene, OR: Cascade Books, 2014.

———. "Embracing Beauty in a World of Affliction." *Republics of Letters: A Journal for the Study of Knowledge, Politics, and the Arts* 5:1 (2017): 1-14. Accessed May 17, 2016, http://arcade.stanford.edu/rofl/embracing-beauty-world-affliction.

———. "How Love for the Image Cast Out Fear of It in Early Christianity." *Religions* 8:20 (2017): 1–15. Accessed May 17, 2016, http://www.mdpi.com/2077-1444/8/2/20.

———. "Making, Breaking, Loving, and Hating Images: Prelude to a Theology of Iconoclasm." *Logos* 16:2 (2013): 15–32.

———. "A Reconsideration of Religious Authority in Christian Theology." *Heythrop Journal* 40 (2014): 467–80.

Cavell, Stanley. *Disowning Knowledge: Six Plays of Shakespeare*. New York: Cambridge University Press, 1987.

———. *Pursuits of Happiness: The Hollywood Comedy of Remarriage*. Cambridge, MA: Harvard University Press, 1981.

"Charlie Hebdo attack: Three Days of Terror." BBC News, January 14, 2015. Accessed March 28, 2016, http://www.bbc.com/news/world-europe-30708237.

Chrétien, Jean-Luc. *The Call and the Response*. Translated by Anne A. Davenport. New York: Fordham University Press, 2004.

———. *Hand to Hand: Listening to the Work of Art*. Translated by Stephen E. Lewis. New York: Fordham University Press, 2003.

———. "Like a Liquid Bond." In *Hand to Hand: Listening to the Work of Art*, translated by Stephen E. Lewis, 130–51. New York: Fordham University Press, 2003.

Chrisafis, Angelique. "Attack on 'Blasphemous' Art Work Fires Debate on Role of Religion in France." *The Guardian*, April 18, 2011. Accessed November 4, 2015, http://www.theguardian.com/world/2011/apr/18/andres-serrano-piss-christ-destroyed-christian-protesters.

Coakley, Sarah. "'Batter my heart . . . '?: On Sexuality, Spirituality, and the Doctrine of the Trinity." *Graven Images* 2 (1995): 74–83.

———. *God, Sexuality and the Self: An Essay "On the Trinity."* Cambridge: Cambridge University Press, 2013.

———. "The Identity of the Risen Jesus: Finding Jesus Christ in the Poor." In *Seeking the Identity of Jesus: A Pilgrimage*, edited by Beverly Roberts Gaventa and Richard B. Hays, 301–19. Grand Rapids, MI: Eerdmans, 2008.

———. "Living into the Mystery of the Holy Trinity: Trinity, Prayer, and Sexuality." *Anglican Theological Review* 80:2 (1998): 223–32.

Coetzee, J. M. "Lesson 5: The Humanities in Africa." In *Elizabeth Costello*, 116–55. New York: Penguin, 2003.

Coles, Robert. "The Doubtful Pilgrim." *New York Times*, June 8, 1997. Accessed September 4, 2015, https://www.nytimes.com/books/97/06/08/reviews/970608.08colest.html.

Constas, Fr. Maximos. *The Art of Seeing: Paradox and Perception in Orthodox Iconography*. Alhambra, CA: Sebastian Press, 2014.

Council of Trent. "On the Invocation, Veneration, and Relics of Saints, and on Sacred Images." In *The Canons and Decrees of the Sacred and Oecumenical Council of Trent*, edited and translated by J. Waterworth, 232–89. London: Dolman, 1848. Accessed July 8 2016, http://thesacredarts.org/newsite/knowledge-base/from-the-holy-see/105-the-council-of-trent-on-the-invocation-veneration-and-relics-of-saints-and-on-sacred-images-1563.

Covolo, Father Enrico dal. "I paradossi iconografici della *Madonna guerriera* e della *Vergine che allatta*: Lo sfondo teologico di una galleria d'immagini." *L'Osservatore Romano*, June 19, 2008, 4.

Cyril of Alexandria. "The Dispensation of the Incarnation." In *Cyril of Alexandria*, by Norman Russell, 160–7. New York: Routledge, 2000.

Danto, Arthur. "The Artworld." *Journal of Philosophy* 61:19 (1964): 571–84.

Danto, Arthur C. "Danger and Disturbation: The Art of Marina Abramović." In *Marina Abramović: The Artist is Present*, edited by Klaus Biesenbach, 28–36. New York: Museum of Modern Art, 2010.

———. "On Art, Action, and Meaning." *New York Times*, June 3, 2010. Accessed April 23, 2015, http://opinionator.blogs.nytimes.com/2010/06/03/on-art-action-and-meaning/.

———."Sitting with Marina." *New York Times*, May 23, 2010. Accessed April 23, 2015, http://opinionator.blogs.nytimes.com/2010/05/23/sitting-with-marina/.

Darnton, Robert. *The Forbidden Best-Sellers of Pre-Revolutionary France*. New York: W. W. Norton, 1995.

Dewey, Bradley R. "Walker Percy Talks About Kierkegaard: An Annotated Interview." *Journal of Religion* 54:3 (1974): 273–98.

A Dictionary of the Older Scottish Tongue (up to 1700). Accessed July 11, 2016, http://www.dsl.ac.uk/entry/dost/oblisment.

Dobuzinskis, Alex. "Nude Virgin Mary Cover Prompts Playboy Apology." *Reuters*, December 15, 2008. Accessed June 18, 2012, http://www.reuters.com/article/2008/12/15/us-playboy-idUSTRE4BE54F20081215.

Donne, John. "The Cross." In *The Poems of John Donne*, edited by E. K. Chambers. London: Lawrence & Bullen, 1896. Accessed April 25, 2013, http://www.bartleby.com/357/107.html.

Ebner, Margaret. *Revelations*. In *Margaret Ebner: Major Works*. Translated and edited by Leonard Patrick Hindsley, 85–172. New York: Paulist Press, 1993.

Elkins, James. *The Object Stares Back*. New York: Simon & Schuster, 1996.

Ellenbogen, Josh, and Aaron Tugendhaft, eds. *Idol Anxiety*. Stanford, CA: Stanford University Press, 2011.

Ephrem the Syrian. *Hymns on the Nativity*. Translated by Kathleen McVey. Mahwah, NJ: Paulist Press, 1989.

Evdokimov, Paul. *The Art of the Icon: A Theology of Beauty*. Translated by Fr. Steven Bigham. Redondo Beach, CA: Oakwood, 1972.

Florensky, Pavel. *Iconostasis*. Translated by Donald Sheehan and Olga Andrejev. Crestwood, NY: St. Vladimir's Seminary Press, 1996.

Francis. "Exposition of the Holy Shroud." Video Message, March 30, 2013. Accessed July 11, 2016, http://w2.vatican.va/content/francesco/en/messages/pont-messages/2013/documents/papa-francesco_20130330_videomessaggio-sindone.html

———. "Message to the Americas for the Feast of Our Lady of Guadalupe," December 11, 2013. Accessed July 11, 2016, http://www.news.va/en/news/pope-francis-sends-message-to-the-americas.

Freedberg, David. *The Power of Images: Studies in the History and Theory of Response*. Chicago: University of Chicago Press, 1989.

Fried, Michael. "Art and Objecthood." In *Art and Objecthood: Essays and Reviews*, 148–72. Chicago: University of Chicago Press, 1998.

Gerö, Stephen. "The Eucharistic Doctrine of the Byzantine Iconoclasts and Its Sources." *Byzantinische Zeitschrift* 68 (1975): 4–22.

Ghorashi, Hannah. "A Look at the Full Scope of ISIS's Destruction of World Heritage Sites." ARTNEWS, November 7, 2015. Accessed March 28, 2016, http://www.artnews.com/2015/11/07/isis-destruction-graphic/.

González de Flores, Aura Rosa, and Jorge Alberto Carías Ortega. *Restauración en Esquipulas*. Guatemala City: Instituto de Antropología e Historia, 1998.
Gray, Sherman. *The Least of My Brothers: Matthew 25:31–46: A History of Interpretation*. Atlanta, GA: Scholars Press, 1989.
Gregory of Nazianzus. Oration 14.40. In *Gregory of Nazianzus*, by Brian Daley. New York: Routledge, 2006.
Gregory of Nyssa. "An Address on Religious Instruction." In *Christology of the Later Fathers*, edited by Edward Rochie Hardy, 268–326. Louisville, KY: Westminster John Knox Press, 1954.
———. *The Life of Moses*. Translated by Everett Ferguson and Abraham Johannes Malherbe. New York: Paulist Press, 1978.
———. *The Life of Saint Macrina*. Translated by Kevin Corrigan. Toronto: Peregrina, 1998.
———. "On the Love of the Poor, 1: On Good Works." In *The Hungry Are Dying: Beggars and Bishops in Roman Cappadocia*, by Susan R. Holman, 195–9. New York: Oxford University Press, 2001.
———. "On the Love of the Poor, 2: On the Saying, 'Whoever Has Done It to One of These Has Done It to Me.'" In *The Hungry Are Dying: Beggars and Bishops in Roman Cappadocia*, by Susan R. Holman, 199–206. New York: Oxford University Press, 2001.
Grillmeier, Aloys. *Christ in Christian Tradition: From the Apostolic Age to Chalcedon (451)*. London: Mowbray, 1965.
Gutiérrez, Gustavo. *Las Casas: In Search of the Poor of Jesus Christ*. Maryknoll, NY: Orbis Books, 1993.
———. *On Job: God-talk and the Suffering of the Innocent*. Maryknoll, NY: Orbis Books, 1987.
Guyer, Paul. "History of Modern Aesthetics." In *The Oxford Handbook of Aesthetics*, edited by Jerrold Levinson, 23–60. New York: Oxford University Press, 2003.
Guyer, Paul. "The Origins of Modern Aesthetics: 1711–1735." In *The Blackwell Guide to Aesthetics*, edited by Peter Kivy, 15–44. Malden, MA: Blackwell, 2004.
Hart, David Bentley. "No Shadow of Turning": On Divine Impassibility." *Pro Ecclesia* 11:2 (2002): 183–206.
Hedley, Douglas. *The Iconic Imagination*. London: Bloomsbury, 2016.
Hickey, Dave. *The Invisible Dragon: Essays on Beauty*. Rev. and exp. ed. Chicago: University of Chicago Press, 2009.
Hollywood, Amy. "Acute Melancholia." *Harvard Theological Review* 99:4 (2006): 381–406.
———. "Practice, Belief, and Feminist Philosophy of Religion." In *Thinking Through Rituals: Philosophical Perspectives*, edited by Kevin Schilbrack, 52–71. New York: Routledge, 2004.
Hunt, Lynn. "Introduction." In *The Invention of Pornography: Obscenity and the Origins of Modernity, 1500–1800*, edited by Lynn Hunt, 9–45. New York: Zone Books, 1993.
Irenaeus. *Against Heresies*. Translated by Alexander Robert and William Rambaut. In

Ante-Nicene Fathers, Vol. 1, edited by Alexander Roberts, James Donaldson, and A. Cleveland Coxe. Buffalo, NY: Christian Literature Publishing, 1885. Edited and revised for New Advent by Kevin Knight. Accessed July 8, 2016, http://www.newadvent.org/fathers/0103.htm.

"The Islamic Veil Across Europe." BBC News, July 1, 2014. Accessed June 28, 2016, http://www.bbc.com/news/world-europe-13038095.

Jasper, David. *The Sacred Body: Asceticism in Religion, Literature, Art, and Culture*. Waco, TX: Baylor University Press, 2009.

Jenson, Robert W. "Christ-Dogma and Christ-Image (1963)." In *Theology as Revisionary Metaphysics: Essays on God and Creation*, edited by Stephen Wright, 171–80. Eugene, OR: Cascade, 2014.

John Chrysostom. "79th Homily on the Gospel of Matthew." In *St. Chrysostom: Homilies on Saint Matthew*, translated by George Prevost and revised by M. B. Riddle, 455–60. Grand Rapids, MI: Eerdmans, 1986.

John of Damascus. *Three Treatises on Divine Images*. Translated by Andrew Louth. Crestwood, NY: St. Vladimir's Seminary Press, 2003.

John Paul II. Address, Pastoral Visit to Vercelli and Turin, Italy, May 24, 1998. Accessed July 11, 2016, https://w2.vatican.va/content/john-paul-ii/en/speeches/1998/may/documents/hf_jp-ii_spe_19980524_sudario.html

———. "Art Must Not Violate the Right to Privacy." In *Theology of the Body: Human Love in the Divine Plan*. Boston: Pauline Books and Media, 1997.

Kahn, Paul W. *Putting Liberalism in Its Place*. Princeton, NJ: Princeton University Press, 2005.

Karlin-Hayter, Patricia. "Iconoclasm." In *The Oxford History of Byzantium*, edited by Cyril Mango. New York: Oxford University Press, 2002.

Karstonis, Anna. *Anastasis: The Making of an Image*. Princeton, NJ: Princeton University Press, 1986.

Kempe, Margery. *The Book of Margery Kempe*. Translated and edited by Lynn Staley. New York: W. W. Norton, 2001.

Kendrick, Walter. *The Secret Museum: Pornography in Modern Culture*. Berkeley: University of California Press, 1997.

Koerner, Joseph. "The Icon as Iconoclash." In *Iconoclash: Beyond the Image Wars in Science, Religion, and Art*, edited by Bruno Latour and Peter Weibel, 164–213. Cambridge, MA: MIT Press, 2002.

———. *The Reformation of the Image*. Chicago: University of Chicago Press, 2004.

Latour, Bruno. *On the Modern Cult of the Factish Gods*. Durham, NC: Duke University Press, 2010.

Lincoln, Bruce, and Anthony Yu. "A Reply to Jean-Luc Marion's 'After "Charlie Hebdo," Islam Must Critique Itself.'" *Sightings*, February 12, 2015. Accessed April 23, 2015, https://divinity.uchicago.edu/sightings/reply-jean-luc-marion's-"after-'charlie-hebdo'-islam-must-critique-itself"-bruce-lincoln.

Lossky, Vladimir. *In the Image and Likeness of God*. Edited by John H. Erickson and Thomas E. Bird. Crestwood, NY: St. Vladimir's Seminary Press, 2001.

———. "The Saviour Acheiropoietos." In *The Meaning of Icons*, by Leonid Ouspensky and Vladimir Lossky, 69–72. Crestwood, NY: St. Vladimir's Seminary Press, 1982.
Lyall, Sarah. "For Her Next Piece, a Performance Artist Will Build an Institute." *New York Times*, October 19, 2013. Accessed April 23, 2015, http://www.nytimes.com/2013/10/20/arts/design/marina-abramovic-is-putting-her-name-on-a-center-in-hudson-ny.html?_r=0.
Lydon, Christopher. "Whose Words These Are: Christian Wiman's 'Wound of Being.'" *Radio Open Source*, January 27, 2011. Accessed November 12, 2015, http://radioopensource.org/whose-words-these-are-christian-wimans-wound-of-being/.
Mahmood, Saba. "Religious Reason and Secular Affect: An Incommensurable Divide?" In *Is Critique Secular?: Blasphemy, Injury, and Free Speech*, by Talal Asad, Wendy Brown, Judith Butler, and Saba Mahmood, 64–90. Berkeley: University of California Press, 2009.
Manker, Rob. "*Time* Magazine Cover Photographer: Image Patterned After 'Madonna and Child.'" *Chicago Tribune*, May 11, 2012. Accessed June 19, 2012, http://articles.chicagotribune.com/2012-05-11/news/ct-talk-time-magazine-cover-0511-20120510_1_chicago-area-breastfeeding-coalition-breast-feeding-parental-rights.
"Marina Abramović made me cry." Accessed April 23, 2015, http://marinaabramovicmademecry.tumblr.com/.
Marion, Jean-Luc. "After the 'Charlie Hebdo' Massacre: Islam Must Open Itself to Critique." *Sightings*, January 29, 2015. Accessed April 23, 2015, https://divinity.uchicago.edu/sightings/after-charlie-hebdo-massacre-islam-must-open-itself-critique-jean-luc-marion.
———. *The Crossing of the Visible*. Translated by James K. A. Smith. Stanford, CA: Stanford University Press, 2004.
Marrati, Paola. "Childhood and Philosophy." *Modern Language Notes* 126:5 (2011): 954–61.
Marval, Pierre, trans. and ed. *Grégoire de Nysse: Vie de sainte Macrine*. Sources Chrétiennes, 178. Paris: Éditions du Cerf, 1971.
McGinn, Bernard. "Late Medieval Mystics." In *The Spiritual Senses: Perceiving God in Western Christianity*, edited by Sarah Coakley and Paul Gavrilyuk, 190–209. Cambridge: Cambridge University Press, 2011.
McGuckin, John. *Saint Cyril of Alexandria and the Christological Controversy: Its History, Theology and Texts*. Crestwood, NY: St. Vladimir's Seminary Press, 2004.
Metropolitan of Nafpaktos Hierotheos. *The Person in the Orthodox Tradition*. Translated by Esther Williams. Levadeia, Greece: Birth of the Theotokos Monastery, 1998.
Miles, Margaret. *A Complex Delight: The Secularization of the Breast, 1350–1750*. Berkeley: University of California Press, 2008.
———. "God's Love, Mother's Milk: An Image of Salvation." *Christian Century* 125:2 (2008): 21–25.
Miller, Perry. *Jonathan Edwards*. 1949. Reprint, New York: W. Sloane Associates, 1959.
Mitchell, W.J.T. "Idolatry: Nietzsche, Blake, Poussin." In *Idol Anxiety*, edited by Josh

Ellenbogen and Aaron Tugendhaft, 56–73. Stanford, CA: Stanford University Press, 2011.

———. *Picture Theory: Essays on Verbal and Visual Representation*. Chicago: University of Chicago Press, 1994.

———. *What Do Pictures Want?: The Lives and Loves of Images*. Chicago: University of Chicago Press, 2005.

Mochizuki, Mia. *The Netherlandish Image After Iconoclasm, 1566–1672: Material Religion in the Dutch Golden Age*. Burlington, VT: Ashgate, 2008.

Mogutin, Slava. "The Legend of Marina Abramović." *Whitewall*, Summer, 2010. Also available at http://slavamogutin.com/marina-abramovic/.

Mondzain, Marie-José. *Image, Icon, Economy: The Byzantine Origins of the Contemporary Imaginary*. Translated by Rico Franses. Stanford, CA: Stanford University Press, 2005.

Moxey, Keith. "Visual Studies and the Iconic Turn." *Journal of Visual Culture* 7:2 (2008): 131–46.

Mure, William. *The Works of Sir William Mure of Rowallan*, Vol. 1. Edited and with notes by William Tough. Edinburgh: William Blackwood and Sons, 1898.

Neer, Richard. "Poussin and the Ethics of Imitation." *Memoirs of the American Academy in Rome* 51–2 (2006/2007): 298–344.

Nietzsche, Friedrich. *Thus Spake Zarathustra*. In *The Portable Nietzsche*, edited by Walter Kaufmann. New York: Viking Press, 1954.

O'Collins, Gerald. *The Tri-Personal God: Understanding and Interpreting the Trinity*. Mahwah, NJ: Paulist Press, 1999.

O'Connor, Flannery. "Parker's Back." In *Flannery O'Connor: Collected Works*, 655–75. New York: Library of America, 1988.

O'Hagan, Sean. "Interview: Marina Abramović." *The Guardian*, October 2, 2010. Accessed April 23, 2015, http://www.theguardian.com/artanddesign/2010/oct/03/interview-marina-abramovic-performance-artist.

Orsi, Robert. *History and Presence*. Cambridge, MA: Belknap Press, 2016.

Ouspensky, Léonide. *The Theology of the Icon*. Translated by Anthony Gythiel and Elizabeth Meyendorff. Crestwood, NY: St. Vladimir's Seminary Press, 1996.

Overmyer, Sheryl. "Three More Jigs in the Puzzle: The Unity of Analogy, Beatitude and Virtue in Thomas' *Summa Theologiae*." *International Journal of Systematic Theology* 15:4 (2013): 374–93.

Peel, Albert, ed. *The Seconde Parte of a Register*, 2 vols. Cambridge: Cambridge University Press, 1915.

Peers, Glenn, ed. *Byzantine Things in the World*. New Haven, CT: Yale University Press, 2013.

Pelikan, Jaroslav. *The Spirit of Eastern Christendom (600–1700)*, Vol. 2. Chicago: University of Chicago Press, 1974.

Pentcheva, Bissera. *The Sensual Icon: Space, Ritual, and the Senses in Byzantium*. University Park: Pennsylvania State University Press, 2010.

Percy, Walker. "The Holiness of the Ordinary." In *Signposts in a Strange Land*, edited by Patrick H. Samway, 368–70. New York: Farrar, Straus and Giroux, 1991.

———. *Love in the Ruins*. 2nd ed. New York: Picador, 1999.
———. *The Moviegoer*. New York: Knopf, 1961.
Powell, Derek. "Pope Francis and the Beautiful Iconoclasm of Washing the Wrong Feet." *Huffington Post*, April 11, 2013. Accessed March 29, 2016, http://www.huffingtonpost.com/derek-penwell/pope-francis-and-the-beautiful-iconoclasm-of-washing-the-wrong-feet_b_3055325.html.
Pseudo-Dionysius. *Pseudo-Dionysius: The Complete Works*. Translated by Colm Luibhéid. Mahwah, NJ: Paulist Press, 1987.
Ratzinger, Cardinal Joseph. "Way of the Cross at the Colosseum." Meditations and Prayers, Good Friday 2005. Accessed July 11, 2016, http://www.vatican.va/news_services/liturgy/2005/documents/ns_lit_doc_20050325_via-crucis_en.html.
———. *Spirit of the Liturgy*. Translated by John Saward. San Francisco: Ignatius Press, 2000.
Ross, James Bruce. "The Middle-Class Child in Urban Italy, Fourteenth to Early Sixteenth Century." In *The History of Childhood*, edited by Lloyd DeMause, 183–228. Northvale, NJ: Aronson, 1995.
Russell, Norman. *Cyril of Alexandria*. New York: Routledge, 2000.
Sahas, Daniel J. *Icon and Logos: Sources in Eighth Century Iconoclasm: An Annotated Translation of the Sixth Session of the Seventh Ecumenical Council (Nicea, 787)*. Toronto: University of Toronto Press, 1986.
Scaraffia, Lucetta. "Quelle Marie troppo umane censurate dall'età moderna." *L'Osservatore Romano*, June 19, 2008, 4.
Schaff, Philip, ed. *St. Augustine: Homilies on the Gospel of John; Homilies on the First Epistle of John; Soliloquies*. Edinburgh: T&T Clark, 1888. Accessed July 8, 2016, http://www.ccel.org/ccel/schaff/npnf107.iii.lxxvi.html.
Serrano, Andres. "Protecting Freedom of Expression, from Piss Christ to Charlie Hebdo." *Creative Time Reports*, January 30, 2015. Accessed July 11, 2016, http://creativetimereports.org/2015/01/30/free-speech-piss-christ-charlie-hebdo-andres-serrano/.
Shiner, Larry. *The Invention of Art: A Cultural History*. Chicago: University of Chicago Press, 2001.
Simpson, James. *Under the Hammer: Iconoclasm in the Anglo-American Tradition*. New York: Oxford University Press, 2010.
Skalova, Zuzana. "The Icon of the Virgin Galaktotrophousa in the Coptic Monastery of St. Antony the Great at the Red Sea, Egypt: A Preliminary Note." In *East and West in the Crusader States: Context, Contacts, Confrontations III: Acts of the Congress Held at Hernen Castle in September 2000*, edited by Krijnie Nelly Ciggaar and Herman G. B. Teule, 235–64. Leuven: Peeters, 2003.
Smith, J. Warren. "Suffering Impassibly: Christ's Passion in Cyril of Alexandria's Soteriology." *Pro Ecclesia* 11:4 (2002): 463–83.
Soskice, Janet Martin. *The Kindness of God: Metaphor, Gender, and Religious Language*. New York: Oxford University Press, 2007.
Steinberg, Leo. *The Sexuality of Christ in Renaissance Art and in Modern Oblivion*. New York: Pantheon Books, 1983.

Steiner, George. *Real Presences*. Chicago: University of Chicago Press, 1989.
Sullivan-González, Douglass. *The Black Christ of Esquipulas: Religion and Identity in Guatemala*. Lincoln: University of Nebraska Press, 2016.
Sun, Feifei. "Behind the Cover: Are You Mom Enough?" *Time*: Lightbox, May 10, 2012. Accessed May 14, 2012, http://lightbox.time.com/2012/05/10/parenting/#1.
Theodore the Studite. *On the Holy Icons*. Translated by Catharine P. Roth. Crestwood, NY: St. Vladimir's Seminary Press, 1981.
Time. Front cover. May 21, 2012. Accessed July 8, 2016, http://content.time.com/time/covers/0,16641,20120521,00.html.
Tolson, Jay. *Pilgrim in the Ruins: A Life of Walker Percy*. New York: Simon & Schuster, 1992.
Tsakiridou, Cornelia. *Icons in Time, Persons in Eternity: Orthodox Theology and the Aesthetics of the Christian Image*. Burlington, VT: Ashgate, 2012.
Turcescu, Lucian. "'Person' versus 'Individual,' and Other Modern Misreadings of Gregory of Nyssa." *Modern Theology* 18:4 (2002): 527–39.
———. "*Prosōpon* and *Hypostasis* in Basil of Caesarea's 'Against Eunomius' and the Epistles." *Vigiliae Christianae* 51:4 (1997): 374–95.
von Balthasar, Hans Urs. *Mysterium Paschale: The Mystery of Easter*. Translated by Aidan Nichols. San Francisco: Ignatius Press, 1990.
von Balthasar, Hans Urs. *You Have Words of Eternal Life*. San Francisco: Ignatius Press, 1991.
Wesselow, Thomas de. *The Sign: The Shroud of Turin and the Secret of the Resurrection*. New York: Dutton, 2012.
West, Christopher. *Theology of the Body Explained: A Commentary on John Paul II's "Gospel of the Body."* Boston: Pauline Books, 2003.
Wiesing, Lambert, ed. *Artificial Presence: Philosophical Studies in Image Theory*. Translated by Nils F. Schott. Stanford: Stanford University Press, 2009.
Williams, Rowan. *The Dwelling of the Light: Praying with Icons of Christ*. Grand Rapids, MI: Eerdmans, 2003.
———. *The Edge of Words: God and the Habits of Language*. London: Bloomsbury Academic, 2014.
———. "Language, Reality, and Desire in Augustine's *De Doctrina*." *Journal of Literature and Theology* 3:2 (1989): 138–50.
———. *Ponder These Things: Praying with Icons of the Virgin*. Franklin, WI: Sheed & Ward, 2002.
———. *Resurrection: Interpreting the Easter Gospel*. London: Darton, Longman & Todd, 1982.
Wiman, Christian. "Every Riven Thing." In *Every Riven Thing*. New York: Farrar, Straus and Giroux, 2010.
Wittgenstein, Ludwig. *Philosophical Investigations*. 4th ed. rev. The German text with an English translation by G.E.M. Anscombe, P.M.S. Hacker, and Joachim Schulte. Malden, MA: Wiley-Blackwell, 2009.
———. *Remarks on Frazer's Golden Bough*. Revised and edited by Rush Rhees. Trans-

lated by A. C. Miles. 1979. Reprint, Atlantic Highlands, NJ: Humanities Press International, 1991.

Wolterstorff, Nicholas. "Would You Stomp on a Picture of Your Mother? Would you Kiss an Icon?" *Faith and Philosophy* 32:1 (2015): 3–24.

Wood, Christopher S. "Iconoclasts and Iconophiles: Horst Bredekamp in Conversation with Christopher S. Wood." *Art Bulletin* 94:4 (2012): 515–27.

Wood, Ralph C. *The Comedy of Redemption: Christian Faith and Comic Vision in Four American Novelists*. Notre Dame, IN: University of Notre Dame Press, 1988.

Yalom, Marilyn. *History of the Breast*. New York: Knopf, 1997.

Yoder, John Howard. *Christian Attitudes to War, Peace, and Revolution*. Edited by Theodore J. Koontz and Andy Alexis-Baker. Grand Rapids, MI: Brazos Press, 2009.

———. "Politics: Liberating Images of Christ." In *The War of the Lamb: The Ethics of Nonviolence and Peacemaking*, edited by Glen Stassen, Mark Thiessen Nation, and Matt Hamsher, 165–80. Grand Rapids, MI: Brazos Press, 2009.

———. *The Politics of Jesus: Vicit Agnus Noster*. 2nd ed. Grand Rapids, MI: Eerdmans, 1994.

———. *Revolutionary Christianity: The 1966 South American Lectures*. Edited by Paul Martens, Mark Thiessen Nation, Matthew Porter, and Myles Werntz. Eugene, OR: Cascade Books, 2012.

Zwingli, Ulrich. *Huldreich Zwinglis Sämtliche Werke*, Vol. 4. Edited by Emil Egli and Georg Finsler. Berlin: C. A. Schwetschke und Sohn, 1905.

INDEX

Acheiropoieta, 124, 137–144, 147–149, 151, 165, 167, 170, 214n39
Aesthetics, 2, 42, 44–45, 160, 190
Abramović, Marina, ix–x, xii
Amphibiousness, 58, 75, 82–85
Andrejev, Vladislav, 120, 122
Andreyev, Dmitri, 185–187
Apophaticism, 8, 58, 76–78, 80–81, 83, 85, 178
Aquinas, Thomas, 82
Arianism, 31, 59, 72–73, 84
Art, ix–xii, 1–2, 4–5, 8, 14, 40–45, 153, 183, 186, 199n75; fine arts, 42; beaux arts, 42; pedagogy of museum, 41–43
Asad, Talal, 11, 37–40, 42
Augustine, 78, 113, 157

Bacon, Francis, 14, 156–158, 160, 162–163, 165–168, 170, 172, 174–176, 212n4, 212n5
Balthasar, Hans Urs von, 3, 123
Basil of Caesarea, 124, 126–127, 142
Belting, Hans, xii, 60, 189n11
Benedict XVI (Joseph Ratzinger), 3, 112, 123, 141, 144–146, 148
Blake, William, 159–161, 168, 213n25
Boehm, Gottfried, 60, 189n11
Breast, 19–23, 25, 46, 116; cultural meanings of, 27–30, 42, 48–49, 196n27; desire and, 27–28; Macrina and, 25–27, 51–52; Mary and, 33–34, 47–48, 54–55, 195n2
Bredekamp, Horst, xi–xii, 3, 7, 60

Bynum, Caroline Walker, 8, 192n21, 215n63

Caravaggio, Michelangelo Merisi da, 25
Caritas romana, 25
Catholicism, 3, 15, 20, 58, 82, 88, 91, 140, 153, 181
Cavell, Stanley, 34–36, 72–73
Chalke Gate, 96, 204n16
Charlie Hebdo, 1, 10–12, 193n36, 213n14
Cheapside Cross, 97
Chrétien, Jean-Luc, 171, 197n41
Christ: crucifixion of, xii, 87–89, 91, 95–96, 98–99, 102–103, 105–106, 112–113, 116, 119, 137, 185; desire, 13–14, 22–23, 25, 27, 33–36, 47–49, 51–55, 154–155, 172–175, 177–179, 183; humanity and divinity, 13–14, 30–34, 48–49, 53, 55, 58–61, 72, 74–75, 78, 82, 84–85, 116, 147, 183; icon and, 59–61, 94, 96, 120, 122, 128, 130–132, 138–139, 145, 183, 185; image of, xii, 12–16, 27, 59, 99, 103, 122, 128, 137, 172–179, 183, 185, 187; imitation of, 100–104, 107–108, 110–111, 125; "least of these" and, 14, 124–125, 127–128, 132–137, 139, 143–144, 149–150, 171; negation and revelation, 7, 13, 15, 52–55, 58, 91, 183–185, 194n42; Nestorianism and, 30–34, 59, 72
Claudel, Paul, 168–169, 171, 214n41
Coakley, Sarah, 135, 196n29, 199n77
Coetzee, J. M., 20–25, 32, 46–48, 50–52, 195n8

Confession, 64, 77, 79–81, 84–85, 148
Constas, Father Maximos, 61, 192n19, 207n77, 209n29
Correggio, Antonio da, 19–20, 21, 48, 50–51
Council of Trent, 20, 28, 41, 50
Credi, Lorenzo di, 18–19, 47–48
Cristo Negro, 14, 118–119, 207n81
Cross, 33–34, 49, 61, 88–89, 100, 109–110, 143–145, 171, 182; absence and presence, 88–92, 116, 182; cosmic, 92, 112–113, 206n61; divine love and, 89, 98–99, 116; idol and, 97–98, 100, 109, 113; image of, 87–88, 96–98, 101–102, 104–106, 109, 111, 173, 205n39; image of iconoclasm, 91–96, 112, 114, 117; Paul and, 95–96; poetry and, 113–115; "spiritual," 114–115
Cyril, 32–33, 49

Danish cartoon controversy, 1, 37–38, 184, 213n14
Danto, Arthur, ix–xii, 199n75
Desire (*eros*): Christ and, 13–14, 22–23, 25, 27, 33–36, 47–49, 51–55, 154–155, 172–175, 177–179, 183; Gregory of Nyssa and, 168–178; human and divine, 29–30, 53–55, 154, 168–178, 199n77; iconoclasm and, 24–25, 156, 158, 161–163, 163–169, 174–178; idolatry and, 154–155, 159–163, 163–168, 171–172, 175; image and, 14, 37–40, 48–50, 159–163, 163–169, 171–178, 198n57; knowledge and, 34–35; literal and literalized, 22–25, 36–40, 47–53, 71–72, 154, 164, 166, 199n76; mother-denial and, 34–36; museum and, 41–43; pornography and, 14, 41, 43–45, 49–51
Diego, Juan, 142–143
Docetism, 31–33, 147
Donne, John, 113–115

Ebner, Margaret, 101, 104–110, 112, 117, 206n54
El Shaddai, 27, 53, 195n19

Ephrem the Syrian, 53
Epiphanius, 121
Eschatology, 109, 116, 126, 136, 142, 143, 158, 169, 171, 174, 176, 178
Eucharist, 47, 54, 88, 105, 108–109, 115, 201n10; image and, 60–61, 82–84, 99; presence and, 88, 181, 183–184
Evdokimov, Paul, 4, 83, 121, 123, 129, 132, 137, 139, 147, 174

Florensky, Pavel, 129
Fra Angelico, 56–58, 74, 84
Francis (Pope), 9–10, 12, 141, 143
Franciscanism, 100–102, 104, 110–111
Freud, Sigmund, 29, 34, 46, 199n77
Fried, Michael, x–xii, 52

Galaktotrophousa, 33–34, 47
Golden Calf, 14, 153–156, 158–163, 168–170, 172–173, 175–176, 178–179, 182
Gregory of Nazianzus, 124, 134, 142
Gregory of Nyssa, 25–26, 81, 116, 124, 127, 133, 135–136, 142, 156; desire and, 168–178, 199n77
Grünewald, Matthias, 86–91, 94, 117–119

Hedley, Douglas, 60, 190n11, 191n10, 215n60
Holy Face, 138–140, 211n60
Holy Spirit, 54, 57–58, 126, 148, 176–177; likeness and, 137–141, 148–149
Homoousios, 13–14, 126–127
Hypostasis, 6, 13, 124–126, 128–130, 132, 136–140, 143–144, 146–147, 149–151, 209n32

Icon, 6, 15, 33, 83, 141, 145, 148–149, 185–186, 200n2; Byzantine controversy and, 59–61, 128, 200n3; Christ and, 59–61, 94, 96, 120, 122, 128, 130–132, 138–139, 145, 183, 185; Holy Face and, 138–139; Holy Spirit and, 138–140, 149–151; presence and, 6, 121–122,

INDEX 231

128–132, 138–139, 146–148, 150–151, 183, 185–187, 190n13, 208n16; resurrection and, 120–121, 207n1; Virgin of the Sign, 84–85; visibility and invisibility, 129–132, 146–147, 165
Iconoclash, 94, 117
Iconoclasm, 8–12, 141, 143, 193n29, 200n1; apophaticism and, 8; Baconian, 14, 156–158, 160, 162–163, 165–168, 170, 172, 174–176, 212n4; Byzantine, 59–61, 96–97, 204n16; cross as image of, 91–96, 112, 114, 117; desire and, 24–25, 156, 158, 161–163, 163–169, 174–178; Flannery O'Connor and, 66, 75–76; iconophilia and, 13–15, 67, 76, 92, 99, 117, 164, 181–186; idolatry and, 12, 64, 76–78, 80–81, 97–98, 117, 119, 145–146, 154, 156, 169–170, 182; of fidelity, 12, 15, 50, 58, 76–80, 85, 109–110, 124, 146–147, 149, 154–156, 158, 160, 167–169, 174, 182, 184–185; of temptation, 13, 15, 24, 34, 77, 99, 112, 124, 149, 154–156, 158, 166, 168–169, 178, 184–185; Protestantism and, 38, 89–90, 95–96, 99–100, 117, 181–182; recent acts, 1–2, 93; Wittgensteinian, 14, 156–158, 169, 162–163, 165, 168–169, 174–175, 177–178
Iconodulia, 6, 9, 33, 58–61, 96, 124, 128–132, 138, 200n1
Iconomachy, 9, 14, 33, 58–61, 73, 82–83, 85, 93, 96, 98, 128, 138, 200n1, 204n16
Iconophilia, 3, 11, 13–15, 58, 61–63, 66–67, 76, 81, 92, 99, 117, 149, 153, 157, 164, 181–186, 200n1
Idol: cross and, 97–98, 100, 109, 113; desire and, 25, 50, 154–155, 159–163, 171–172, 175; icon and, 128–132, 150; iconoclasm and, 12, 64, 76–78, 80–81, 97–98, 117, 119, 145–146, 154, 156, 169–170, 182; image and, 1–3, 5–8, 58–59, 67–68, 75–78, 92, 101, 109–110, 124–125, 128, 153–154, 164–167, 169–170, 172, 175, 182, 215n60; mental, 156–158, 212n5;

presence and, 124–125, 130–132, 145, 155–156
Image: agency and, xi, 159, 198n57; blasphemy and, 36–40; desire and, 14, 37–40, 48–50, 159–163, 163–169, 171–178, 198n57; ecumenism and, 3–4, 15–16, 185–186; free speech and, 36–40; gaze and, 8, 47–48, 58, 62,67, 124, 145–146, 150, 164–166, 168, 173, 176–177, 179, 182; idol and, 1–3, 5–8, 58–59, 67–68, 75–78, 92, 101, 109–110, 124–125, 128, 153–154, 164–167, 169–170, 172, 175, 182, 215n60; likeness and, 4–8, 111, 116, 124–126, 128–132, 134–144, 146–150, 192n15; saints' lives as, 99–101; negation and, 4, 6–8, 12,–15, 47–48, 50, 52, 76–77, 82, 84, 88–89, 91, 116–117, 146, 174–175, 179, 182–186, 211n75; onomatopes and, 5; picture and, 4–5, 60, 192n13, 201n14, 213n12; presence and, xi–xii, 13, 60, 66–70, 75–76, 82–83, 122, 124, 129–132, 148, 164, 166, 176–179, 181–187; prototype and, 6, 12, 25, 29, 37–38, 50, 67, 111, 124–125, 128, 130–131, 139, 183, 202n34, 208n15; resurrection and, 148–150; spectacle and, 5, 91, 124–125, 133–134, 173; token and, xi, 5, 124–124, 129–132, 147
Irenaeus, 30–31, 83, 113
Isenheim altarpiece, 86–89, 91, 118
Islam: image and, 2, 4, 10–12, 157, 184

Jasper, David, 129, 131
John Chrysostom, 127, 208n11
John of Damascus, 6, 78, 208n15
John Paul II, 141–142, 199n79

Kant, Immanuel, xi, 42, 60
Kempe, Margery, 101–104, 106–110, 112, 117, 205n44
Kenosis, 8, 129
Kierkegaard, Søren, 79, 201n16
Klein, Melanie, 29

232 INDEX

Koerner, Joseph Leo, 94, 114, 117

Las Casas, Bartolomé, 93–94, 117–119
Latour, Bruno, 94, 156, 163–169, 173, 176
"Least of these," 14, 124, 127–129, 132–137, 139, 142–144, 147–150, 158, 171, 208n11
Likeness, 5–6; Holy Spirit and, 137–141, 148–149; image and, 4–8, 111, 116, 124–126, 128–132, 134–144, 146–150, 192n15, 192n19
Lossky, Vladimir, 78, 83, 129–130, 138
Louvre Museum, 2, 42, 44
Luther, Martin, 89, 91

Macrina, 25–27, 51–53
Mahmood, Saba, 37–38, 40, 42
Mapplethorpe, Robert, 9–10, 12, 213n14
Maria lactans, 19–20, 23, 25, 27–29, 33, 41, 45, 47–51, 53, 196n30
Marion, Jean-Luc, 10–12, 67–68, 76–77, 91, 96, 100, 111, 123, 155–156, 163, 165–169, 173, 202n34
Mary, 14, 21–23, 27–28, 46, 54–55, 57, 102–103, 108, 142; image of, 7, 14, 19–20, 142–143, 150, 182; *Maria lactans*, 19–20, 23, 25, 27–29, 33, 41, 45, 47–51, 53, 196n30; Nestorianism and, 30–34; *Maria orans*, 84–85, 150–151; Virgin of Guadalupe, 20, 140, 142–143, 147, 195n6
Mary Magdalene, 122–123, 136, 140, 144–146
McGuckin, John, 32
Michelangelo, 41, 43, 45, 50
Mitchell, W.J.T., 60, 156–157, 158–163, 168–169, 175, 189n11, 198n57, 212n8, 213n12
Monaco, Lorenzo, 53–54
Monophysitism, 59, 72–73, 84, 200n6
Moses, 96, 145, 153–155, 159, 161, 163, 169–173, 175–179
Muhammed, 1–2, 10–12, 14, 37, 184, 193n36
Mure, William, 97–98, 100, 102, 104, 109, 113–114, 117
Museum, 2, 10, 40–43, 93–94, 191n9; secret museum, 41, 43–44, 198n61

Neer, Richard, 159–162, 167, 214n30
Nestorius, 30–33, 35–36, 59, 72–73, 197n39, 200n6
Nietzsche, Friedrich, 159–161, 163, 168, 213n29
Nikephoros, 129

O'Connor, Flannery, 14, 58, 61–62; "Parker's Back," 63–65, 68, 70, 75–77, 80–81, 84; images and, 70, 75–76
Orsi, Robert, 181, 212n10
Our Lady of Fergusson, 150–151
Ousia, 125–126, 128
Ouspensky, Leonid, 4, 129–130, 146, 209n21

Paul (Apostle), 95–96, 116, 127, 176
Percy, Walker, 14, 58, 61–62; angelism and bestialism, 71–73; image and, 62–63, 66–68, 75; *Love in the Ruins*, 71–72; *The Moviegoer*, 62–75, 77–80, 84; transcendence, 62–63, 68–70, 78
Piss Christ, 2, 14, 93–94, 98
Plato, 45, 60, 70, 84, 112, 157, 162
Platonism, xi, 70, 84
Poor. *See* "least of these"
Pornography, 14, 40–41, 43–45, 48–50, 67, 199n70, 199n76
Poussin, Nicolas, 152–156, 159–164, 167, 169, 178–179, 214n30
Presence, ix–xii, absence and, 6–8, 14, 75–76, 90–91, 118, 122, 181, 183–185 129–132; Eucharist and, xi, 82–83; 87–88, 90; icon and, x, 146–148, 151, 190n13, 192n17, 208n16, 209n23; image and, 4, 13, 24, 41, 60, 66–70, 75–76, 82–83, 122, 124, 129–132, 138–139, 148, 162, 164, 166, 176–179, 181–187, 189–190n11, 190n14, 192n17
Prosopon, 124–129, 132, 134–137, 139–140, 143–144, 147, 149–151
Protestantism: images and, 38, 89–90, 92, 94–95, 98–99, 117, 128, 181–182

Pseudo-Dionysius, 78, 213n11, 214n46

Ratzinger, Joseph. *See* Benedict XVI
Resurrection, 88, 106, 116, 122–123, 129–131, 135–137, 139–140, 144–145, 155, 159–160, 173, 183; Icon of, 121–122; imaging, 14, 123–125, 128, 131, 136–137, 148–150, 207n1

Serrano, Andres, 2, 93, 204n10
Seventh Ecumenical Council, 33, 59
Shroud of Turin, 140–141, 147–148, 210n51, 211n60
Silence, 83, 106, 109, 121–122, 123, 136, 149
Simpson, James, 9, 98, 100
Sin, 64, 78, 81, 88, 95, 112, 116, 133, 141, 158, 172–174
Sinai, 154, 155, 162, 163, 168–179
Suffering, 100, 102–107, 112, 115, 133, 205n38, 206n54

Theodore the Studite, 130, 192n16, 192n17, 208n15
Thérèse of Lisieux, 69, 81
Transfiguration, 130, 132, 137, 145–146, 151, 155, 209n21

Trinity, 54–57, 126–127, 194n42, 201n10, 208n8

Veil of Veronica, 140–141, 143–144, 147, 211n60
Virgin of Guadalupe, 20, 140, 142–143, 147, 195n6, 210n56, 211n58
Visibility: divine, 12, 14, 33, 55, 57–59, 61, 91, 121, 123–125, 129–132, 139, 176, 187; invisibility and, 64–71, 75–78, 80–81, 3–85, 91, 111, 116, 123–125, 129–132, 144, 146–151, 156, 164–168, 171, 173, 176, 183, 187, 209n29; "least of these" and, 132–137
Visual studies, xi, 60, 189–190n11

Williams, Rowan, 85, 136–137, 206n61
Wiman, Christian, 113, 115
Wittgenstein, Ludwig, 14, 156–158, 169, 162–163, 165, 168–169, 174–175, 177–178, 212n8, 212n9, 212n10

Yoder, John Howard, 3, 99–104, 107–113, 207n63

Zwingli, Ulrich, 97

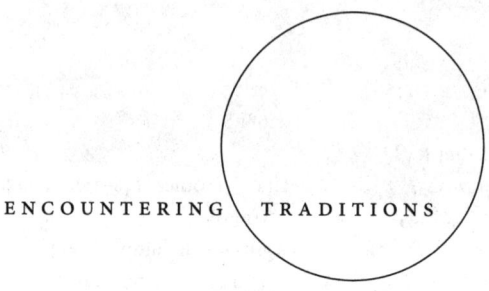

ENCOUNTERING TRADITIONS

Shaul Magid, *Hasidism Incarnate: Hasidism, Christianity, and the Construction of Modern Judaism*

Ted A. Smith, *Divine Violence: John Brown and the Limits of Ethics*

David Decosimo, *Ethics as a Work of Charity: Thomas Aquinas and Pagan Virtue*

Francis X. Clooney, SJ, *His Hiding Place Is Darkness: A Hindu-Catholic Theopoetics of Divine Absence*

Muhammad Iqbal, *Reconstruction of Religious Thought in Islam*

The possibility that our fear comes from awe — that absence necessarily draws us into the true, that ~~it is necessarily revel~~ absence is revelatory. I take Dr. Carnes' reminder to be a call to resist the ease with which we let these dichotomies rest in convenient opposition to one another.